# CITIZEN TOUSSAINT

# *CITIZEN TOUSSAINT*

by Ralph Korngold



HILL AND WANG · NEW YORK

FIRST PAPERBACK EDITION MARCH 1965

Manufactured in the United States of America
1234567890

# FOREWORD

On May 23, 1799, Edward Stevens, Consul General of the United States of America to the French colony of St. Domingo,* wrote to General Thomas Maitland, Commander in Chief of the British Expeditionary Force to the same colony, warning him that the British colony of Jamaica, along with the United States of America, was in danger of invasion by the armed forces of St. Domingo under the command of General Toussaint Louverture. The paragraph relating to the threatened invasion reads: –

> The Agency of Saint-Domingo had received positive orders from the Executive Directory to invade both the Southern States of America and the Island of Jamaica. Gen. Toussaint Louverture was consulted on the best mode of making the attack.

General Maitland did not burst out laughing at the notion that the Negro army of Toussaint Louverture might invade the American continent. A British army of 20,000 well-trained and excellently equipped soldiers had been decisively defeated by Toussaint Louverture, and Maitland had orders to evacuate. Nor did the American Secretary of State, Timothy Pickering, regard the matter as a joke. Stevens wrote to him: "His [Toussaint Louverture's] army amounts to 55,000 men, of which 30,000 are of the line and disciplined. The remainder are militia."

This, for the New World, was a formidable army. The largest

* That part of the island now called "Haiti" was then called "St.-Domingue" by the French and "St. Domingo" by Englishmen and Americans. "*San* Domingo" will be used to designate the Spanish part. The island as a whole will be referred to as Haiti, the name given to it by the aboriginal Indians.

force Washington had ever commanded had not exceeded 20,000 men.

Stevens likewise informed the Secretary that the real ruler of St. Domingo was not the French Directory or its Agent, but Toussaint Louverture: "The Agent does nothing at present but what he is desired to do. The whole machine of Government, both civil and military, is regulated and guided by the General-in-Chief."

Since in 1812 the British did not find it difficult to land an army in the United States, there is reason to believe that with the aid of the French fleet Toussaint could have done the same. He might have proved a more formidable adversary than the British, since thousands of plantation slaves undoubtedly would have joined him. The invasion plan included seizure of all ships in Haitian waters for use as transports. The American Government took the matter sufficiently to heart to forbid American ships to depart for Haitian ports. However, while the French Directory desired Toussaint to invade the United States and Jamaica, he himself had no inclination to do so. He was far more interested in gaining his independence from France. Hence, on June 13, 1799, he made a secret treaty with Great Britain and the United States, in which appears this clause: "No expedition shall be sent out against any of the possessions of his Britannic Majesty and of the United States of America."

## 2

The foregoing should convince the reader that the role played by Toussaint Louverture upon the political stage of his time was not a minor one. Not only was he an exceedingly capable military leader, governor and administrator, but the country he ruled was, in relation to the rest of the world, far more important, then, than now. The exports of the island compared favorably with those of the United States. Toussaint's army and yearly revenue were larger than those of any European power of the second rank. The two principal cities of the colony – Cap Français and Port Républicain (Port-au-Prince) – were almost as large as New York. Cap Français was incomparably better built than any American city. Toussaint wrote with pardonable pride to Napoleon Bonaparte: "The colony of St. Domingo, of which I was commander, enjoyed the greatest tranquillity; agriculture and commerce flourished. The island had attained a degree of splendor it had never before witnessed. And all this – I dare say – was my work."

A number of measures for which Napoleon has received great praise were anticipated by Toussaint. Beauchamp does not hesitate to say: "His [Toussaint Louverture's] political performance was such that, in a wider sphere, Napoleon appears to have imitated him."

## 3

Toussaint Louverture was fifty-nine when he died. His father lived to be 106, and might have become even older had he not been killed by the French. Hence there is reason to believe that but for Toussaint's removal to a foreign climate and prison, he might have reigned for another score of years. Would he have been satisfied with peacefully ruling Haiti while slavery continued to exist on all other islands in the Caribbean? Napoleon did not think so, and said that unless Toussaint was overthrown "the sceptre of the New World would sooner or later pass into the hands of the Blacks." Bonaparte's brother-in-law, General Leclerc, Commander in Chief of the French Expeditionary Force, wrote to the Minister of Marine: "It is here and now that the issue is being decided whether Europe will preserve any colonies in the West Indies." His Chief of Staff, General de Lacroix, wrote: "The sword of Damocles hung suspended by a thread and threatened the prosperity of Cuba and Jamaica. Only the whim of a Haitian chief kept it from falling." Napoleon had but to threaten to recognize Toussaint and to give him a free hand, to have the British withdraw their objections to his expedition.

It is, therefore, no rash assumption that but for the treachery of his own generals, the Liberator of Haiti might have become the Liberator of the West Indies. His overthrow had significance for the United States and for every nation with colonies in the New World. It was an event of prime importance to the white race as well as to the Negro race. None of his successors possessed either his ability or his vision. The danger to white supremacy in the West Indies died with him.

## 4

It was not Toussaint's intention to help the United States of America acquire the Louisiana Territory, which doubled the area of the country and made possible further expansion westward; but there is reason to believe that but for the Negro general the Territory might have remained a French colony.

Napoleon's ambition was to build a great colonial empire. The keystone of that empire was of course to be the incomparable colony of St. Domingo, from which France is said to have derived more profit than all other nations derived from their combined colonies in Asia, Africa and America. As long as Toussaint Louverture remained in power, St. Domingo was a French colony in name only. In reality it was an independent state, having its own constitution, making its own laws, maintaining its own army and negotiating treaties with foreign powers. Even the last link, the Agent or Commissioner, had disappeared. The first step in Napoleon's colonial program was, therefore, to plan the elimination of Toussaint Louverture. The second was the retrocession by Spain, to the French Republic, of the Louisiana Territory, for – says Henry Adams – "St. Domingo, like all the West Indies, suffered as a colony under a serious disadvantage, being dependent for its supplies chiefly on the United States, – a dangerous neighbor both by its political example and its commercial and maritime rivalry with the mother country. The First Consul hoped to correct this evil by substituting Louisiana for the United States as a source of supplies for St. Domingo."

So, in August 1800, Napoleon sent Berthier to the Court of Madrid to negotiate the retrocession of the Territory. He received assurance that it would be ceded, and the following year sent his brother-in-law, General Leclerc, at the head of the most powerful army that had ever crossed the Atlantic, to St. Domingo to subdue Toussaint Louverture. Had Leclerc succeeded, Napoleon would have carried out his project, and the Louisiana Territory would have remained a French colony.

But Leclerc did not succeed. Napoleon's plan suffered shipwreck as a result of Toussaint Louverture's stubborn resistance and his foresight in arming virtually the entire Negro and mulatto population of St. Domingo. "Louisiana could not be made useful until St. Domingo should be thoroughly subdued," says Henry Adams. Having lost St. Domingo, Napoleon lost interest in the Louisiana Territory and sold it to Jefferson. But it was Toussaint Louverture and the Negroes and mulattoes of St. Domingo who gave Jefferson his opportunity.

Salvador de Madariaga gives credit to the Jewish people for having produced the man who discovered America. If the United States of America stretches from Canada to the Gulf and from the Atlantic to the Pacific, some credit for this is due to a member of the Negro race.

## 5

This is not a fictional biography, and no attempt has been made to have Toussaint appear better or wiser than is warranted by the evidence. But no estimate of Toussaint's character and accomplishments would be just if it failed to consider that he was a slave for forty-seven years out of the fifty-nine years of his existence. If Washington, Jefferson and Lincoln had had such a handicap to contend with, who knows if they would have attained his stature? Certain it is that slavery would have left its mark upon them, as it did upon him.

"It is for slaves to lie, for freemen to speak truth," wrote Apollonius. Duplicity and mendacity are the natural weapons of the weak and helpless. Toussaint Louverture's liberal use of these weapons should be ascribed to habits formed in slavery. This mitigating circumstance cannot be cited in defense of such honored figures in the white Hall of Fame as Queen Elizabeth and Napoleon Bonaparte. Of Queen Elizabeth a distinguished historian has written: "Nothing is more revolting in the queen, but is more characteristic than her shameless mendacity. A falsehood was to her an intellectual means of meeting a difficulty." As for Napoleon, his perfidy has seldom been equaled. The reader will find documentary evidence of it in this volume.

Still another excuse may be offered for Toussaint. Says Cardinal Newman: "Almost all authors, Catholic and Protestant, admit that *when a just cause is present*, there is some kind of verbal misleading which is not sin." * It is now generally conceded that Toussaint's cause was just. Whether the kind of "verbal misleading" he practised is in conformity with good ethics the reader may decide for himself.

If no man is a hero to his valet, neither is he to his biographer. All human idols have feet of clay, though of varying friability. This, however, does not deter the biographer of Toussaint from agreeing with Beauchamp, who pronounces the Negro leader to have been "one of the most remarkable men in an age rich in remarkable men."

RALPH KORNGOLD

* Italics, Newman's.

# CONTENTS

Capacity to learn comes with dependence on education; and as that animal which at birth is most incapable and immature is the most teachable, so too those human races which are most precocious are most incorrigible, and while they seem the cleverest at first prove ultimately the least intelligent. . . . It is perhaps the duller races, with a long childhood and a brooding mind, that bear the hopes of the world within them, if only nature avails to execute what she has planned on so great a scale.

GEORGE SANTAYANA

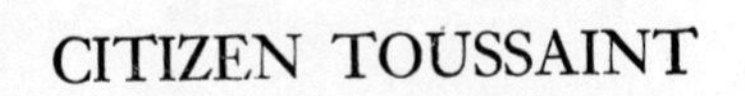
CITIZEN TOUSSAINT

# *PART ONE*
# *Haiti Before Toussaint*

## CHAPTER I
## The Paradise of God

Columbus had tasted the joy of discovery. He had set foot in the New World and had taken possession for his king "with proclaiming heralds and flying standards, no one objecting." In Cuba he was told of an island to the east where there was an abundance of gold. The natives called it "Haiti" – The Land of Mountains. On December 5, 1492, Columbus set sail for the island with two caravels. That same evening he sighted it and saw a beautiful bay, sheltered by a high bluff, "like the bay of Cádiz." Adverse currents prevented him from entering until the following morning, when he named it Môle St. Nicolas, in honor of the saint of that day. Since, however, the natives had taken fright and remained undiscoverable, Columbus drew up anchor the following day and sailed northward along the coast to explore other parts of the island.

The more he saw of it, the better he liked it. In some ways it reminded him of Spain, so he called it "Espagnola," later Latinized to the diminutive Hispaniola – Little Spain. Still later the French were to call it "St. Domingue," after the city Columbus' brother founded on the island.

In letters to his two friends and patrons, Luis de Sant Angel and Gabriel Sanchez, and in his journal, Columbus is enthusiastic about Haiti, which he calls "the most beautiful thing in the world," and "the most pleasant place in the world." Once he refers to it as "the Paradise of God," and writes: "Here I will dwell, I and my children, here I shall remain and the last remnant of my days be spent, and here I will be buried."

If Columbus was pleased with the island, he was equally pleased with its inhabitants. To read him one might think that this was indeed paradise, inhabited by beings unaffected by the fall of man. To the King he wrote: "They are loving people, without covetousness. I declare to Your Highness that there is not a better country nor a better people in the world than these. They love their neighbors as themselves and their speech is the sweetest and gentlest in the world, and always with a smile."

It must be acknowledged that the conduct of the Haitian Indians toward Columbus and his companions merited the Admiral's flattering opinion of them. On the night before Christmas, the sea being motionless, the rudder of Columbus' flagship, the *Santa María*, was entrusted to a boy. An imperceptible current carried the ship towards the coastal reefs, which it struck with a thundering noise. Columbus, who had given strict orders not to give the rudder to such inexperienced hands, rushed on deck, only to discover that the ship was irretrievably lost.

No sooner had the "king" of that region, whom Columbus had visited the previous day, heard about this shipwreck than he hastened to the Admiral's assistance with a large force of men. Nothing could be done to save the ship, but all the cargo and the stores were saved and placed under shelter in several houses the "king" ordered cleared for that purpose. He visited Columbus the following day and besought him "with tears in his eyes" not to grieve over the loss, as he would do what he could to compensate him for it. Columbus informs us that not the smallest article was stolen, although the ship was loaded with gewgaws dear to the heart of an Indian.

The fact that the Indians believed the Spaniards to be visitors from heaven may, in part, have accounted for their exemplary behavior, but travelers who visited the island when much had happened to dispel that illusion, likewise assure us that the

Haitian Indians were simple, mild and humane. "More like children than men," says Jefferys. Columbus tells us that they were whiter and handsomer than any aborigines he had yet seen and that the skin of some was "as white as any that could be seen in Spain."

Haiti was divided into five kingdoms, each ruled by a hereditary absolute king called a "cacique." The caciques do not appear to have been tyrannical or bellicose. When a difference arose between them they met and usually managed to reach an agreement without resort to arms.

## 2

The West Indian historian Bryan Edwards has said: "The whole story of mankind affords no scene of barbarity equal to that of the cruelties exercised by the Spaniards on the inoffensive natives of the Leeward Islands." Listen to the Dominican friar Bartolomé de Las Casas, future Bishop of Chiapa, who was an eyewitness: –

> I once beheld four or five Indian chiefs roasted on a slow fire, and as the victims poured forth screams which disturbed the commanding officer in his slumbers, he sent word that they should be strangled. But the officer on guard (I know his name, and I know his relations in Seville), would not suffer it; but causing their mouths to be gagged, that their cries might not be heard, he stirred up the fire with his own hands and roasted them till they expired.

When Columbus discovered Haiti, the island – which is about the size of Ireland – had a population estimated at from 1,000,000 to 3,000,000. When forty-three years later Oviedo visited the island, there were not over 500 of the original inhabitants left. What could have been the reason for the cruel extermination of a people of whom Las Casas says "They never committed against the Spaniards any one mortal offence punishable by the law of man"?

The Spanish adventurers who flocked to Haiti had only one aim in view: They wanted gold and colonial products. They had been trading with the natives, giving them leather thongs, bits of glass, mirrors, earthenware, strings of beads, etc., in exchange for their gold, but the Indians could not use an unlimited supply of such treasures and had no desire to engage in gold mining as a regular occupation. They regarded gold as a sacred metal and before going in search of it used to purify themselves by fasting and continence, neither of which appealed to them. As for cultivating the soil on a scale requiring long hours of labor in the hot sun, they had not the slightest inclination to do so. The Spaniards were as indolent as the Indians, but far better armed and skilled in the art of warfare. Moreover, they possessed horses, unknown to the Indians and greatly feared by them. They defeated the Indians, enslaved them and compelled them to work for them.

When the Indians had been conquered, they as well as their land were divided among the Spanish grandees and lesser adventurers. The Spanish government collected a twenty-five-per-cent tax on exports, but as long as Indians were plentiful, slaves could be had for the asking. Indians were regarded as a natural resource, and in newly settled countries natural resources are usually wasted. Raynal says that Castilian gentlemen went out shooting Indians for pleasure and considered the hunting poor if they did not kill at least a dozen — "one for each apostle."

If the Indians perished by tens and by hundreds of thousands, the white colonists prospered. Mines and plantations were developed. The ports of the island were crowded with proud galleons bringing manufactured products from the mother country and carrying away rich colonial produce. For many of the colonists the dream of wealth came true. Some returned to Spain and spent in riotous living the wealth wrung from the Indians. Others built fine houses, imported costly furniture and clothing and set out to found a colonial aristocracy. Oviedo wrote to Charles V that there was not a city in Spain comparable with Santo Domingo City, where there were mansions surpassing in size, splendor and comfort the palaces in which royalty lived in the mother country.

But the reservoir of Indian slave labor was not inexhaustible. One day the Spaniards discovered that it was beginning to run dry: 40,000 Indians were imported from the Bahamas to replenish the stock. The wanton killing of natives was stopped. When all this proved inadequate, Negro slaves were imported. But the African slave traffic was as yet poorly organized and a labor shortage soon made itself felt. Here a plantation, there a mine had to be abandoned. Exports and imports began to drop alarmingly. Many of the colonists gave up in disgust and moved to Mexico or Peru.

More misfortunes came when England and Holland fitted out privateers to prey upon Spanish commerce. The waters around Hispaniola began to swarm with them to such an extent that a galleon stood little chance of arriving at its destination unless convoyed by a man-of-war. The government was obliged to close all the ports of the island, except Santo Domingo City. In 1586, Sir Francis Drake captured the city and held it for nearly a month. Before leaving he decided to reduce it to ashes, and had made a promising beginning when the citizens ransomed the remainder by paying him 80,000 pieces of eight.

The Spanish colony never regained its former prosperity. Agriculture was almost entirely abandoned, and the inhabitants became ranchers and herdsmen. In the seventeenth century the western part of the island was lost to France.

# CHAPTER II

## The Buccaneers

In 1625 some English and French adventurers took possession of the island of St. Christopher, one of the smallest of the Leeward Islands. They had been on the island five years and were feeling thoroughly established, when the Spanish admiral Don Federico de Toledo came to pay them an unwelcome visit. When the visit was over, the surviving members of the colony found themselves at sea in open boats, with no particular aim in view except to get away as far as possible from the admiral's barking cannon.

The early history of the fugitives is somewhat obscure. The preponderance of evidence indicates that they first landed on the northwest coast of Hispaniola, a wild and uninhabited country. The Spaniards had introduced horses, cattle and pigs into the island. These had rapidly multiplied and great herds ranged the savannas. So the fugitives, who were well armed, did not lack sustenance. They had learned from the Indians how to preserve meat without salt, which was costly and hard to obtain. The meat was cut into strips, cured in the sun and then smoked over a green-wood fire. The process was called "boucanning," hence the settlers became known as "buccaneers." The rude sheds in which they lived and smoked their meat were called "boucans."

Shortly after the fugitives came to Hispaniola some of them decided that there was a more lucrative way of making a living than hunting the bull and the boar and selling hides to smugglers. A few miles from the coast was the small island of Tortuga. It was cigar-shaped, with a north coast inaccessible even to a canoe and a south coast that had only one narrow harbor, easily defended. The more venturesome among the buccaneers decided to seize Tortuga and use it as a base for piratical operations.

A garrison of twenty-five Spaniards stationed on the island was ordered to leave and obligingly complied. The adventurers now built a small ship, and, luck being with them, had soon captured several from the Spaniards. Their success attracted others and Tortuga became a veritable breeding place for pirates. They became known as "filibusters" or "freebooters," terrorized the Spanish Main and extended their operations as far as the Pacific.

Many others of the buccaneers now moved to Tortuga to trade with the freebooters, and as time progressed abandoned hunting for agriculture. The Spaniards, however, were now fully awake to the danger of the situation and made persistent efforts to get rid of the intruders. They recaptured Tortuga several times and waged a war of extermination on the buccaneers. One finds on the map of Haiti such names as River of the Massacre, Plain of the Massacre, Mountain of the Massacre, all of which antedate the Haitian Revolution and are a reminder of the bloody encounters between Spaniards and buccaneers. But try as they might, the Spaniards were unable to dislodge their enemies permanently and new recruits kept constantly arriving.

When not fighting the Spaniards, the buccaneers kept in trim by fighting among themselves. Some were French, some English and some Dutch. The Dutch, being a small minority, made no bid for leadership, but the French and the English constantly fought for supremacy, with now one, now the other faction having the better of an argument that lasted forty years. By 1664, however, the French were firmly in the saddle, owing to the support of their home government. Then France took charge of the colony and d'Ogeron de la Bouère was appointed Governor.

## 2

The French Government now made an attempt to people the colony with Frenchmen. It sent over indentured servants, called *engagés*. They were given free passage, but had to sign an agreement promising to work three years for whoever wished to purchase their services. They were inhumanly treated. Du Tertre tells of fifty dying in the service of a single master. Finally it was decided to send convicts. It was comparatively easy for a poor man to become a convict in those days, so those transported were not necessarily desperate characters.

The first Governor, d'Ogeron, convinced that a colony without women did not have much of a future, had asked that women be sent; he received two consignments of fifty. "They were," says de Wimpffen, "vixens from the Salpêtrière [the women's prison in Paris], sluts picked up from the gutter, shameless hussies whose language was as vile as their morals." Nevertheless d'Ogeron had no difficulty in disposing of them to the highest bidder, and they were considered such prizes that their employers usually married them. But the young women were such a handful that, after several more shiploads had arrived, a harassed governor sent this plaint to the Minister of Marine: "It were better to send no more women than the kind we have been getting. They ruin the men's health and cause them so much worry as to drive them to an early grave – not to speak of all the other mischief with which they disturb peace and order."

Immigrants who began flocking to the colony, intent on making a fortune, were almost equally undesirable. "Colonial life, it is true," writes the Intendant Mithon, "does not usually attract the cream of the population, but what we get here is riffraff from every part of the world, whom licentious conduct or a spotted past have forced to emigrate."

# CHAPTER III

## St. Domingo Comes of Age

UNTIL the middle of the seventeenth century the principal products of St. Domingo had been cocoa, indigo and tobacco. In 1644, the Brazilian Jew Benjamin Dacosta introduced sugar cane from Java into the Antilles and brought about a great economic revolution. Sugar cane might have been profitably grown on small farms had independent mills been erected. But there appeared instead large sugar plantations that had their own mills and were manufactories as well as agricultural establishments. To produce sugar in this fashion required a great outlay of capital. Vast estates swallowed up the small farms. "More than four thousand people have left whose land is now owned by twelve or fifteen sugar plantations," wrote in 1680 the Intendant Patoulet. Indentured servants no longer sufficed. Negroes were imported in ever greater numbers.

By 1789 nearly 1,000,000 Negroes had been imported – over 40,000 in 1787 alone, not counting some 3000 smuggled in to avoid the head tax. A great variety of African tribes were represented. Moreau de Saint-Méry enumerates thirty, differing as widely from one another in physical and mental characteristics as a Nordic from a Semite. There were Senegalese, "strong, well-made, tall and ebony-hued"; copper-colored Fulahs, with straight hair and Caucasian features; Angolese, who, says du Tertre, "smelt so horribly that the air was tainted for a quarter of an hour after they had passed"; cannibal Mondongos, with teeth filed to sharp points. There were Bambaras, tall, insolent and given to thieving; Aradas, proud, but excellent agriculturists; Congos, small and active, but prone to run away; Nagos, kind and docile; Mines, resolute and capricious; Ardras, talkative and quarrelsome; Ibos, good field workers, but easily despairing and apt to hang themselves; and many others. Urged by the whips of drivers and under the supervision of white overseers, this vast army of Negroes did a prodigious amount of work. Towns grew into cities, and new towns and villages sprang up. Roads and bridges were built, aqueducts and irrigation works constructed. The broad savannas, where wild cattle and horses had ranged, were transformed into sugar and cotton plantations separated by hedges of citron and lime. Mountain slopes were cleared and became coffee plantations. Nearly a quarter of a million acres were under cultivation. There came a time when two thirds of all French import and export trade was with St. Domingo. The combined imports and exports of the colony reached the astounding total of 716,000,000 livres; 1000 merchant vessels, employing 80,000 sailors, were required to carry the tonnage to and from the mother country. At the time of the Revolution there were nearly 800 sugar plantations, about half that many cotton and indigo plantations, and 3000 coffee plantations. Where land was unfit for cultivation cattle and pigs were bred. Says H. E. Mills: "In 1789 St. Domingo had attained a height of prosperity not surpassed in the history of European colonies. It supplied half Europe with sugar, coffee and cotton."

About the middle of the eighteenth century the French nobility went into decline. Money was needed to restore some of the proudest blazons of France to their former luster. So the Ségurs, Noailles, La Rochefoucaulds, Rohans, Chabans, Guy-d'Arseys – all that was *Vieille France* – formed alliances by marriage with the purse-proud planters of St. Domingo. A young noble's colonial bride might betray in speech and manner her descent from a buccaneer and a Paris prostitute, but an income of 200,000 livres easily compensated for such shortcomings. Many nobles came to live in the colony and a veritable squirearchy was created. In the neighborhood of Le Cap alone some 200 nobles lived on their estates. "Sire, your Court has become Creole by alliances," a delegation from St. Domingo said proudly to Louis XVI.

## 2

There sprang up a legend concerning life in the colony that has not died to this day. To be "a St. Domingo planter" was considered equivalent to being a nabob. The average Frenchman imagined life in the colony as a cross between Mardi Gras and Arabian Nights. Visiting planters were responsible for this fantastic notion. One arrived in Paris with an exotic retinue of mulatto and Negro servants. He established himself in the most elegant suite of the leading hostelry and entertained like an oriental potentate. It is not unlikely he was spending a ten years' income to indulge his vanity, but Paris did not know that. When he described his colonial country residence one received the impression of a tropical Trianon, and when he enlarged upon the attractions of the colony's two principal cities, Cap Français and Port-au-Prince, Paris looked drab by comparison. No wonder that when in 1790 Baron de Wimpffen landed in the heart of Port-au-Prince, he imagined himself in one of the meaner suburbs and went looking for the metropolis he had heard described in such glowing terms. The disillusioned baron commented that St. Domingo's famed capital reminded him of a Tartar camp.

Cap Français, or "Le Cap," as it was colloquially called, would have been less disappointing. It compared favorably with most European cities of the second rank. The colonists referred to it as "the Paris of the New World." The streets were straight, narrow and for the most part paved, a luxury few European cities permitted themselves. There were several fine squares, two of them embellished with fountains. The houses were of hewn stone, transported at great cost from Europe. The majority had two stories and wrought iron balconies, which were sometimes gilded. There were many public buildings, several churches, two large hospitals, a theater, a bathing establishment where men and women could enjoy each other's company at the bath, cafés, gambling houses and innumerable brothels.

Le Cap had over 20,000 inhabitants and a large floating population. The streets were filled with a noisy and colorful crowd – mulatto women, with towering headdresses and fantastic earrings; Negresses with vivid-colored turbans; richly dressed Creole women; planters, dressed in white and wearing broad-brimmed straw hats; fortune seekers, sailors, officers and soldiers of the garrison. There were men on horseback, women in sedan chairs carried by Negroes or horses, or one might see "an elegant carriage, drawn by horses or mules of different colors and sizes, with ropes for traces, covered with the most filthy trappings and driven by a postilion glittering with gold – and barefoot."

It was an animated spectacle, but there was something factitious about it, as if it were a stage setting. There was a feverishness in the atmosphere, which extended into the country, where the planters lived in houses that obviously were a makeshift, devoid of architectural beauty and scantily furnished. There was, in fact, hardly a white man in St. Domingo who did not look forward to the time when he would be able to leave the colony and go to live in France. "All wish to be gone," says Raynal, "everyone is in a hurry; these people have the air of merchants at a fair."

## 3

The colony was divided into three provinces: the North, West and South. The North Province was the oldest, best developed and most densely populated. Its capital was Cap Français. The West Province was almost twice as large, but not as fruitful or well developed. The capital was Port-au-Prince, which was likewise the seat of the colonial government. The South Province, with the town of Les Cayes for capital, had been colonized last, was little developed and sparsely settled.

In 1789 there were approximately 39,000 whites, 27,000 "free people of color" (commonly called "mulattoes"), and 452,000 slaves in the colony. An undetermined number of the "free people of color" were Negroes, and about ten per cent of the slaves were mulattoes. Some of the free people of color owned slaves, but a free Negro would not have attempted to own a mulatto slave, who would have preferred death to such a humiliation.

St. Domingo was governed by officials sent over from France. There was no self-government even in municipal affairs. At the head of the government were the Governor and the Intendant, appointed by the King and responsible to the Minister of Marine. The Governor, usually a bluff old soldier, commanded the garrison, the colonial militia, the gendarmes, the squadron. He promulgated the laws and gave land concessions. The Intendant, generally an astute man of the law, had charge of the judiciary and managed the finances. It was a dual government that worked badly. Because of his control of the armed forces, the Governor was more powerful, but he and the Intendant were sufficiently equal to be at loggerheads most of the time. Under these two principal functionaries served a host of minor officials, who imitated the quarrel of their superiors. On one point, however, all were agreed: they, too, had no intention of remaining permanently in the colony and wished to make as much money as possible in a minimum of time. Graft and corruption were rampant. St. Domingo boasted one of the most extravagant and expensive governments in the world.

But it was not the dishonesty of the government officials that worried the colonists. Perhaps under the circumstances they preferred them to be dishonest. A dishonest official could more easily be induced to temper the severity of the Colonial Pact, that instrument of the Devil, the very thought of which could raise the temperature of a colonist. The Pact permitted the colonists to sell only to France and to buy only from France. Now, France could use barely a fourth of their exports. All the rest was bought by French merchants, for resale elsewhere. Millions that the colonists could have made went into the pockets of the French traders. When it came to imports – if a colonist wanted flour from Philadelphia, he had to get it by way of Bordeaux! For many articles he paid double what he would have paid had he been able to buy in the open market. As a result of all this, officialdom and the colonists were far from being friends. The planters looked enviously at the United States of America, whose example they would have liked to imitate.

# CHAPTER IV

## The Whites

THE most substantial part of the population were the Creole * planters – the *Grands Blancs.* The typical Creole planter was taller than the average Frenchman, handsome and romantic-looking – dark-eyed, ebony-haired, olive-skinned. He possessed a feline grace, due to a childhood spent in the open, unencumbered by much clothing. He was courageous and open-handed. At one time he had been famed for his hospitality, but towards the close of the eighteenth century that trait had in a large measure disappeared. Against this meager catalogue of virtues there was a long list of defects and vices. Montesquieu calls the St. Domingo planters "ferocious, proud, quarrelsome, voluptuous and cruel." Baron de Wimpffen charges them with

* Originally a Creole was a person of European descent born in the French or Spanish West Indies. Later *any* person born there was called a Creole. Thus there were *Creole* Negroes and *African* Negroes, i.e. Negroes born in Africa.

being "irascible, capricious, willful and imperious." Both believed the planters to have developed their least admirable traits of character in the exercise of absolute power over their slaves.

The Creole planter's wife was often a charming creature, if seldom sylphlike. Large dark eyes, abundant and glossy black or brown tresses, an ivory complexion, fine teeth, graceful languor, drawling and melodious speech captivated the newcomer. Usually she could be found lying in a hammock or on a couch, reading a French novel, receiving the attentions of an admirer or listening to naughty ballads, sung in Creole by a mulatto slave girl. Another slave girl, at the foot of the couch, might be supplying her with her favorite excitation, which consisted of having the soles of her bare feet tickled with a feather. The charm of this Arabian Nights scene would be rudely shattered if the lady lost her temper. At such a time she might spit at her slave girls, pinch them, or abuse them in language reminiscent of her ancestress who had made a forced journey to the colony. If a girl protested she stood a good chance of being flogged. Practically all authorities agree that Creole women were more cruel to the slaves than the men. Says Descourtilz: "They order and witness with perfect equanimity the most inhuman punishments inflicted upon the slaves and appear completely insensible to cries of mercy or to the effusion of blood."

An American girl, Miss Hassall, who made a prolonged visit to the colony, wrote to her friend Aaron Burr, former Vice President of the United States: "The Creole lady divides her time between the bath, the table, the toilette and the lover. The *faux pas* of a married lady is so much a matter of course, that she who has only one lover, and retains him long in her chains, is considered a model of constancy and discretion."

## 2

The government officials and army men in the colony kept aloof from the Creoles, who returned their dislike with a vengeance. When in 1760 Count d'Estaing, Governor of St. Domingo, made a tour of the colony, he found it advisable to make long detours to find accommodations with free mulattoes and Negroes. In a letter he speaks of the "shameful reception and humiliating disappointments" he experienced at the houses of some of the planters and warns his compatriots not to rely on Creole hospitality.

The relationship between the planters and the bourgeois of the cities was little more cordial. The bourgeois – bankers, merchants, lawyers – were usually Frenchmen representing concerns with whom the planters did business and to whom, as a rule, they owed money.

The largest class of whites were known as *Petits Blancs*. In the country they were small farmers, overseers and handicraftsmen – descendants of the *engagés*, not quite free from the obloquy that had attached to their ancestors; in the cities the class consisted of a miscellaneous lot of rapscallions – gamblers, gaming establishment and bawdyhouse keepers, cardsharps, soldiers of fortune, small shopowners and tavernkeepers, all of whom considered physical labor beneath the dignity of a white man. If they condescended to keep a shop and could not afford to buy slaves, they hired them. They considered it a crying injustice for anybody with Negro blood to have more than they. The free mulattoes were reasonably well protected in the ownership of their property, though in little else, and the *Petits Blancs* avenged themselves by heaping humiliations upon them. In this they were encouraged by the planters, who were glad to see the dissatisfactions of propertyless whites directed into racial channels.

Ecclesiastics were fairly numerous in the colony and their reputation was of the worst. "Perhaps nowhere in Christendom have the clergy so profaned their sacred calling," said in 1863 the Haitian Minister of Public Worship, Lizaire. The Archbishop of Port-au-Prince, Gailloux, mournfully declared: "For the honor of the Church I wish I could wipe out their [the priests'] shame with my tears and plunge their acts into eternal oblivion." Many of the priests had concubines and children, with whom they lived openly. "He is a good father, even if he is a bad priest," was said in defense of one of them. The clergy were usually monks who had broken their vows, or priests who had disgraced themselves in France and had been relegated to the colony instead of being unfrocked. Their religious influence was naturally small.

But it was not the debauchees among the clergy who incurred the wrath of the colonists. The priests upon whom the colonists heaped anathema and whom they charged with every conceivable crime were a half-dozen men who, like Father Delahaye, came to the colony because of their genuine sympathy with the Negroes. When the slave rebellion broke out these priests committed the unpardonable sin – they ranged themselves on the side of the rebels.

# CHAPTER V

## Mulattoes and Mulattresses

THE colloquial term "mulatto" designated all persons of mixed white and Negro blood. There were, however, thirteen subdivisions – *mulâtre*, *griffe*, *quarteron*, *tierceron*, *métis*, *mameluc*, and more. A mulatto's social standing depended in a large measure on the amount of white blood in his veins.

Haitian historians tell us that in the early days of the colony mulattoes had enjoyed near-equality with the whites. There had been an unwritten law that the child of a white man and a slave woman became free at the age of twenty-four. Many planters had not regarded their mulatto offspring as slaves at any time and had endowed them with considerable property.

Whites and mulattoes had met on a friendly footing and marriage between them had been frequent. The change in racial relations is supposed to have taken place when white women began arriving in the colony in considerable numbers. They were nearly always poor and discovered to their chagrin that white men preferred their propertied mulatto sisters. It is even claimed that, apart from property considerations, white men found mulattresses more attractive. The white women managed to exhibit such scorn for miscegenation (at least of a legal character) that the men became infected and racial barriers sprang up.

Mulattoes could not hold public office or practice any of the learned professions. Even some of the skilled trades were closed to them. They had to serve three years in the militia and to provide their own equipment. In church, at the theater, in a public conveyance, they had to occupy special seats. They were not allowed to wear certain kinds of clothing and jewelry and could not ride in a carriage. If they rode on horseback, they had to dismount before entering a city or town. It was forbidden to address them as "*Monsieur*" or "*Madame.*" A white man could insult or beat a mulatto with impunity. A complaint to the authorities would have been useless and woe to him if he tried to retaliate: a mulatto who raised his hand against a white man ran the risk of having his hand cut off. This law had, it is true, fallen into desuetude, but shortly before the Revolution a free mulatto was sold into slavery for having struck a white man.

With practically every avenue of social advancement, except the acquisition of property, barred to them, the mulattoes of St. Domingo did what the Jews had done under similar circumstances – they devoted themselves to amassing wealth. In 1790 they put forth the claim that one third of the land and one fourth of the slaves belonged to them. The claim has been called into question, but a report the Administrators of the Colony sent in 1755 to the Minister of Marine, appears to confirm it. We read: –

Their economical way of living enables them to lay aside each year a good part of their earnings and thus accumulate considerable capital. When a property is auctioned, they bid it up, until the price has reached astronomical figures. The whites, not possessing as much money as they, cannot buy it, or if they do, find themselves ruined. In many districts the finest estates have fallen into their hands. They are arrogant because they are rich and in proportion to their riches. Unless appropriate measures are taken, the time is not far distant when they will succeed in forming alliances with the most distinguished families in the kingdom, so that a mulatto might actually become a member of a family in which his mother had been a slave.

Wealthy mulattoes sometimes managed to cross the color line. Napoleon's dislike for the colored race may, in part, have been due to the fact that he did not relish having a mulatto brother-in-law. A sister of the Empress Josephine had married a mulatto named Castaigns. There were some two hundred white men in the colony married to mulattresses. In 1788 a royal edict forbade marriage between whites and mulattoes or Negroes.

Mulatto slaveowners identified their interests with those of the white planters and had the reputation of being even harder taskmasters than their white colleagues.

## 2

The St. Domingo census of 1774 lists over seven thousand mulattresses, five thousand of whom are listed as white men's concubines. Since there were twice as many white men as white women in the colony this is not surprising. A mulatto concubine was, for that matter, as necessary to a married planter as to a bachelor. She was the link between the plantation house and the slave quarter. Where two or three white men lived on a lonely plantation in the midst of a hundred times that many slaves, the link was indispensable. The safety of the planter and of his family often depended on the loyalty of the concubine.

Mulattresses had the reputation of being vain, extravagant and lascivious, but also of being kind, generous and compassionate. They were far more skillful than their white sisters in attracting men and in keeping them interested. They possessed greater gaiety and vitality, were better-natured and less exacting. White women found their taste vulgar, but men liked the originality with which they dressed and arranged their hair.

Once the white women of Le Cap struck a telling blow at their rivals by prevailing upon the authorities to issue a decree forbidding mulatto women to appear in public wearing silk clothing and without a handkerchief knotted about the head. The Abbé Grégoire says that guards were stationed in the streets and at the doors of churches who tore the clothes off mulattresses wearing the forbidden finery "until they were dressed only in their modesty." The mulatto women struck back by ceasing to go out. The result upon trade was so disastrous that the merchants demanded and obtained the revocation of the decree.

# CHAPTER VI

## The Slave Traffic

As early as 1503 a few Negroes had been transported from Guinea to Hispaniola and sold into slavery. Much hardier than the Indians, they were incomparably better suited for plantation work. The old Spanish historian Herrera says: "The African prospered so much in the colony that it was the opinion that unless a Negro should happen to be hung he would never die, for as yet none had been known to perish from infirmity." And we are assured that "The work of one Negro was more than equal to that of four Indians."

In 1516 Charles V granted a patent to a Flemish favorite to import annually 4000 Negroes into Haiti, Cuba, Jamaica and Puerto Rico. The courtier had no intention of engaging in the traffic himself, but sold his patent to Genoese merchants, who disposed of it to Portuguese.

The slave trade was at first poorly organized, or rather not organized at all. Captains trading along the African coast usually brought a few Negroes along with their cargo of gold, ivory and gum. As the demand for slaves increased, it was found that to be really profitable the traffic should be organized. Hence, along the west coast of Africa, from Cape Verde to the equator, "slave factories" were established.

A "slave factory" was a combined fort and trading post. Within the fortified enclosure were the soldiers' barracks, offices, warehouses, living quarters of officials, etc. Here the slaves were accumulated and kept until the arrival of the slave ship. The man in charge of trading operations was the factor. He remained at the fort and directed the activities of junior factors, scattered in the interior, who kept a steady flow of slaves moving towards the factory. By exciting the cupidity of a chieftain they often induced him to condemn scores of his own subjects to be sold into slavery. By displaying a clasp knife, a string of beads, a bright piece of cloth before the eager eyes of primitive people, they would get a husband to sell his wife, parents to sell their children, children to sell their parents.

It has been estimated that in the course of three centuries – from 1500 to 1800 – thirty million Negroes were taken from Africa and sold into slavery. One million of these were brought to the French colony of St. Domingo. Moreau de Saint-Méry estimates that in 1789, at the outbreak of the Revolution, two thirds of the slaves in the colony were African-born.

## 2

Negro slave traders drove the slaves to the factory, yoked together neck to neck with heavy forked poles and linked together with chains. Through blazing heat, through torrential rain, through dense jungles and over the parched African plain, fording streams infested by crocodiles, lashed by the whips of the drivers, stung by insects, torn by briars, the black men, women and children toiled on towards the factory. Here they were herded into "trunks" – barracks devoid of furnishings or sanitation – to await the coming of the slave ship.

Testimony before a Select Committee of the House of Commons proves that as many as six hundred slaves were loaded into a vessel of one hundred and twenty tons. The male slaves, completely naked, had a chain running from wrist to ankle. They were driven into the hold and forced to lie down on wooden shelves, built one above the other. The space allotted to each was "not over a foot and a half in width and five feet and six inches in length." Since the distance between the shelves was found to be "two feet in many cases and two feet and a few inches in the rest," the testimony of the captain who said: "They had not so much space as a man in a coffin," was not a mere figure of speech. Each slave was now fastened to a ringbolt in the floor, or to an iron bar running the entire length of the shelf. Women and children were not chained, but had little more space.

The voyage lasted from five weeks to eighty days, depending on the wind and the location of the factory. The reader will be reminded of the Black Hole of Calcutta and wonder why the consequences were not equally disastrous. The reason was that the slaves were frequently taken out on deck for exercise. The exercise consisted in making them jump up and down in their chains. This was called "dancing" by the slave traders. If they refused to dance they were beaten with a cat-o'-nine-tails.

The average death rate during the voyage was between seven and eight per cent, but in some cases half the cargo was lost. Taking into account those who died on the way to the factory, in the trunks, in the raging surf when the light boats upset that carried the Negroes to the ship, on arrival at their destination and during the "seasoning process," not more than half the slaves purchased by the factors lived to work on a plantation.

# CHAPTER VII

## Household Slaves and Field Slaves

On their arrival at Le Cap, the principal slave mart of St. Domingo, the slaves were herded into barracks at some distance from the city. An inspection of these barracks, made in 1784 by order of the Minister of Marine, is stated in the official report to have "revealed a revolting scene of dead and dying strewn pell-mell in filth."

When a slave was purchased he, or she, was branded on the breast with the owner's initials. The practice had been abandoned throughout the West Indies, but persisted in St. Domingo. A report submitted by the St. Domingo planters to the French National Assembly after the outbreak of the slave rebellion assures us, however, that the condition of the Negroes in the colony left little to be desired. The report says: –

> Let any fair-minded and well-informed person compare the deplorable state of the Negroes in Africa with the mild and pleasant lot of those in our colonies. Guaranteed against want; supplied with comforts unknown to the greater part of the peasants of Europe; secure in the enjoyment of their property (for they had property and it was sacred); nursed in times of sickness at a cost and with a care unknown in the vaunted hospitals of England; protected and respected in the infirmity of old age; at ease in respect to their children, their relatives and their friends; subjected to a labor proportioned to the strength of each individual; enfranchised when they merited it – such was the true, unvarnished picture of the lot of our Negroes.

One is reminded of Lincoln's query why those who vaunted the advantages of slavery to the slaves never applied for the privilege of becoming slaves themselves.

The report admits that some slaveowners abused their power: –

> Not that we would deny that there did exist among the planters a very small number of hard and ferocious masters. But what was the lot of these wicked men? Abhorred, detested by men of character, ostracized, discredited, they lived in disgrace and dishonor, and died in misery and despair.

## 2

Consideration of the lot of the slaves makes it necessary to separate them into two principal groups – household slaves and field slaves.

Authorities agree that household slaves were, as a rule, not ill-treated; but they were as much at the mercy of their masters as the field slaves, and the testimony before the Select Committee contains accounts of hair-raising cruelties inflicted by sadistic masters upon household slaves. Granted that in the case of household slaves such treatment was exceptional, yet the fact remains that it did take place and that the slaves had no redress.

Household slaves were usually Creole Negroes. They were a privileged class among the slaves and looked down upon the field slaves, most of whom were African-born. They sometimes obtained their freedom, either for faithful service, or for amorous satisfaction given to the master or mistress. A free Negro was practically always a former household slave or the descendant of one.

A planter's social standing depended in a large measure on the number of household slaves kept by him. Moreau de Saint-Méry says that most St. Domingo planters kept from four to eight times as many as they needed. When a planter gave a formal dinner there was often a slave behind every chair, so that much needed circulation was impeded. Under these circumstances household slaves were not overworked. In fact, they were idle most of the time. Each had some small special task to perform and if ordered to do anything else felt that he was imposed upon. "The generous hospitality with which travelers were received on the island and the sight of the many more or less indolent and smiling household slaves busily engaged doing nothing, have betrayed such travelers into attempting an apology of slavery," says Peytraud.

When the master was good to him, the household slave sometimes developed a genuine affection for him. When the slaves rose in revolt many planters and their families were saved by their household slaves. But not the least remarkable feature of the St. Domingo slave uprising was that household slaves whom their masters had treated with every consideration nevertheless felt their solidarity with the field slaves. Having led their masters to safety, they usually joined the rebels.

## 3

The field slaves were the proletariat of the slave world. On their arrival at the plantation they were assigned to one of three principal groups. The first comprised vigorous men and women; the second, the old, the weak, adolescents and women with child; the third was composed of children, whose work mainly consisted of gathering grass for the cattle.

The field slaves were wakened before sunrise by the cracking of the whips of the drivers – mulatto and Negro freedmen. The whip-crack was the most characteristic sound on a St. Domingo plantation. It gave the signal to rise in the morning, to kneel for prayer, to commence or to cease work. "The cracking of whips, suppressed cries of pain, the dull moaning of Negroes take the place of the crowing of the cock. It is to such infernal sounds as these that I awakened from sleep the morning after my arrival in St. Domingo," writes de Wimpffen.

The workday was exceedingly long. The Negroes were in the field from dawn until sunset, without any respite except the time necessary to swallow their food. "They have no more than three or four hours' sleep, especially in harvest time," says du Tertre. Governor de Gallifet writes: "The majority of the colonists force their Negroes to work beyond human endurance, all day and the greater part of the night." Witnesses before the Select Committee testified that "the slaves work as long as they can keep awake or can stand on their legs."

If the slave worked at the mill, failing to keep awake might have serious consequences. A hand or arm might be caught in the machinery, or the sleep-drugged unfortunate might fall into a cauldron of boiling sugar. To keep the slaves awake the overseer frequently ordered them to sing, which appears to have misled superficial observers.

For their many hours of toil the slaves were entitled to food, clothing and shelter. The Black Code specified that adult slaves were to receive a weekly ration of two measures and a half of manioc, or three of cassava, and two pounds of salted beef, or three of fish. The law, however, was disregarded. In St. Domingo only one planter out of every four gave any rations whatever to his slaves. Planters in the French colony had adopted a system originating in Brazil which relieved them of all responsibility to feed or clothe their slaves. Each Negro family was assigned a plot of land on which to raise fruit and vegetables for its private consumption. Whatever surplus the slaves had they could sell in town on Sunday, and purchase meat, fish and clothing. To enable them to cultivate their land they were given Saturday as well as Sunday free. In 1782, Baron de St. Victor, who was far from being an abolitionist, wrote: "Three fourths of the masters of St. Domingo do not feed their slaves and rob them of all the leisure to which the law entitles them. It is too much! Sooner or later despair will drive these unfortunates to extremes."

His prediction came true within a decade. The Negroes of

St. Domingo did not, as is generally supposed, rebel to obtain their liberty. At the beginning of the rebellion not even Toussaint Louverture believed emancipation possible. Their principal demand was for one additional day a week in which to cultivate their allotments of land.

Hunger was so prevalent among the St. Domingo slaves that many spent part of the night roaming the country in search of food, that is, robbing the gardens of Negroes on neighboring plantations and those of small white farmers and free mulattoes. The Intendant Patoulet wrote to the Minister of Marine that measures should be taken to compel the planters to feed their slaves, which would "bring relief to people harassed and often ruined by slaves who steal and pillage, hunting food wherever they can, because their masters do not feed them."

Testimony before the Select Committee shows that in the British West Indies those too old to work "had no food except what they could get from such relations as they might have had." It is hardly to be supposed that in St. Domingo, where even able-bodied slaves were not fed, things were different. The claim of the planters that the slaves were "protected and respected in the infirmity of old age," would, if true, confer credit upon the relations of the superannuated slaves, but hardly on the slaveowners. It was likewise shown that many planters did not care to have such useless slaves around and "drove them forth to plunder, beg or steal."

# CHAPTER VIII

## Man's Inhumanity to Man

In theory the slaveowner's power over his slave was limited. The Black Code forbade the master to inflict corporal punishment upon his slave for anything except laxness in his work, and then only to a very limited degree. All other offenses were to be punished by the authorities, whom no one ever accused of undue leniency towards the slaves. But the law was not and could not be enforced. Plantations were often far removed from the nearest community. Besides, masters felt that punishment inflicted in the presence of their slaves was more effective.

Slaves had the right to complain to the authorities, but Governor Gallifet and other colonial officials frankly admitted that this provision of the law was meaningless. Hilliard d'Auberteuil, who did not wish to abolish slavery, but to reform it, writes: "Negroes die daily in chains and under the lash. They are beaten, strangled, burned to death without any legal formality. Every act of cruelty against them remains unpunished. In St. Domingo any white man can ill-treat a Negro with impunity. The situation is such that the Negroes may be said to be the slaves not only of their masters, but also of the general public. An injury done to a slave is considered by the magistrates only from the point of view of the pecuniary damage suffered by the owners."

In 1786, the King of France, aroused by the reports of colonial officials, issued an edict which did honor to his intentions. Slave-owners were forbidden to administer more than fifty lashes to a slave. Violators were to be fined 2000 livres for the first offense and at the second violation were to be enjoined from owning slaves. If a slave died as a result of punishment inflicted by his master, the penalty was death.

The fact that so severe an edict was deemed necessary proves that the situation was serious. Unfortunately this law, like nearly all others designed to humanize slavery, proved ineffective. The edict was put to the test in 1788, when the planter Le Jeune committed such cruelties against his slaves that fourteen of them, in fear of their lives, ran to Le Cap to seek protection. The magistrates went to the plantation. They found that Le Jeune had killed four slaves and had put two Negresses to the torture. The women were laden with chains, their feet, legs and buttocks horribly burned, their wounds festering. One had an iron collar fastened tightly around her neck, preventing her from swallowing. Both died as a result of the ordeal.

A warrant for Le Jeune's arrest was issued, but he disappeared. The Governor and the Intendant wrote in a joint report to the Minister of Marine: – "On the 23rd of March we received a petition from a group of citizens – by no means those worthy of least respect – declaring their solidarity with the Sieur Le Jeune and demanding that the slaves who denounced him should each receive fifty lashes." The case was tried and Le Jeune acquitted. The government appealed, but the Supreme Court, showered with demands, threats and petitions, confirmed the acquittal. "In a word," writes the Intendant, "it would appear that the safety of the colony depends on the acquittal of the Sieur Le Jeune."

## 2

The most common form of punishment was flogging. The whip with which the punishment was administered is thus described in the Abstract of Evidence of the Select Committee: "The whip is generally made of plaited cow-skin, with a thick, strong lash. It is so formidable an instrument in the hands of some overseers, that by means of it they can take the skin off a horse's back. He [the witness] has heard them boast of laying the marks of it in a deal board and has seen it done. On its application to a slave's back, he has seen blood spurt on the first stroke."

Other witnesses testified that "at every stroke a piece of flesh was drawn out," that "it will even bring blood through the clothes," that "such is the effusion of blood as to make their frocks, if immediately put on, appear as stiff as buckram," that "the incisions are sometimes so deep you may lay your fingers in the wounds."

Other punishments considered legitimate were branding the

slave upon the cheek, putting him in irons or in the stocks, making him wear an iron collar (often with projections extending high above the head, to make escape into the forest impossible), cutting off one or both ears. A disciplinary expert in St. Domingo advised cutting off the nose instead of the ears, to prevent Negroes from hiding the mutilation by wearing a handkerchief.

Notwithstanding the premeditated destruction of court records in St. Domingo, the list of well-authenticated "extraordinary" punishments is found to include: throwing the slave alive into a flaming furnace; suspending him by arms and legs over a slow fire; burying alive; burying up to the neck and smearing head and face with burnt sugar, to attract flies and other insects; tying into a bag and drowning; rubbing the body with sugar and pouring spoonfuls of ants into all the bodily cavities; stuffing into a barrel into which nails had been driven and rolling down a mountainside; ladling boiling sugar over the victim's shaven head; forcing him to eat human excrements; hanging by the ears, or with head down; amputating the genitals; stuffing gunpowder into the rectum and causing it to explode (this was a favorite form of punishment and went by the name of *brûler un peu de poudre au cul d'un nègre*); applying fire to the genitals, crucifying, etc.

There is abundant evidence to show that no matter how barbarous a planter's conduct towards his slaves, he had no reason to fear ostracism. Baron de Wimpffen wrote in 1790 from St. Domingo to a friend: "A woman whom I have seen, a young woman, one of the most beautiful on the island, gave a formal dinner. When a platter with cakes that had not turned out well was served, she became infuriated and ordered her Negro cook seized and thrown into the furnace in which the fire was still burning. This horrible termagant, whose name I withhold out of consideration for her family, still daily receives the homage of society, for she has wealth and beauty."

Indeed, it appears that barbarous conduct towards one's slaves evoked admiration and heightened a man's repute. On July 18,

1791, Guiton, an agent of the *Club Massiac*, the famous planters' club in Paris, wrote a letter to Billard, the president of the club, in which he says: –

> If a man is needed who does not scruple to cut off heads, Citizen General de Caradeux (Commander of the district of Port-au-Prince) is the man to put in charge. When he was manager of the Aubry plantation he chopped off about fifty. So that the lesson might not be lost, he had them stuck upon pickets, all along the plantation hedge, as another might plant palms, and as if it were the most natural decoration in the world.

## 3

In St. Domingo the death rate among the slaves exceeded the birth rate by two and a half per cent. Had the traffic been abolished and slavery been maintained, the Negroes would have disappeared in forty years as completely as the Indians. "There is hardly a plantation in the colony," says Frossard, "where the number of slaves can be maintained without annual purchases." This, we are assured by the apologists of the slaveowners, was because the planters preferred buying slaves to breeding them, as pregnancy interfered with the work. To this argument, which bears little relation to truth, Leroy-Beaulieu has added the further argument that "by some fundamental law of nature slavery hinders man's reproductive capacity, as captivity does that of wild animals." Whether this be true or not, it has no bearing on the situation in St. Domingo, where the birth rate was not low, but remarkably high – between eight and nine per cent. The Negroes are a prolific race. With or without encouragement, they continued to breed.

The reason thousands of Negroes had to be imported annually to bridge the gap between birth and death rate, was due not to a low birth rate, but to an appallingly high death rate. In his report to the French National Assembly, Garran-Coulon gives the annual death rate among the slaves of St. Domingo as eleven per cent – "higher," he says, "than the death rate during many a bloody battle." Frossard says that it was one-third higher than the death rate in the hospitals of Lyons. *Every year one ninth of the slaves in St. Domingo died.* It would have had to be an extraordinary birth rate to have kept pace with such slaughter. It is interesting to note that the population, which slavery would have exterminated in forty years, trebled in the thirty-eight years following the abolition of slavery, although the importation of Negroes had entirely ceased.

How could such a wanton waste of life have been in the interest of the planters?

Light is thrown upon this matter by testimony before the Select Committee. Plantation managers testified that experience had shown it to be profitable to amortize a slave in seven years and during that period to drive him to the limit of his endurance. If at the conclusion of that period he died or became useless, it did not matter; he had been amortized; a new slave could be bought to take his place. A Jamaican super-efficiency expert called Yeman testified that in his opinion even better results could be obtained by exhausting the slave in four years.

## 4

Something can and should be said in defense of the planters. It is only the exceptional man who is endowed with creative imagination enough to resist appearances with gifts in their hands. The average man is the dupe of such appearances. It should also be considered that few of the planters came in direct contact with the field slaves. Usually they employed managers. Ignorance they could not plead, but they could have pleaded that their susceptibilities were not directly engaged. And they could have pleaded that acts of cruelty to which we become accustomed not only fail to shock us, but may even become a source of enjoyment – witness the attraction of the arena at Rome to all classes of Roman citizens.

The owners of the largest plantations did not live in St. Domingo, but in France. Some were cultured men, and it is but reasonable to suppose that on their rare visits to the colony they were shocked by what they saw. But unless one is a born altruist, does one quarrel with a manager who makes one's capital yield twenty-five per cent or more? Does one even risk interfering with him?

The resident planters were, with few exceptions, anxious to leave the colony and live in France, an ambition seven out of every ten were able to satisfy. Undoubtedly there were some who were painfully affected by the wretched lot of the field slaves, by the enormous mortality rate. But the method the managers were using was known to give the best financial results. Should one condemn oneself and one's family to perpetual exile in the colony to make the slaves more comfortable? Should one see one's friends and neighbors depart while one remained behind? No! One owed it to oneself and to one's children to flee this brutalizing atmosphere as quickly as possible. In the meantime one shut one's eyes to what went on in the sugar field and in the mill, and found comfort in benevolence towards the household slaves.

As for the managers – in a colony where the proprietors were either absentee owners or anxious to be gone, it was inevitable that ruthless men, able to produce rapid results, should have replaced those whose milder methods proved less remunerative. There were a few exceptions. Sometimes a big-hearted planter hired a humane manager and told him he was willing to take the consequences of a milder policy. Such men, not the Le Jeunes, had to fear the ostracism of their colleagues, for their methods created greater dissatisfaction among the slaves of neighboring plantations.

# CHAPTER IX

## What Sort of People Were the Slaves?

ONE can glean from the authorities almost any opinion one wishes about the Negro slaves. Does one desire support for the claim that they were by nature indolent? One can find it in the writings of Moreau de Saint-Méry, who says: "The Africans were indolent and lazy." Does one prefer to represent them as industrious? One can quote Hilliard d'Auberteuil, who says: "They are industrious when not discouraged." De Charmilly considers them timid; de Reille says: "They have great courage before real danger," but maintains that they were of "mediocre intelligence." In this he is contradicted by d'Auberteuil, who says: "I know of no other race possessing greater natural intelligence."

Perhaps it is safest to take the opinion of a comparative outsider, a man of keen intelligence and few prejudices, who spent many months in the colony, was neither a slaveowner nor an abolitionist, and numbered many planters among his friends – de Wimpffen. In a letter to a friend he writes: –

> One will find among the Negroes some that are good, some that are bad, some that are admirable, others who are detestable. The example of Creole Negroes who have shown themselves capable of acquiring art and virtue when their masters have pointed the way and have given them the opportunity, proves that the inferiority of the African is largely a matter of education. It seems absurd to believe that the comparatively slight physical difference which distinguishes the average white man from the average Negro should prove an insurmountable obstacle for the latter to attain the norm of intelligence and perfection of which the former is capable.

Many of the defects and vices of which white contemporaries of the Negro slaves complain have no racial significance, but were the result of slavery. White men kept in slavery would have developed similar characteristics, just as mulatto slaveowners acquired characteristics peculiar to the slaveowner. When Aristotle said: "Slavery excludes any kind of virtue," he may have been exaggerating, but he had white slaves, not black, in mind. De Charmilly, one of the few who differentiates between racial and slave characteristics, lists among the latter indolence, gluttony, dishonesty, falsehood and vindictiveness.

## 2

If one thing is characteristic of the African race, it is its amazing ability to wring a few drops of joy from the most hopeless situations – to laugh, to sing, to dance in the face of injustice and tyranny, to mock the oppressor by a gaiety all his power cannot buy him. The Negro has the ability to live in the moment. It is a power children have and philosophers have vainly striven to attain through the power of the intellect. To banish the phantoms of past and future, to know nothing but the moment and its intensity of pleasure or pain – what liberty!

The field slaves laughed and sang and danced whenever they had the least excuse or opportunity. When Alexander von Humboldt wrote after his voyage to the West Indies: "Every evening the slaves of both sexes were to be seen dancing in festive circles – and the sound of music and the voice of gladness were heard on all sides," he proved not that he understood what was happening in the Antilles, but that he did not understand Negro character. "They sing on their deathbeds," wrote the amazed du Tertre. "They advanced against us singing, for the Negro sings everywhere and makes songs about everything," wrote Lamour-Delafosse about the soldiers of Toussaint Louverture. Captains of slave ships related before the Select Committee how Negroes sang in the holds of ships amidst corpses. "Their bodies," writes du Tertre, "might be subjected to the terrible ordeal of slavery, but their souls have remained free."

They loved dancing even better than singing. Their favorite dance was the *chica*, which is of phallic origin. "Their passion for it," writes Father Labat, "surpasses all imagination. All take part in it, the old, the young, even children barely able to stand. One might think they had danced it in their mothers' wombs."

The dance orchestra was composed of two drums, one long, the other short. They were of hollowed logs, with goat- or sheepskin stretched over the openings. A man or boy would sit astride each drum and beat upon the sheepskin with the tips of his fingers and the ball of his hand. One player beat fast, the other slow. The rhythmic sound thus produced had a hypnotic quality. It was like the pulsating of the blood in one's veins. The drums were often supplemented by the twanging of a four-stringed instrument resembling a violin, and always by the clapping of hands, the shaking of small hollowed gourds in which dried grains of maize were rattling, and weird, seemingly discordant chanting that yet obeyed some primitive law of harmony.

At the commencement of the dance, the two sexes, arms akimbo, would face each other in two rows, some distance apart. Then the dancers would begin swaying slowly, in rhythm to the music. First the shoulders, then the hips, finally the whole body would sway, twitch and shake. Slowly the two rows would now advance towards each other, stopping now and then to engage in more violent contortions. At last men and women, boys and girls, would stand face to face, eye probing into eye. They would provoke, invite, taunt each other with look, gesture and movement – circle around each other, sometimes stopping to rub bellies and thighs together, after which they would recoil, as if violently repulsed, or resoundingly slap each other's buttocks. Then the music would break off suddenly, and when a moment later it recommenced, the rows would have reformed and would fall back slowly, to come to a final halt and begin a fresh advance. This was repeated over and over, sometimes for hours, and however tired or hungry a slave might be, he found strength to join in the dancing.

## 3

The planters and their managers considered the Christian religion dangerous doctrine when taught to a slave. Says Giraud-Chantrans: "The slaveowners of St. Domingo, far from being worried about their slaves living without religion, are pleased. In their opinion the Catholic religion contains elements that might generate ideas of equality in the mind of the Negro." Their opinion was shared by officialdom in the French Antilles. Governor de Fénélon of Martinique wrote to the Minister of Marine: "I arrived in the Antilles favoring instruction which the principles of our religion command, but I became convinced that the security of the white population requires keeping the Negroes in profound ignorance."

The law, however, required the planters to acquaint the Negroes with the principles of the Catholic religion and to have them baptized. Baptism took place in this manner: –

A hundred or so Negroes, freshly arrived from Africa, would be herded into a church. Whips cracked and they were ordered to kneel. A priest and his acolytes appeared before the altar and Mass was said. Then the priest, followed by an acolyte carrying a basin with holy water, walked slowly down the aisle and with vigorous swings of the aspergillum scattered the water over the heads of the crowd, chanting in Latin. The whips cracked again, the slaves rose from their knees and emerged into the sunlight, converts to the Christian religion.

It is therefore not surprising that when the Negroes felt in need of religious consolation they turned to their African religion, known as "voodoo" or *vodun*.

Volumes have been written about the voodoo religion, which is a combined nature and ancestor worship. Voodoo or *vodun* means God, and is a generic name for all the gods of the voodoo pantheon. Some of these, the *rada*, are nature gods, with dominion over the sky, the earth, the sea, the soul, etc.; others, the *petro*, are deified ancestors, who intervene with the nature gods on behalf of the worshiper and may be compared with the saints. There is a host of spirits, called *loa*, whose power is limited, but who can work only good. They may be compared with the angels and often exercise the function of guardian angels. The chief god is *Damballa*, whose symbol is the serpent.

Slave traders being no respectors of persons, there was no lack of voodoo priests and priestesses in the colony. The priests, called *huñgans*, and the priestesses, called *mambus*, continued to exercise their calling. By day they might be indistinguishable from other slaves, but at night, officiating at a voodoo ceremonial in the depth of the forest or in some lonely ravine, they were important personages, representatives of a religion as old as the human race.

When the planter and his overseers had retired for the night and all was quiet on the plantation, there often could be heard – so faintly that only an African ear could catch it – the far-off throbbing of the voodoo drums. Soon dark figures cautiously emerged. Unerringly guided by the sound, they found their way to where the voodoo priest or priestess, fantastically arrayed, waited before an improvised altar. On the altar, in the midst of gourds filled with offerings of corn, cassava, figs, oil and so on, stood the carved image of a serpent.

The ceremony varied in accordance with the occasion, but there was usually a blood offering, the animals most frequently sacrificed being pigeons, hens, roosters, goats or pigs. Some writers have claimed that human sacrifices took place occasionally, but the evidence is not convincing and the statement is emphatically denied by Negro scholars.

When the animal had been sacrificed, the worshipers drank of the blood, which was usually mixed with rum and sometimes with gunpowder. Under the influence of the pulsating beat of the drums, the religious exultation and the strong drink, there took place a ritual dance that had some terrifying aspects. As the dance progressed the participants lost control over their bodies, which apparently became the playthings of invisible hands that shook, jerked and twisted them, as if they were rag dolls. The head swung limply, as if the neck had been broken, the eyes bulged and stared, the lips foamed. Now and then a ghostly manipulator relinquished his prey, which immediately collapsed; or a dancer suddenly stiffened and toppled over like a ninepin. At the conclusion of the dance the priest and his entire congregation might be lying in a coma.

The fact that the Negroes possessed a religion and a priesthood of their own, so that slaves from different plantations met secretly in the forest, was of immense significance in the events that were to come. Some of the voodoo priests used their influence to arouse the slaves to revolt. Long before Toussaint Louverture methodically organized the rebellion, chants of revolt and prayers invoking the aid of the voodoo deities against the white man were heard in the nocturnal gatherings.

# CHAPTER X

## How the Slaves Fought Back

So effective was the terror maintained by the planters that until the great insurrection of 1791, such slave rebellions as took place in St. Domingo were negligible. It is claimed that in 1757 a bold attempt was made by the Negroes to capture Le Cap, but the evidence is somewhat doubtful. If, however, the slaves did not rebel, it was not from lack of inclination. They fought back as best they could, with such weapons as were at their disposal — suicide, poison, conspiracy.

"They kill themselves, hang themselves, cut their own throats, often for trifling reasons, usually with the object of injuring their masters," writes Father Labat. There were suicide pacts, when a dozen or more slaves on a plantation would hang themselves simultaneously, as if heeding Seneca's counsel: "You complain of being a slave? See that tree? Freedom hangs from its branches."

Suicide was favored by the belief, current among the Negroes, that death was a form of migration to Africa. If a slave died, his relatives never said "He is dead," but "He has gone away." As it was virtually impossible to keep a slave from destroying himself if he had a mind to do so, the owners faced a difficult problem, which they met by taking advantage of a Negro superstition. Most of the Negroes believed that when a corpse is mutilated the disfigurement persists in after-life. Hence, when a slave killed himself, the master cut off the head and hands, or the nose and ears, as a warning to his remaining slaves. Since spending eternity deprived of such useful organs had obvious disadvantages, most slaves preferred to live out the short span of their existence.

## 2

The weapon the slaveowners dreaded most was poison. "Poison," writes Xavier Eyma, "is the offensive as well as the defensive weapon of the slave." There were over a quarter of a million cattle in the colony, but so many died of poisoning that the industry was considered extremely hazardous. Le Pole, a celebrated veterinary at Le Cap, wrote a monograph on the subject, in which he says: "It is not without reason that a million [sic] slaves whom the masters have entrusted with the care of cattle, have died under the lash or at the stake." In 1777 a Negro named Jacques was burned at the stake for having poisoned over a hundred head of cattle. An official memorandum, addressed in 1726 to the Minister of Marine, says: "It would be impossible to believe to what extent the Negroes make use of poison if there were not a thousand examples on every hand.

There are few colonists who have not suffered loss and many have been ruined."

Slaves often killed fellow slaves to injure their masters. On the Larnage plantation, in 1737, one hundred slaves died of poisoning out of a total of one hundred and fifty. The planter Le Jeune, who was prosecuted for his cruelty towards his slaves, lost, in the course of two years, fifty-seven Negroes and thirty mules by poison. His father, in the course of twenty-five years, lost over four hundred slaves in the same manner, fifty-two dying during a six-month period.

The poison commonly used was arsenic. It was easily procurable, since the planters were forced to use large quantities of the drug in combating the dreaded sugar ant. The household slaves of doctors and apothecaries did a thriving business selling arsenic and other poisons to those unable to supply themselves any other way. The slaves, however, had numerous sources of supply. They used dogwood root, black-eye, ground glass, chopped horse's tail. One of the commonest poisons used was germ-laden earth taken from graves. No less an authority than Pasteur has warned against the dangers of cemetery soil, so the instinct of the slaves did not deceive them. "There appear," says Peytraud, "to have existed veritable secret associations of slaves to manufacture, distribute and administer poison to the cattle and to the colonists."

It is easy to understand the effect of all this on the nervous systems of the slaveowners. Some of the gruesome punishments inflicted upon slaves were undoubtedly the result of hysterical fear. Many a planter who had a stomach ache imagined himself poisoned and tortured a slave to force him to confess. It is claimed that colonists sometimes died as a result of a toxic condition produced by the imagination.

## 3

Poison figures in what is claimed to have been the boldest attempt made by the Negroes before the Revolution to throw off the yoke of slavery. A Negro named Macandal is the supposed originator of the plot. While Macandal's attempt to poison the white inhabitants of Le Cap is credited by historians, it must be said that documentary evidence is lacking. A semi-official memorandum, written in 1779 (twenty-two years after the supposed attempt), gives the story of the plot, but furnishes no proof. The records of Macandal's trial show that he was accused of being "a seducer, profaner and poisoner," but no evidence of any such widespread conspiracy as is related in the memorandum was introduced. There is good reason to believe that the author of the memorandum accepted without questioning a legend to which the poisoning obsession of the colonists had given birth.

Macandal, who, whatever the truth about the poison plot, must be regarded as Toussaint Louverture's principal forerunner, was a Maroon chieftain. Maroon Negroes were fugitive slaves or the offspring of fugitives. They lived in inaccessible camps in the mountains and supported themselves by hunting and pillaging. They made the roads unsafe and sometimes attacked lonely plantations, driving off the cattle and taking the slaves with them. A colony of several thousand Maroon Negroes, living in the mountains along the Spanish border, became such a menace that, in 1784, the government made a treaty with them, recognizing their independence for a promise of good behavior.

Macandal, the most famous of their chieftains, was an African Negro, born in Guinea. He had been a slave on the Lenormand plantation near Le Cap. Having lost a hand in the mill, he was put to guarding cattle, which gave him ample time to reflect. About the year 1751, he escaped and soon rose to leadership among the Maroons. What to his predecessors had been merely a means of obtaining booty, was to him guerrilla warfare intended to free the Negroes from white domination. He held meetings in the woods and Negroes would walk miles and risk severe punishment to hear him speak.

According to the memorandum before mentioned, Macandal resolved, in 1757, to capture Le Cap. Lacking military strength, he decided to use poison. He had thousands of packets of poison distributed among the Negroes of the city, with instructions that on a given day they were to poison any food or beverage the whites were likely to absorb. When the white population was in the throes of death, he would descend from the mountains with his warriors and kill the survivors. The plot was discovered and frustrated in the nick of time.

Like many another prophet, Macandal had a tragic end, due to a weakness common in the profession – love of strong drink, women and dancing. In his wild retreat he kept a well-assorted harem, and when he heard about a dance on some plantation near where he was encamped, it was hard for him to remain away. He ran comparatively little risk in attending such dances, for no Negro would betray him, and few white men had ever seen him.

One Sunday he attended a dance at the Dufresne plantation near Le Cap. It so happened that the paramour of a Negro on the plantation had been seduced by the prophet and had followed him into the forest. The deserted lover forgot his awe of the holy man and betrayed his presence to the manager. The white man distributed a large quantity of rum among the dancers and soon all, including the prophet, were helplessly drunk. Macandal was seized, securely tied and taken to the office. A messenger was sent on horseback to notify the authorities at Le Cap. It was night, so the manager and a white assistant took turns in keeping an eye on the prisoner and his Negro guards. The manager dozed off, awakening just in time to see Macandal disappear through a window.

The escape availed the Negro little. Dogs trailed him, he was recaptured and lodged in prison at Le Cap, where he died at the stake, in March, 1758. As the flames licked his body, he wrenched himself loose from the chains that bound him, but collapsed in the fire and gave up the ghost. His followers claimed that he had metamorphosed himself into a mosquito and had flown away, to resume human shape later.

# CHAPTER XI

## The Revolution Comes to St. Domingo

THE absentee slaveowners living in Paris had formed a club known as the "*Club Massiac.*" When, in May 1789, the States-General was called to meet at Versailles, the members of the club felt that the colony should send commissioners to negotiate what might be termed "dominion status." The resident planters, while no less anxious to obtain self-government for the colony, thought better results could be obtained by electing deputies to the new representative body. Defying officialdom, which did not consider the colony entitled to representation of any kind, they called an election. In each province invitations were sent to planters considered socially and financially eligible to attend a gathering at the house of one of their number. The *Almanach de Gotha* must have been used as a guide, for the eighteen Deputies chosen (six from each province) all boasted noble lineage. They were provided with a *cahier* embodying the grievances of the planters and proposing a remedy. The principal grievances were of course the Colonial Pact and lack of self-government; the remedy proposed was a Colonial Assembly elected exclusively by the great landed proprietors.

Now, the members of the French National Assembly, which emerged from the States-General, were, with few exceptions, solid property owners or respectable members of the bar. They had no intention of upsetting the apple cart and having the mob scramble for the apples. A mountain of oratory frequently produced a legislative mouse. Some had itching palms, a discomfort the planters were prepared to allay. With the help of the Colonial Committee, the Deputies from St. Domingo managed to get what they wanted – a Colonial Assembly the manner of whose election assured control by the great landed proprietors.

## 2

The free mulattoes had elected a Commissioner, Julien Raimond, to look after their interests in France. He was a wealthy and cultured young mulatto who had been residing in Paris for some time. Although a slaveowner, he favored a gradual abolition of slavery and had many friends in the *Société des Amis des Noirs*, the French abolitionist society – to which such important men as Lafayette, Brissot, Clavière, Grégoire and Robespierre belonged. Granting civic rights to the mulattoes seemed to them a step in the right direction, and when Raimond made his plea before the National Assembly he did not lack supporters. There can be no doubt that when the Colonial Assembly was created it had been the intention of the National Assembly to grant the mulattoes civic rights, but the decree was so ambiguously worded that it could be interpreted either way. When the election was called the mulattoes were bluntly told that they would not be permitted to vote.

Now, there was a mulatto in Paris less patient than Raimond. His name was Vincent Ogé. His widowed mother possessed a plantation near Dondon, in the North Province, and owned a number of slaves, but Ogé favored abolition, although not in the immediate future. For the present he was mostly concerned about the injustice done to the mulatto caste. He decided to return to St. Domingo and organize the mulattoes into an armed body capable of defending their rights. The *Club Massiac*, however, got wind of his project and was sufficiently powerful to make it impossible for any man of color to embark at a French port. But the *Amis des Noirs* were not without influence themselves and with their help Ogé finally reached London, where he was received by Clarkson, Secretary of the English Abolitionist Society. With Clarkson's help he crossed the ocean to Charleston, where American abolitionists arranged his passage for St. Domingo and furnished him money with which to buy arms.

Before leaving France, Ogé had purchased a colonel's commission in the army of the Duke of Luxembourg, which gave him the right to wear a natty gold-braided uniform calculated to impress. He had acquired the uniform, but the commission was intercepted by agents of the *Club Massiac*, who forwarded it to the authorities at Le Cap, together with Ogé's portrait and the urgent request that he be arrested as soon as he set foot on the island. He managed, however, to elude the police and reached his mother's plantation, where his two brothers and his principal lieutenant Jean Baptiste Chavanne received him enthusiastically.

Chavanne, who had fought at Savannah, was of the opinion that in order to succeed they must call the Negroes as well as the mulattoes to arms, but Ogé recoiled from so bold a step. When they had recruited some three hundred men and had armed them with muskets landed from an American sloop, Ogé wrote three somewhat highfaluting letters – to the Governor, to the Provincial Assembly and to the Commander of the Le Cap garrison. He assured them that his only intention was to have the decree of the National Assembly respected, but that if force was used against him he would repel it. He then marched his followers to Grande-Rivière, a short distance from Le Cap, and entrenched himself.

General Vincent at the head of 800 men sallied forth from Le Cap to teach the mulattoes a lesson. He was worsted during a skirmish and beat a hasty retreat. General Cambefort took the field with 1500 men and artillery. Against such an overwhelming force Ogé and Chavanne could not hold out. Their force was scattered and many prisoners fell into the hands of the whites. The two leaders and a few followers escaped to the Spanish colony, but were handed over to the French.

The trial of the rebels lasted two months and made a profound impression. Thirteen were condemned to the galleys; twenty-one sentenced to be hanged; Ogé and Chavanne were to be broken on the wheel.

Ogé broke down and wept when the sentence was pronounced, but he did not beg for mercy and did not make a confession implicating others, as stated by Bryan Edwards, who confuses Vincent with his brother Jacques. There exists a confession signed by Jacques Ogé, but Garran-Coulon has proved beyond a shadow of a doubt that it is a forgery.

# CHAPTER XII

## The Mulattoes Rebel

OGÉ dead was more formidable than Ogé living. When news of his martyrdom reached Paris, there was a gasp of horror, followed by a cry of indignation. The debate on the question in the National Assembly was one of the most heated to which Paris had ever listened. But fear lest the colony throw itself into the arms of England had a sobering effect. The decree of May 15, 1791, resulting from the debate, was remarkably moderate. It did little more than confirm the right of the free mulattoes to vote and to be elected to office. But it did something the previous decree had failed to do; it left no room for equivocation and provided that three Commissioners should be sent to watch over the observance of the decree.

The storm created in Paris by the news of Ogé's martyrdom was, however, as nothing compared with the hurricane provoked in St. Domingo by the apparent determination of France to have the free mulattoes enjoy civic rights. The colonists united in denouncing the meddlers. In the Provincial Assembly of the North Province motions were made to seize French ships in the harbor, to confiscate the property of Frenchmen, to place an embargo on French goods, to call the colonists to arms, to lower the national colors, to hoist the British standard! The streets were littered with national cockades, impulsively torn from headgear and trampled underfoot. Persecution of the mulattoes gained in intensity. Governor Blanchelande, at his wit's end, suspended the decree.

## 2

The mulattoes felt their cup was full to overflowing. In the West Province, they gathered for self-defense. What made the situation especially serious was that the whites in that province were engaged in a particularly bitter quarrel. At Port-au-Prince the Democrats were in control. Governor Blanchelande had been forced to flee to Le Cap. Royalists, who had established headquarters at La-Croix-des-Bouquets, now proposed to the mulattoes to make common cause against their mutual enemy. The proposal was accepted. The Royalists supplied most of the officers, the mulattoes most of the men, and there came into existence a well-organized mulatto army, four thousand strong.

If party strife had made the Royalists careless about caste lines, the mulattoes, too, were carried away by their passion. Mulatto slaveowners armed their slaves. Negroes on surrounding plantations became interested and offered to enlist. They, too, were given arms and a regiment was created composed entirely of Negroes and nicknamed "the Swiss."

The white and mulatto armies were about evenly matched. On the side of the Democrats was the garrison of Port-au-Prince, the white militia and a force the municipality had recruited from the floating population and named "the Filibusters." They had superior equipment, but lacked capable leadership. When the two forces clashed the white militia turned and fled, the Filibusters added nothing to the valorous tradition of their name, and the troops of the line, their flanks exposed, were cut to pieces or taken prisoner.

But now the leaders of both sides began to reflect. Could they afford to continue their strife and see Negroes desert plantations in ever greater numbers? Slaves with arms in their hands! Slaves tasting victory over their masters! It would never do. A white delegation came to the mulatto camp with an offer to negotiate. A pact was made. The whites solemnly promised to respect the decree of the National Assembly and acknowledged that Ogé and his friends had been "the unfortunate victims of passion and prejudice." A contingent of the mulatto army was to enter Port-au-Prince, not as conquerors, but as brothers in arms.

The mulattoes entered the city and were received with apparent enthusiasm. One saw whites and mulattoes walking arm in arm, drinking together in taverns. But there remained the question of the black Swiss. Was it not to the best interest of all that they be returned to their masters? The mulattoes agreed.

## 3

So the slaves were disarmed and sent back to the plantations they had deserted. How their masters received them, how they proceeded to quench the flame that had been lighted in their breasts, we can well imagine. There were, however, some two hundred slaves so obviously spoiled by their heroic adventure that to allow them to mingle with their fellows would be foolhardy. They were put aboard a ship, with provisions to last three months, and the captain was instructed to convey them to the far-off Mexican coast. When the ship got as far as Jamaica, the captain saw a lonely bay he thought would do equally well. He disembarked his human cargo and sailed away.

It was not long before the British governor heard about the

unauthorized landing. He had the new arrivals rounded up and conveyed to Le Cap. Here they were transferred to another ship and sent to Môle St. Nicolas. On the bay where Columbus had once dropped anchor now stood a strongly fortified town. The commander would not allow the Negroes to land. They should be taken to Port-au-Prince.

That night the ship lay peacefully in the bay, its rigging outlined against the starry sky. Sometime during the night boats filled with armed men put off from shore and moved towards the ship. They drew alongside. The men climbed aboard. The hatch was lifted. Men with lanterns went down the ladder into the thick, foul atmosphere of the hold, where the Negroes lay in chains. The glint of steel; startled eyes gazing up at the intruders. Then, one by one, the Negroes were sent up the ladder, taken to the bow of the vessel. A stunning blow on the back of the head, then the collapsing body was seized and thrown overboard.

Towards morning the armed men departed. When the town awoke the ship lay peacefully in the bay, its rigging outlined against the cerulean sky. For many days thereafter carrion crows circled about the beaches, where black bodies washed up.

Cain, where is thy brother Abel? Mulattoes, where are the black Swiss who fought for liberty by your side? The mulattoes had not wanted this. It was not they who had killed. But in the years to come a phantom regiment would rise up to accuse them. It fought against them in the bitter quarrel that later divided the mulattoes from the Negroes.

The betrayal availed the mulattoes little. Their triumph was short-lived. The National Assembly, alarmed by the clamor in the colony and urged by the *Club Massiac*, repudiated the decree granting the mulattoes civic rights. The whites at Port-au-Prince, expecting the support of the Home Government, repudiated the pact they had made. In the disorders that followed the city was swept by flames.

Yet, if slavery was to be maintained, unity was more than

ever necessary between slaveowners, of whatever complexion. For that which they had dreaded for a hundred years or more had finally come to pass. The black flood was upon them! In the North Province the slaves had risen.

The man responsible for the uprising, under whose leadership the slaves gained their liberty and successfully defended it against the planters, against the British, against the Spaniards, against the armies of Napoleon, was Toussaint Louverture – the First of the Blacks.

# *PART TWO*

# *Toussaint's Climb to Power*

## CHAPTER I

## Toussaint on the Bréda Plantation

On the heights overlooking Le Cap and the blue Caribbean, in the district called Haut-du-Cap, was the Bréda plantation, one of the largest and best managed in the North Province, worked by over a thousand slaves. Its owner, the Count de Noé, who had inherited the property from his uncle, the Count de Bréda, lived in France. He was benevolent by nature and had instructed his manager, Béager, to be considerate to his slaves. His instructions were obeyed, and the Bréda slaves were treated with comparative humanity.

Among the Negro freedmen employed on the plantation was one whose name was known to Negroes far and wide. He was, indeed, somewhat of a phenomenon. Not only could he read and write, but he was reputed to know Latin, a reputation somewhat exaggerated, for his knowledge of the classical tongue was confined to a few liturgical phrases. He was besides versed in plant lore and could brew curative potions for man and beast. This extraordinary Negro was named Pierre Baptiste Simon. He had acquired his knowledge in the service of the Jesuit Fathers, who had conducted a school at Le Cap. When the Jesuits were banished from the colony, they had freed their slaves.

Pierre Baptiste was a full-blooded Negro of the Arada tribe. We do not know if he was a Creole Negro or was born in

Africa. If the latter, then he must have been transported to St. Domingo and sold to the Jesuits when still of tender years, for he eschewed voodooism and was a devout Catholic. Before coming to the Bréda estate he had worked on another plantation, where he had had two children by a household slave. When he left to seek employment elsewhere he had to leave his family behind.

On the Bréda plantation Pierre Baptiste took for helpmate a Negro slave woman named Pauline, by whom he had eight children, five boys and three girls. The eldest of the boys was François Dominique Toussaint, born, presumably, in 1744, on All Saints' Day.*

## 2

In his boyhood Toussaint, who remained lean and wiry all his life, was so thin that his playmates called him *fatras-bâton*—thrashing-stick. But he was far from being a weakling. He could run and climb with the best and was an excellent swimmer. Very early in life he learned to ride horseback and became so expert that in his manhood he was sometimes referred to as "the Centaur of the Savannas." Once, when still a child, he fell off a horse and broke his finger. His father's skill being unequal to setting the bone properly, one finger of his right hand ever after curved upward like a question mark.

Toussaint's father farmed a tract of land on shares, and while he never earned enough to enable him to buy the freedom of any of his children, Toussaint seldom went hungry. Pierre Baptiste was, however, unable to shield his family from all the unpleasant consequences of slavery: Toussaint's sister Geneviève was sold to a planter in the South Province when she was a little girl and he did not see her again until he was past fifty. Toussaint's mother died when he was still a boy and his father took a new female companion, Pélagie. Toussaint's foster mother was

* See Appendix concerning Toussaint's parentage and date of birth.

good to him and he later bought her freedom and took care of her in her old age.

In the family circle Negroes spoke their tribal tongue, but all, or nearly all, knew Creole – a mixture of French, Spanish and Negro dialects. Toussaint's father taught him to speak, read and write French, but Creole remained the language in which he expressed himself with greatest facility. He learned to write a legible hand, but his orthography remained poor. He likewise acquired the few liturgical phrases that had established his father's reputation as a Latinist and throughout his life enjoyed rolling them off his tongue. They never failed to excite the wonder and admiration of his Negro listeners.

While still a slave Toussaint did considerable reading. That he was acquainted with Roman history is evident from his memorandum to Napoleon and from several letters. He read Epictetus in a French translation and the influence of the noble Stoic upon his character is unmistakable. Raynal he read when in his thirties. It is not known if he ever read Machiavelli, but he later practised many tricks of statecraft the astute Florentine would have approved.

## 3

When Toussaint was in his teens he was put to guarding cattle, which gave him time for study and reflection. The manager of the Bréda plantation, Béager, and his successor, Bayon de Libertat, did not share the opinion, held by most planters, that slaves should be kept in ignorance. Most of the books Toussaint read he obtained from them. Some may have been lent him by the parish priest, for Toussaint had embraced the Catholic religion with great fervor and all his life sought the company of priests.

He remained small of stature and by Caucasian standards was far from being an Adonis. A description of him in the prison register of the Fort de Joux informs us that he was five feet two inches tall, very black, lean and wiry, with large expressive eyes, broad uptilted nose, thick lips, long pointed chin and long teeth, covered with tartar. The upper and lower incisors are reported missing, but we know that he lost them in middle age, during a siege of St. Marc, when hit in the mouth by a spent cannon ball. Whether as a result of success and power he acquired an impressive bearing, or whether he always had it, we do not know; but white men accustomed to meeting the great ones of the earth were impressed by him. General Vincent said of him: "Nobody can approach Toussaint without fear or leave him without emotion." Rainsford speaks of his appearance in dithyrambic terms. His ugliness, like Lincoln's, appears to have had a quality that attracted some and repelled others.

In his character, as in that of most slaves, there was a tendency to dissimulate. If convinced that a man meant to deal fairly with him, he kept his word loyally; if convinced of the contrary, he met perfidy with perfidy. He despised flattery when it was offered to him, but did not disdain using it when dealing with someone who appeared susceptible to it. He could exercise extreme patience and self-control, but was careless of consequences once his temper was aroused.

When he was eighteen his love for horses led to his appointment as a stable boy. During a dispute with Béager about a horse, he struck the manager. For a slave to strike a white man could have the gravest consequences. If the blow resulted in effusion of blood – even so much as a nosebleed – the death penalty could be imposed. It was to the credit of Béager that he chose to overlook the incident.

During Toussaint's career as a slave only one instance of ill-treatment by a white man has been recorded. Toussaint was returning from church, dressed in his best and reading his breviary, when he found himself confronted by a white man carrying a heavy stick. The man was of those who wished to keep the Negroes in ignorance. With a blow of his stick he struck the book from Toussaint's hand and laid on so cruelly that the

Negro was covered with blood. The Haitian historian Madiou claims that Toussaint refused to allow his bloodstained coat to be cleaned and took to wearing it every day, until, at the beginning of the insurrection, he met the wielder of the stick and stabbed him to death.

## 4

Toussaint did not marry until he was forty.* "I chose my wife myself," he is quoted as saying. "My masters wished me to marry a dashing young Negress, but in a matter of this kind I always managed to resist pressure contrary to my own idea of what constituted a happy union."

The woman he chose, Suzanne Simon, a relative of his father, was neither young nor dashing. She was five years his junior, of ample proportions and the mother of a four-year-old boy, Placide Séraphin Clère, the offspring of a mulatto. Planters in the French Antilles did not wish their slaves to contract legal unions. When a slave was legally married members of his household could not be sold separately. Hence only one Negro couple in five thousand was legally married. Toussaint and Suzanne were not among these exceptions.

Béager had died and his place had been taken by Bayon de Libertat, a man of kindly disposition and liberal tendencies, with whom Toussaint was on the best of terms. The new manager had made Toussaint his coachman and had allotted him a plot of land, which the Negro farmed on shares. In a statement quoted by a traveler Toussaint paints a somewhat idyllic picture of his existence: "We went to labor in the field, my wife and I, hand in hand. Scarcely were we conscious of the fatigue of the day. Heaven always blessed our toil. Not only did we swim in abundance, but we had the pleasure of giving food to Blacks who needed it. On the Sabbath and on festival days we went to church – my wife, my parents and myself. Returning

* Presumably. In 1801, when he was fifty-seven, his eldest son was sixteen.

to our cottage, after a pleasant meal, we passed the remainder of the day in the family circle, and we closed it by prayer, in which all took part."

Some allowance should be made for Toussaint's inclination to make his period of bondage appear as little degrading as possible; nevertheless, it is obvious that his condition was incomparably better than that of the average field slave and superior to that of most household slaves. Indeed, from a letter written by him to the Directory in July, 1797, it appears that de Libertat had granted him what was known in the colony as *liberté de savanne*, under which the slave, while legally remaining the property of his master, enjoyed most of the privileges of a freeman. Some Negroes preferred this to unconditional liberty, as it assured them of the master's protection. Toussaint writes: "Twenty years ago the yoke of slavery was lifted from my shoulders by a man who placed duty towards oppressed humanity ahead of the advantages to be derived from wringing all possible profit from an unfortunate fellow being."

Thus Toussaint and Suzanne lived contentedly enough. Two children were born to them, Isaac and Saint-Jean. Slavery weighed lightly upon him and his family; and had it not been for the sufferings of his fellow slaves, he might have never struck a blow for liberty and have found consolation for his condition of bondage in these words of his favorite philosopher, who himself had been a slave: "Man is not the master of man, but death is, and life and pleasure and pain; for if he comes without these things, bring Caesar to me and you will see how firm I am. But if I shall release myself from my masters, that is from the things by means of which masters are formidable, what further trouble have I, what master have I still?"

## 5

Toussaint was thirteen when the Negro prophet Macandal died at the stake at Le Cap. He must have heard Macandal's death and teachings discussed in the Negro quarter, and it may well be that this set him to thinking about the injustice done to his race. Or perhaps, when reading the history of Rome, he was thrilled by the story of Spartacus. He was twenty-six when the Abbé Raynal published anonymously his famous *Histoire philosophique et politique des établissements et du commerce des Européens dans les deux Indes*, and nearly forty when that work appeared under the author's own name. Hence it was in his maturity that he read these words: –

> Nations of Europe, your slaves will break the yoke that weighs upon them. The Negroes only lack a leader. Where is that great man to be found? He will appear, we cannot doubt it; he will show himself to raise the sacred standard of liberty and to gather around him his companions in misfortune. More impetuous than the mountain torrents, they will leave behind them on all sides the ineffaceable signs of their resentment. The old world as well as the new will applaud him. The name of the hero who will have re-established the rights of the human species will be blessed forever.

To Voltaire this was "*du réchauffé avec de la déclamation,*" but to Toussaint the words must have had a prophetic ring. In a letter to the Directory, dated August 26, 1797, he writes: "I was born in slavery, but I received from nature the soul of a freeman. Every day I raised up my hands to God to implore Him to come to the aid of my brethren and to shed the light of His mercy upon them."

He might have been less patient had he himself suffered more, but then his heart would have been filled with rancor against the white race and his vision would have been blurred. Now they were not. He remained free from race hatred. He knew that the Negroes were oppressed not because they were Negroes, but because they were weak. Epictetus and millions of other white men had been slaves. The chieftains who sold war prisoners and even their own subjects into slavery were of the same race as their victims. White planters were often cruel, but mulatto planters were said to be even worse.

Toussaint would not have agreed with Macandal that the whites should be banished from the island. He believed the Negroes needed the whites to teach them many things. He was conservative by nature and the abolition of slavery appeared to him for a long time an ideal that could not be realized for many years. In the meantime he would have been satisfied with reasonable reforms, such as Hilliard d'Auberteuil and other white humanitarians advocated. He told General Vincent that even after the rebellion was in full swing, he would have been in favor of terminating it had the planters been willing to grant reforms and to give liberty to only sixty of the principal leaders.

In common with most Negroes, Toussaint looked to the King of France for improvement in the condition of the slaves. The edicts for their protection had, in fact, all come from the King and his ministers. Had those edicts been obeyed the lot of the slaves would have been bearable. He hoped that someday the King's wrath would be kindled and he would send an army strong enough to compel the planters to obey the law and to bring about drastic reforms.

But the years went by and the King did not act. Toussaint was no longer young. His crinkly hair, gathered into a little pigtail and tied with a ribbon, was profusely streaked with gray. He drove his master's carriage, sitting on the box in livery and barefoot. He worked the land and had charge of the tools at the sugar mill. He brewed potions from plants he gathered in the mountains and distributed them to Negroes who came to seek relief from bodily ills. Occasionally he read a book lent him by de Libertat or by the parish priest. He was nearing the half-century mark and his life seemed almost over. Yet he had not even begun the career that was to make him famous.

# CHAPTER II

## Toussaint Organizes the Insurrection

WHEN Baron de Wimpffen visited St. Domingo in 1790, few things astonished him more than the recklessness with which the colonists discussed revolutionary happenings in France in the presence of their household slaves. Creole nonchalance and pride were responsible. The colonists considered it below their dignity to exercise caution, lest it be imagined that they stood in fear of their slaves. Thus, unwittingly, they themselves became the principal disseminators of the revolutionary seed among the Negroes.

Imagine a formal dinner at a plantation house, with a slave in attendance behind every chair. Letters and newspapers have arrived from France, and the host describes with dramatic emphasis how his uncle or cousin has had to flee with his family because his scoundrelly peasants have burned down his castle, have looted his stores and will no longer recognize him as their lord. The narrator expresses the opinion that if the said uncle or cousin had made a liberal use of the whip such outrages could not have occurred. Others tell of similar misfortunes that have befallen their relatives. One asks if those present have read the shameful proclamation of the Rights of Man, which asserts that all men are created free and equal. Another remarks that if the *Amis des Noirs* had their way, this would even apply to Negro slaves! All join in denunciation of the National Assembly, and even of the King – who, if he were not utterly spineless, would have his soldiers arrest the whole pack of traitors and shoot them.

The household slaves listen, standing barefoot behind each chair, passing the highly spiced Creole dishes and pouring the sparkling wines of France. Their expression does not change, but something in them has been kindled. Many have relatives among the field and mill slaves, to whom they pay an occasional visit. They sit with them around the fire, laid on the earthen floor in the center of the cabin, and tell the exciting news they have heard. The field slaves listen; one, more thoughtful than his fellows, remarks that if the people of France have gained their freedom, then, obviously, they, too, must have been slaves. Whereupon the idea germinates in the minds of several that the black slaves of St. Domingo ought to follow the example of the white slaves of France.

A secondary but important source of propaganda was the sailors from the French merchant vessels. All, or nearly all, had imbibed the wine of the New Freedom and had found it good. On shore leave in the colony they partook of other intoxicants, and, the mixture having mounted to their heads, they harangued Negroes, telling them that by virtue of the sacred Rights of Man they were now free and the equals of their masters. Anybody who pretended otherwise was an aristocrat and a traitor, and would eventually be dealt with by the National Assembly, unless the Negroes chose to deal with him themselves. The Negroes compared this with what they had already heard, and believed it; so that, as early as October 1789, François Raimond wrote to his brother, the Mulatto Commissioner in Paris: "The Revolution has penetrated here, most of all among the Blacks. To them the national cockade stands for liberty and equality. They were ready to revolt, but several have been sent to the scaffold and things have quieted down again."

Toussaint knew about these abortive attempts, which confirmed him in his belief that revolt would be futile. Except for their machetes – long-bladed, swordlike knives with which the sugar cane was cut – the Negroes were unarmed. What chance would they have against troops of the line? And even if they managed to overcome the garrison, they would be crushed by armies sent from France. He was too old to be reckless. He preferred to wait. What did he expect? He probably did not know himself, yet he was to say later: "I felt I was destined for great things." Destiny, he somehow felt, would show him the way. In the meantime, when some hot-blooded young Negro would suggest to him that the time had come to rebel, Toussaint would say in Creole: "*Doucement allé loin,*" or "*Patience bat la force.*" They were his favorite proverbs.

## 2

When the National Assembly passed the measure granting civic rights to the mulattoes, officialdom in the colony was forced to support it, whatever its private views might have been. In doing so it ran afoul of the colonists. Never before had relations between them been so strained. Governor Blanchelande's action in suspending the decree improved things but little. The colonists knew that the trend of public opinion in France would eventually force the issue. They longed for independence and were in open revolt. Blanchelande had been forced to flee from Port-au-Prince, where blood had already flowed. The situation in Le Cap was becoming equally alarming. In this emergency the harassed government party decided to make use of a technique that had been employed with considerable success in France by the Third Estate.

Whenever the Third Estate had wished to obtain concessions from the King and his supporters, it had made use of the Paris populace and the peasants to frighten them. Supposedly spontaneous popular outbursts, such as the storming of the Bastille, the march of the women on Versailles, the peasant revolt, were in reality carefully staged performances, ordered and paid for by financiers like Laborde, Boscary and Dufresnoy, by wealthy merchants and industrialists. In practically every case they accomplished their immediate purpose. There was, however, a fly in the ointment. When the actors were no longer needed, they refused to be dismissed and eventually staged a series of performances of their own, not at all to the liking of the original promoters. In the summer of 1791, however, the danger of this was not as obvious as it was to become a year later, and Governor Blanchelande and the government party decided to employ a similar expedient. They arrived at the conclusion that the best way to cure the colonists of their hankering for independence was to stage a slave rebellion.

A slave rebellion would make the colonists realize that the support of the mother country was indispensable to them. They would realize that they were too few in number to keep the slaves in subjection without outside help. Loss of life and destruction of property were of course unavoidable to teach them that lesson, but if things were allowed to drift, blood was bound to flow anyway, and it might well be the blood of the officials. Since the officials owned few slaves and possessed little property in the colony, they were not incurring a great deal of risk. If the movement got out of hand reinforcements from France would restore order. The principal difficulty was to find a Negro sufficiently capable to organize the revolt and to keep it under reasonable control.

## 3

The manager of the Bréda plantation, Bayon de Libertat, was out of sympathy with the attitude of the colonists. For lack of any other group with which to affiliate, he found himself drawn to the government party. They welcomed him and admitted him to their counsels.

One day a government official called on him and disclosed the hazardous plan. He explained that an exodus rather than an insurrection was intended. The slaves were to leave the plantations and take refuge in the mountains, where they were to remain until the signal was given for them to return. They would be rewarded with a few badly needed reforms.

Céligny-Ardouin, the first Haitian historian to shed light on this phase of the insurrection, claims that Toussaint overheard the conversation and offered his services. It appears more probable that de Libertat recommended him. Anyway, he and the government official were brought face to face and this agreement was made: –

Toussaint was to organize the insurrection, but was not to be held responsible for the consequences and was to receive a safe-conduct, signed by Governor Blanchelande, guaranteeing him immunity.

The government troops were only to feign an attack upon the slaves, who were to receive supplies by way of the Spanish colony.

Before returning to the plantations the slaves were to be granted an additional free day a week and the abolition of the whip.

Toussaint and all the principal leaders were to be given their freedom.

To give the Negroes greater confidence, the news was to be spread that the reforms had already been granted by the King, but that the planters refused to carry them out; also, that an army was on the way from France to force the planters to obey the edict.

A number of spurious copies of a Paris newspaper were to be placed in Toussaint's hands, in which the supposed edict and the news concerning the army was to appear in print.

Toussaint's statement in his memorandum to Bonaparte that at the outbreak of the insurrection he possessed 648,000 francs makes it evident that a considerable sum of money was placed at his disposal.

## 4

It was the night of August 14, 1791. The scene was a glade in a dense forest, known as Bois Caïman,* on the Lenormand plantation at Morne-Rouge, where Macandal had been a slave. Several smoking torches illuminated the scene.

* See "Meeting in the Bois Caïman" in Appendix.

On the ground, in a half-circle, some two hundred Negroes and a mulatto were seated. The Negroes were without exception gang-foremen – two from nearly every plantation in the Plaine-du-Nord and the surrounding parishes. More than a hundred plantations were represented. Many of the Negroes had walked the greater part of the day, which was a Sunday, to attend the meeting and would walk again a large part of the night to be back at their work before dawn.

Toussaint was not present and remained in the background during the entire first phase of the insurrection. Apparently he wished to reserve himself. He had created the elaborate organization probably as much for the purpose of controlling the rebellion as for setting it on foot, but undoubtedly realized that during its first phase, when discipline was necessarily lax, excesses might be committed which would ruin the reputation of any man connected with that phase. So, having constructed the insurrectionary machine, he allowed others to take charge, while he watched and waited.

The night was sultry. Occasionally there was a spasm of lightning and the distant muttering of thunder. A tall Negro of commanding appearance, who had been in conversation with the mulatto, arose. His name was Boukmans. He was a Jamaican Negro, a voodoo priest and gang-foreman on the Turpin and Flaville plantation, in the parish of Acul. He addressed the meeting in Creole, telling the delegates that the King, who was their friend, had issued an edict granting the slaves an additional free day a week, so they might have time to work their land allotments and feed themselves and their families properly. They would thus be working two days a week for themselves, four for the planters, and have their Sundays free. But would the planters agree to this? No! They had ignored the King's edict, as they had ignored the Black Code and all other edicts the King had issued for the protection of the slaves. This time, however, the King was resolved to be obeyed. An army was on its way from France to enforce the law and to punish the planters.

But the Negroes should not wait like helpless children for the soldiers to come and hand them their rights. They should strike a blow themselves. They should abandon the plantations and take refuge in the mountains.

He now turned to the mulatto and asked him to read the King's edict and the order concerning the army. The mulatto produced a copy of the spurious newspaper the government party had fabricated and read the supposedly official documents. The reading greatly impressed the gathering, and Boukmans now called on the delegates to express their views.

Some were of the opinion that the insurrection should be timed to coincide with the arrival of the army. Boukmans, who knew that the documents were spurious, opposed this and received the support of the delegates from the parishes of Acul and Limbé. Then some of the delegates became wildly enthusiastic and proposed that the insurrection begin that very night. This was rejected as impractical, and the evening of August 22 was set as the date on which the rebellion was to take place.

This matter having been settled, it was now fitting to invoke the favor of the gods and offer a suitable sacrifice. Boukmans led the delegates down a narrow path towards another glade, where before Damballa's altar stood a tall, gaunt, gray-haired priestess. At her feet, securely tied, lay a black pig. It was as if the elements wished to contribute to the impressiveness of the scene, for as the *mambu* raised a long, gleaming knife and her assistants untied and held the pig, there was a jagged flash of lightning, followed by a loud clap of thunder. She plunged the knife into the animal and expertly slit its throat and belly, while her assistants caught the blood in hollowed gourds and added rum and gunpowder. The vessels then passed from hand to hand and each delegate drank of the mixture, while Boukmans, his arms raised to the sky, where now lightning flash followed lightning flash and the thunder roared and rumbled, intoned this prayer: –

"The God who created the sun, which gives us light, who

rouses the waves and rules the storm, though hidden in the clouds, He watches us.

"He beholds the misdeeds of the whites.

"The white man's God inspires him with crimes; our God calls upon us to do good works.

"But though our God is merciful, He wishes us to be avenged.

"He will direct our arms and aid us.

"Throw away the symbol of the God of the whites – that God who gloats over our suffering – and listen to the voice of liberty, which finds an echo in our hearts."

## 5

On August 22, 1791, at about ten o'clock in the evening, there was great commotion in the Negro quarter of the Turpin and Flaville plantation. Men, women and children swarmed from their cabins. The women and children were laden with the family possessions, sufficiently scant not to be burdensome; the men grasped their machetes with an air of resolution. Some had tied the knife to a pole, constructing a vicious-looking glaive. Boukmans surveyed the scene and issued orders.

The plantation manager and his white overseers came running, whips in hand. What they saw filled them with consternation. The passive, bovine creatures of that afternoon seemed transformed. No longer did they bend their backs meekly to receive the cutting lash. The looks they cast at the white men spoke of defiance. "The great only seem great to us because we are on our knees – let us rise!" the French publicist Loustallot had written. Having risen from their knees the slaves suddenly realized that their oppressors were far less formidable than they had seemed.

The manager and his overseers retreated and barricaded themselves in the plantation house. But the Negroes had no intention of molesting them. Chattering noisily in Creole and in Negro dialects they poured out of the plantation gate, behind their leader. There was a moon and stars, but torches helped to light the way, making visible the exaltation of the Negroes, as they set out on their great adventure.

The first stop was made at the Clément plantation. The Negroes here had been expecting them and received them with cheers. They were ready to depart. The two groups of slaves held a meeting and each elected a leader. Boukmans was confirmed as the leader of the Turpin and Flaville slaves; the Clément Negroes chose a man named Auguste. The augmented stream now swept onward towards the Tremes plantation.

The Tremes slaves joined with enthusiasm. A white carpenter employed on the estate ventured too close and a shot was fired in his direction. He tried to escape, but was caught and brought before the leaders, who ordered him released. Then the march was resumed towards the Noé plantation.

These details, taken from the report of the special committee appointed by the Colonial Assembly, prove that in its initial stages the movement was remarkably orderly and that neither the burning of the plantations nor a massacre of the whites was originally intended. The trouble started on the Noé plantation. Here, too, the slaves joined immediately, but they felt this was a golden opportunity to settle old scores. The manager and the white refiner were slain; a doctor and his wife, who lived in the plantation house, were not harmed. The slaves invaded the house to search for firearms. Other objects took their fancy and they began to loot. Someone touched a torch to inflammable material and within a few minutes smoke and flame belched forth. This released a spirit of destruction. Building after building flamed. Negroes armed with torches ran into the adjoining fields and set fire to the dry sugar cane.

It was then that Toussaint's elaborate organization collapsed. Either the leaders lost control of their followers, or themselves became infected. The burning of the Noé plantation turned the exodus into an orgy of destruction. Flames leaped up on all the surrounding plantations, to be answered by flames throughout the Plaine-du-Nord and on the mountain sides, where were the coffee plantations. A luminous haze drowned out the moon and the stars. The North Province was doomed.

## 6

A hundred thousand slaves were in revolt. Within two months 220 sugar plantations, 600 coffee plantations, 200 cotton and indigo plantations ceased to exist. Clouds of smoke, from which fiery tongues were leaping, hung over the mountains, giving them the appearance of volcanoes in eruption. "The most striking feature of the terrible spectacle," writes Carteau, "was a rain of fire composed of burning cane-straw, which whirled thickly before the blast, like flakes of snow, and which the wind carried, now towards the harbor and shipping, now over the houses of the city." The richest agricultural section of the island – perhaps the richest in the world – became a scorched and blackened waste. "We arrived in the harbor of Le Cap," writes Bryan Edwards, "at evening of September 26, and the first sight which arrested our attention as we approached was a dreadful scene of devastation by fire. The noble plain adjoining Le Cap was covered with ashes, and the surrounding hills, as far as the eye could reach, everywhere presented to us ruins still smoking and houses and plantations at that moment in flames."

Two thousand whites and five times that many Negroes were slain. Both sides committed atrocities. Delirious with freedom, thirsting for revenge, drunk with the rum they were able to obtain in abundance, the slaves indulged in an orgy of violence. Women and girls were raped before the eyes of husbands and fathers by Negroes who, even in their delirium, were perhaps not unmindful of the fact that their own wives and daughters had been at the mercy of white men's lust. In their report to the French National Assembly the planters tell of a man placed between two boards and sectioned with a saw; of another who was crucified and whose arms and legs were hacked off with an ax. Shocking as is this testimony, it is not more so than the atrocities which witnesses before the Select Committee accused planters of committing in cold blood. The worshipers of voodoo, but recently emerged from the jungle, could hardly have been expected to be more humane than the followers of the Nazarene, inheritors of an ancient civilization.

Yet, strange to say, they *were* more humane. The Negro leaders (as we shall see) executed one of their number guilty of atrocities. One searches in vain for a similar example in the white camp. "By killing our women you compel us to kill yours," was the vain appeal the Negro leaders Jean-François and Biassou addressed to the white general Cambefort.

## 7

Governor Blanchelande and the government party were in the unenviable position of men who, wishing to burn underbrush, have started a forest fire. They were forced to intervene. With the troops at their disposal they established fortified lines, called "cordons," with which they managed to confine the rebellion to the North Province. To police the Plain the Governor had to rely on the white militia, but the planter régime had benefited so small a portion even of the white population that the members of the militia were not in the least disposed to risk their lives in defense of the planters and their property. Blanchelande wrote to the Minister of Marine: "This city contains a very large number of poor and dissatisfied whites, who would welcome disorder in the hope of bettering their lot by plunder. They have clearly shown their evil intention by their formal refusal to fight the rebels."

When the militia was finally coaxed and bribed into patrolling the Plain, their method consisted of shooting all Negroes they encountered or taking them to Le Cap to be tortured. "This city," wrote a British officer, "presents a terrible spectacle, surrounded by ditches and palisades; the streets blocked by barricades and the squares occupied by scaffolds on which captured Negroes are tortured – the whole forming a picture of devastation and carnage."

The principal result of the efforts of the militia was that thousands of Negroes who had had no intention of joining the insurrection were forced to seek safety in the rebel camp.

# CHAPTER III

## Peace Negotiations

BOUKMANS was captured during an attack on Le Cap and died at the stake. The head of the voodoo priest, stuck upon a pike, grinned derision outside a city gate. Toussaint still kept aloof from the insurrection, waiting for the situation to clarify itself. Two new leaders, Jean-François and Biassou, were beginning to forge an army out of the Negro hordes now roaming the North Province.

Jean-François, who styled himself "Grand Admiral and Commander in Chief," was a Creole Negro of pleasing appearance. His master, the planter Papillon, had treated him well, but Jean-François, preferring freedom, had escaped into the mountains and had spent several years with the Maroon Negroes. There can be no doubt that he and Biassou owed their elevation to the government party. The Procurator Gros quotes Jean-François as saying: "It is not I who have appointed myself General of the Negroes. Those possessing the power to do so have conferred that title upon me." A letter written to Jean-François by Don Alonzo, a high Spanish functionary, in the early days of the insurrection, furnishes further proof. The Spanish officials at that time collaborated with their French colleagues, and Don Alonzo wrote: "I am sorry I did not know that you lacked ammunition. Had I known, I should have sent it to you. You will receive this aid and anything else you might ask as long as you defend the interests of the King."

The French, not the Spanish, King was meant. The Negro general's standard was white, with, on one side, the French coat of arms and the words "*vive le Roi,*" and on the other, "*Ancien Régime.*"

Jean-François played his role with gusto. He wore an elegant gray uniform with yellow facings, large gold epaulettes and a black cordon, embroidered with white fleurs-de-lis. On his breast shone the cross of the Order of St. Louis. A plumed and cockaded hat, shining top boots with tinkling spurs and a huge cavalry sword completed his costume. When he reviewed his army he would be seated in an open carriage, drawn by six plumed horses and surrounded by a bodyguard of twelve mounted Negroes in natty uniforms with fleur-de-lis insignia.

His fellow-commander Biassou, who had adopted the title of "Generalissimo of the Conquered Territories," did not look nearly as impressive, being small of stature, ill-shapen and extremely ugly. He had been a slave belonging to the Fathers of Charity, at Le Cap. Religious orders had the reputation of treating their slaves well. Theirs were the only agricultural establishments in the French Antilles on which the birth rate exceeded the death rate. They not only did not find it necessary to import slaves, but in the words of a cynical Governor, "were able to export some of their own manufacture."

A third leader, undoubtedly self-appointed, was Jeannot. His master, the planter Bullet, had treated him with the utmost brutality, and the results were now apparent. Judged by standards which the whites adopted during the race war, Jean François and Biassou were not exceptionally bloodthirsty; Jeannot, however, hated the whites with an intensity bordering on insanity. He had assumed the significant title of "Grand Judge," and in the manner of Citizen-General de Caradeux decorated his camp with severed heads stuck upon pikes. He had adopted as his banner the body of a white infant impaled upon a pole and hanged his white prisoners upon trees, from hooks stuck under their chins, after first boring out their eyes with a corkscrew. He was known to cut the throat of a prisoner, scoop up the blood with both hands, drink it, and with half-closed eyes murmur ecstatically: "Ah, my friends, how sweet, how good this white blood! Let us take full draughts. Let us swear irreconcilable revenge against our oppressors. Peace with them – never! So help me God!"

Monstrous as was Jeannot, he did not lack sincerity. He reminds one of Marat, who combined unquestionable sincerity and pity for the oppressed with an unbalanced nature and a hate for the oppressors that betrayed him into constant incitements to massacre. As for Jean-François and Biassou, the French Commissioner Sonthonax was undoubtedly right when he said that they were more interested in becoming slaveowners themselves than in freeing the slaves. When there was no loot to dispose of and subsidies were slow in arriving, they did not hesitate to sell Negroes into slavery to the Spaniards, under the pretext that they were "*mauvais sujets*," whom they otherwise would have to execute. Among the "*mauvais sujets*" were the wives and children of their own soldiers.

## 2

In sharp contrast with the splendid array of the two principal generals, the Negro soldiers were dressed in rags or wore only loincloths. A few wore clothing they had looted, which varied from ballroom finery to underwear of both sexes. About one in three had some kind of firearm – an old musket or pistol, for which ammunition was seldom available. The rest were armed with machetes, iron-pointed sticks, broken or dented swords, or pieces of rusty iron hoops. The cavalry was mounted on a heterogeneous collection of draft horses, saddle horses and mules. There were a few cannon, but the artillerymen knew so little about handling them that they were known to put the powder in front of the ball. To compensate for the paucity of equipment and training there was a superabundance of general officers. There were few who confessed to any lower rank than captain and the number of generals was bewildering.

Besides these more or less organized forces there were numerous bands roaming the country and warring in the primitive manner of their African ancestors. An anonymous contemporary author gives this description of their mode of combat: –

The Negroes never mass in the open: a thousand Blacks will never await in line of battle the attack of a hundred whites. They first advance with a frightful clamor, preceded by a great number of women and children singing and yelling in chorus. When they have arrived just out of gunshot, the most profound silence suddenly falls, and the Negroes range themselves in such a manner that they appear six times as numerous as they really are. The man of faint heart, already daunted by their apparent number, is still further awed by their posturing and grimacing. All this time the ominous silence continues; the only sounds coming from the magicians, who now begin to dance and sing with demoniac contortions. These men are working their incantations, confident that the bullets cannot touch them and wishing to prove to their followers the power of their magic charms. The attack now takes place with cries and howlings.

## 3

A week or two before the outbreak of the rebellion, the manager of the Bréda plantation, de Libertat, had been obliged to go to Le Cap for a prolonged stay. Before leaving he called Toussaint and told him he relied upon him to maintain order on the plantation. He especially recommended to him the safety of Madame de Libertat. Toussaint promised to do his best and kept his promise. When the insurrection broke out and plantations flamed on all sides, the influence of the middle-aged Negro saved the Bréda estate from a similar fate, and the slaves remained at their work. But Toussaint realized that this could not last. The Bréda Negroes were being constantly solicited to join the rebellion, and the white militia from Le Cap made it dangerous for them to remain. Besides, Toussaint reached the conclusion that the time had now arrived when his presence at rebel headquarters was indispensable.

One day, about a month after the outbreak of the insurrection, he called his younger brother Paul and told him to put the horses before the carriage and be ready to drive to Le Cap. Then he went to see Madame de Libertat and informed her that he could no longer guarantee her safety and she must join her husband in the city. He helped her pack her valuables, and when the servants had loaded the boxes onto the carriage and she was seated within, Paul climbed to the coachman's box and drove off.

Toussaint had already informed his family that they must prepare to leave. He accompanied them across the frontier to the Spanish colony, where he established them in comfortable quarters. Then he returned to St. Domingo and immediately went to the Gallifet plantation, at Grande-Rivière, where Jean-François and Biassou had their headquarters.

## 4

Toussaint found several white men at Negro headquarters. One was the Procurator Gros, who told him, undoubtedly with a twinkle, that he (Gros) was a prisoner. There were four priests – Fathers Bienvenu, Sulpice, Boucher and Delahaye. The colonists have made various accusations against them, among others that they acted as procurers for the Negro generals among white women prisoners. All, however, were instrumental in saving the lives of numerous white persons. Father Delahaye is known to have been a man of unblemished character, whose feeling for the Negroes was not unlike that of Las Casas for the Indians.

Jean-François and Biassou being jealous of their authority, it was decided that Toussaint should occupy himself with the sanitary service and should bear the title of "Doctor to the King's Armies." The sanitary service even in the best organized European armies was deplorable at that time and we can well imagine what it must have been in the Negro army. Voodoo priests and medicine men took care of the sick and wounded. If patients became too numerous, the problem, according to one authority, was solved by carrying them into a building and setting fire to the premises. With his genius for organization Toussaint must have improved matters considerably, but he held the office only a short time. Capable men were scarce, and Biassou soon placed him in command of a part of his army.

The court-martial and execution of Jeannot took place shortly after Toussaint's arrival at headquarters and we are justified in assuming that he was responsible for the decision. On two occasions during his future career he ordered the execution of a subordinate guilty of atrocities towards the whites. He undoubtedly pointed out to Jean-François and Biassou that policy as well as decency demanded that Jeannot's career be brought to a close. A counsel was held and the task of punishing Jeannot entrusted to Jean-François. The camp of the fanatic was surrounded during the night. He was taken prisoner, brought before a drumhead court-martial and sentenced to be shot. He had been recklessly brave in battle, but now all courage deserted him. He threw himself at the feet of Jean-François and offered to work for him in chains the remainder of his existence if his life were spared. Father Bienvenu, who had accompanied the expedition, approached the condemned man with a crucifix. Jeannot clutched the priest's cassock and implored his protection. Force had to be used to get him to release his hold, and he was dragged cursing and screaming to a tree, to which he was tied. He continued to wail and to implore until the muskets spoke. Jean-François had Jeannot's body suspended from a hook and departed with his men.

## 5

Three Civil Commissioners – Roume, Mirbeck and Saint-Léger – were known to be on their way from France, and it was believed that an army would soon follow. It seemed, therefore, the part of wisdom to come to an understanding with the planters before the arrival of reinforcements deprived the Governor of an excuse for his inactivity. It also appeared advisable to make Draconian demands that left ample room for bargaining. A counsel was held in which the Procurator Gros and the priests participated. A letter was drawn up to the Governor in which the Negroes made this declaration: –

That they had taken up arms in defense of the King, whom the whites kept imprisoned in Paris, because he had wanted to liberate the Blacks, his loyal subjects;

That they demanded this liberation and the restoration of the *ancien régime;*

That if these demands were granted, the whites would not be harmed, but after being disarmed could return to their dwellings.

Negro emissaries carrying a white flag delivered the letter at one of the city gates.

A second letter was even more uncompromising. It began with the statement that it had not been the intention of the Negroes to throw off the yoke of slavery – "We did not wish to abandon our masters." The insurrection was the result of cruel ill-treatment – "Those who, next to God, should have proved our fathers, have been tyrants, monsters unworthy of the fruits of our labor." But now that the yoke had been discarded, the Negroes would not "throw themselves like sheep into the jaws of the wolf. No, it is too late! God who fights for the innocent, is our guide; He will not abandon us. Accordingly, this is our motto – Death or Victory!" Great as have been the wrongs they have suffered, they do not thirst for vengeance and are willing to make peace, "but on condition that all the whites, whether of the plain or of the mountains, shall quit Le Cap without a single exception. Let them carry with them their gold and their jewels; we seek only liberty – dear and precious object!" The letter ends with the words: "Victory or death for Freedom!"

This epistle was undoubtedly written by Father Delahaye, whom Carteau calls "the most ardent apostle of the liberty of the Blacks." It was signed: "All the Generals who compose our Army."

Governor Blanchelande, who must have found it somewhat difficult to play his dual role convincingly, replied that if the Negroes wished peace, they must surrender their leaders and return to the plantations. This reply, made to preserve appearances, was of course not taken seriously and soon after a third communication was prepared, this time addressed to the Colonial Assembly, which alone had the power to come to an agreement with the rebels. It bears all the earmarks of having been written by a man possessing legal training and must be attributed to the Procurator Gros. It is far more moderate in tone than either of the two preceding documents and argues at great length why the rebels were entitled to benefit from the amnesty decree the King had recently issued as his contribution towards a better understanding between whites and mulattoes. The remaining demands – presented viva voce by two mulatto emissaries – were substantially the same as had been agreed on between Toussaint and the government party: liberty for four hundred of the principal leaders, an additional free day a week for the slaves, and prohibition of the use of the whip. According to Toussaint's own statement to General Vincent, a reduction of the number of enfranchisements to fifty or sixty would have been acceptable.

It has been well said that "whom the gods would destroy they first make mad." So moderate were the demands that had the planters possessed the power to crush the revolt, the cost of doing so would have far exceeded any benefit they could have derived from such a course. Indeed, the Negro leaders were themselves far from certain that their followers, having tasted liberty and become conscious of their strength, would be willing to agree to the proposed terms. But the Colonial Assembly was not disposed to make any concessions. They received the emissaries haughtily and dismissed them contemptuously, after informing them that the rebels must submit unconditionally. For those who showed themselves truly contrite they might consider clemency.

The two mulattoes were about to depart disconsolately, when they were informed that the Civil Commissioners, who had arrived, wished to see them. They answered the summons and were received with amiability. The Commissioners listened with obvious sympathy and gave the emissaries a letter, addressed to the Negro leaders, in which they proposed that Jean-François meet them at the St. Michel plantation, a short distance from Le Cap. While this has the appearance of a *mise en scène* in which the Assembly and the Commissioners collaborated, subsequent developments proved that the Commissioners acted entirely on their own responsibility and that the Assembly disapproved of their conciliatory attitude.

The two mulattoes now returned to Negro headquarters, where they gave an account of their reception by the Colonial Assembly. Biassou flew into a violent rage and ordered that all white prisoners be shot instantly. Toussaint intervened. He and Jean-François were not on the best of terms, but his influence with Biassou was great and he managed to have the order recalled. The mulattoes now went on with their story and the atmosphere cleared perceptibly when they produced the letter the Commissioners had given them.

## 6

On the appointed day, Jean-François, attired in his gaudiest uniform and accompanied by several Negro officers, rode to the St. Michel plantation. He had no sooner passed through the entrance gate than his horse's bridle was seized by a man brandishing a whip. The man – none other than Jeannot's former master, the planter Bullet – swung the whip, and the heavy lash seared the face of the Negro general. Biassou would probably have drawn his sword and split his assailant's head, but Jean-François was of a milder disposition. He warded off the blows as well as he could, but swung his horse about, intending to return to Negro headquarters. But the Commissioners made their appearance, the choleric Bullet was led away and the Negro leader prevailed upon to remain. Saint-Léger, who was of Irish extraction, showed himself so amiable that Jean-François, quite overcome, sank on one knee before him, saying he wished to pay homage to the only white man he had ever met who seemed to be truly humane.

The negotiations, however, did not advance the cause of peace, since the Commissioners lacked power to reach an agreement without the consent of the stiff-necked Colonial Assembly. Jean-François, however, was induced to promise the release of his white prisoners. He asked that the whites reciprocate at least to the extent of releasing his wife, imprisoned at Le Cap. The Commissioners promised to do their best, but it is not certain that they obtained her release. The Negro leader departed, convinced that the Commissioners were well-intentioned, but lacking in authority.

When Jean-François gave an account of the interview at Negro headquarters, the disappointment was keen. Biassou objected to surrendering the prisoners, but Toussaint supported Jean-François and it was agreed that two hundred should be released. Fearing that they might be massacred by roaming bands of Negroes, Toussaint accompanied them to the city with an armed force. The prisoners testified that they had been well treated.

Jean-François and Biassou now dictated a letter to the Commissioners which does them little credit. They explained that, most of the rebels being African-born, it would be impossible to induce them to resume the yoke of slavery without the co-operation of all the chieftains. This could only be obtained if the chieftains themselves were given their freedom. Even then the Negroes would probably claim that they had been betrayed and would refuse to comply, but if the King's forces would occupy the open country, the writers would undertake "to hunt down the obstinate Blacks, who refusing obedience will infest the woods."

Even this did not satisfy the Colonial Assembly and the negotiations came to a close. Toussaint continued to co-operate with Jean-François and Biassou, but his mind was now made up concerning the necessity of abolishing slavery altogether.

# CHAPTER IV

## Emancipation

THE choice now left to the rebels was to return to the plantations on the planters' own terms or to continue the struggle. What their lot would have been had they chosen the first course we can well imagine. The number of executions would undoubtedly have far exceeded the number of enfranchisements sought by the Negro leaders during the negotiations. And since it was the policy of the planters to increase the pressure in proportion to the danger threatening them, the condition of the slaves would have surpassed in horror anything the West Indies had yet witnessed. The Negro leaders had proposed a less barbarous form of slavery; the planters forced Patrick Henry's slogan upon the Negroes.

The planters believed that hunger would eventually force the Negroes to surrender. Thousands, indeed, died of hunger, but other thousands hurled themselves with the courage of desperation against the cordons held by the government forces. The Cordon of the East gave way, and the plain of Fort-Dauphin suffered the same fate as the Plaine-du-Nord. Plantations went up in flames, hundreds of people were massacred and many more Negroes joined the ranks of the rebels. The peninsula of the Môle was overrun. Biassou penetrated into the suburbs of Le Cap and captured one of the forts. Naked Negroes, armed only with machetes, charged the cannon of the fort with a fanaticism that awed the defenders.

Toussaint took part in many of these operations, but his principal preoccupation, now and for some time to come, was to discipline, train and equip his men, whose number then did not exceed a few hundred. Knowing little about military training, he availed himself of the services of two white prisoners – a retired officer, whom he had saved from a massacre, and a former militiaman from Le Cap. It was not long before he perceived that classical military exercises were ill adapted to the character of his people and to the circumstances under which he had to combat. He modified the training, exercising his men especially in guerrilla tactics. Later, however, he developed exercises for mass attack, which are thus described by a British officer, Captain Marcus Rainsford: –

Each general officer had a demi-brigade, which went through the normal exercises with a degree of expertness I had seldom before witnessed. They performed, excellently well, several manoeuvres applicable to their method of fighting. At a whistle a whole brigade ran three or four hundred yards, and then, separating, threw themselves flat on the ground, changing to their backs and sides, and all the time keeping up a strong fire; after this they formed in an instant again into their wonted regularity. This single manoeuvre is executed with such facility and precision, as totally prevents cavalry from charging them in bushy or hilly country. Indeed, such complete subordination prevailed – such promptitude and dexterity, as must astonish any European soldier who had the smallest idea of their previous situation.

General Pamphile de Lacroix, Chief of Staff of Napoleon's expedition to the island, pays this tribute to the discipline maintained by the Negro leader: –

Never was a European army subjected to severer discipline than Toussaint's. Officers commanded pistol in hand and had the power of life and death over their subordinates. It was remarkable to see these Africans, the upper part of their bodies bare and equipped only with an ammunition bag, a sword and a musket, give the example of the strictest self-control. Returning from a campaign during which they had lived on a few ears of corn, they would, when quartered in a town, not touch any of the provisions exposed in the shops or brought in by the cultivators. They trembled before their officers and were respectful to the inhabitants. The manner in which he succeeded in disciplining these barbarians was the supreme triumph of Toussaint Louverture.*

In a letter addressed to his generals during his campaign against the British, Toussaint has this to say concerning discipline: –

I invite you to maintain the strictest obedience and discipline among your troops. These are the two military virtues which in ancient times made the Romans the most martial people on earth. They are the virtues that have enabled our country's European armies to gain victory over their enemies. It is only by adhering to them that we can hope to be victorious.

* How remarkable Toussaint's accomplishment was may be judged when we compare de Lacroix's statement with the report of the French Army authorities during Napoleon's occupation of Moscow: –

"The Emperor is extremely displeased that despite the strict orders to stop pillage, parties of marauding Guards are continually seen returning to the Kremlin. Among the Old Guard disorder and pillage were renewed more violently than ever yesterday evening, last night, and today. The Emperor sees with regret that the picked soldiers appointed to guard his person, who should set an example of discipline, carry disobedience to such a point that they break into the cellars and stores containing army supplies. Others have disgraced themselves to the extent of disobeying sentinels and officers and have abused and beaten them."

## 2

For a long time ill-feeling had existed between Biassou and Jean-François. Biassou knew himself to be more daring and resourceful, but he lacked that intangible something called personality. White men as well as Negroes felt attracted to Jean-François and repelled by Biassou, who resented his rival's assumption of superior authority. There were bitter quarrels, during which, on several occasions, their swords flew from their scabbards. They now decided to separate, each assuming jurisdiction over a part of the territory.

Toussaint preferred the crude Biassou to the vain Jean-François. The latter saw in Toussaint a dangerous rival, and once, on some pretext or other, had him placed under arrest. Biassou's threatening attitude secured his release. When the parting came Toussaint went with Biassou. They established headquarters at Tannerie, which Toussaint fortified in accordance with plans drawn by himself. He had a moat dug around the entire town, into which water from a near-by stream was led. Behind the moat was a sturdy palisade. The gate was re-enforced with heavy copper plates, capable of resisting artillery fire. White engineers who later inspected these fortifications marveled at the fact that they had been constructed under the direction of a man possessing no special training.

Biassou was Toussaint's chief in name only. The Negro leader later wrote to Don Joachim García, Governor of the Spanish colony: "I gave an account of my operations to General Biassou, not because I considered myself his subordinate, but to avoid unpleasantness, he being a man of violent and quarrelsome disposition."

Then, for nearly a year, the situation in the North Province remained virtually unchanged. The Negroes controlled the open country and most of the villages, the whites remained in possession of Le Cap and other fortified towns.

## 3

In September 1792 an important event took place. Three new Civil Commissioners – Sonthonax, Polverel and Ailhaud – arrived from France. What made their arrival far more significant than that of their predecessors was that they had been given dictatorial power and were accompanied by an army of 6000 men, commanded by capable generals.

When hereafter we speak of the Commissioners we must leave Ailhaud out of the reckoning. He was a timid soul whom St. Domingo terrified. As soon as opportunity offered he returned to France, giving ill-health as a pretext. Sonthonax, an energetic but emotional and none too scrupulous lawyer, was the moving spirit of the Commission. The middle-aged Polverel was honest and capable, but lacked the driving power of his colleague.

The colonists were not altogether pleased with the new arrivals. Radicalism was on the ascendancy in France. The new National Assembly had once more voted to grant civic rights to the mulattoes, and the Commissioners were instructed not to permit any infringement of the new law. Considering the seriousness of the Negro insurrection, one might have expected the colonists to have somewhat modified their attitude towards the mulattoes. Admitted to equality with the whites, the free mulattoes, many of whom in their resentment were giving aid and comfort to the rebels, would have made common cause with the colonists. But the colonists had learned nothing and had forgotten nothing. They remained uncompromising.

The Colonial Assembly received the Commissioners with great ceremony. The president, Daugy, made a welcoming speech, in which he said that "the existence of the Negroes as freemen is physically incompatible with that of your European brothers." The colonists, he said, had not imported half a million Negroes into St. Domingo for the purpose of making them French citizens.

Sonthonax replied that it had never been the intention of the National Assembly to free the slaves and that if such an ill-advised measure were ever proposed he would oppose it. Later he said in a proclamation that the Colonial Assembly alone had the privilege of dealing with the Negro problem.

The Commissioners had a twofold task to perform – to insure the enjoyment of civic rights to the mulattoes and to crush the Negro rebellion. Had the colonists been willing to co-operate in settling the first problem, it is not impossible that the second might have been settled, for during the short period in which the French army took the field against the Negroes, it scored important victories. Tannerie and the headquarters of Jean-François were captured. The Negro generals had to flee into the mountains with the remnants of their forces. As for the Negro hordes that fought under the leadership of voodoo priests and African chieftains, they fared even worse. The crack regiments of Generals Rochambeau and Laveaux created such havoc among them that at one time 14,000 came to the white headquarters offering to submit. But the attitude of the colonists, combined with happenings in France, made it impossible for the Commissioners to undertake a vigorous campaign.

## 4

The Colonial Assembly was opposed to solving the mulatto problem in the way the French National Assembly wished to have it solved. Its solution was to terrorize the mulattoes as well as the Negroes. This was contrary to the instructions the Commissioners had received and impractical from the military viewpoint. Yet so bitter was the opposition of the Colonial Assembly and of the colonists that, to maintain order in the cities and guard against the machinations of the very people they had come to protect, the Commissioners were forced to immobilize a good part of their army. They were fighting on two fronts.

Finding it impossible to collaborate with the elite of the colony – the *Grands Blancs* – they turned to the *Petits Blancs* for support. They expected the little people to be more democratic in their sentiments. They were bitterly disillusioned. Persecuting the free mulattoes had too long served to compensate the *Petits Blancs* for their social and economic inferiority. Max Beerbohm has wittily remarked: "If he would have his ideas realized, the Socialist must first kill the Snob." Wretchedly poor as were many of the *Petits Blancs*, their snobbery was dear to them. They were "aristocrats of the epidermis." The idea that the free mulattoes should have the same civic rights as they was intolerable to them. In desperation the Commissioners dissolved the Colonial Assembly and the Jacobin Club they had organized and turned for support to the mulattoes. They gave them arms and formed them into legions – the Legion of Equality, the Legion of the West, the Legion of the South.

This, however, got them into fresh difficulties. The officers of their army had been taken to the bosom of the colonial aristocracy and had quickly adopted the prejudices of their hosts. They resented the idea of having to treat mulatto officers as their equals. There were unpleasant incidents, detrimental to morale and discipline. When in February 1793 the head of Louis XVI fell on the guillotine and news of the execution reached the colony, the army disintegrated. Most of the officers were royalists, and as republican France was now at war with Spain, scores of them deserted and went to join the Spaniards. Some offered their services to the Negro generals and helped them reorganize their shattered armies. Malaria still further paralyzed the activities of the white army. And then came the event that forced the Commissioners to abandon the cause of the colonists altogether, and turn for support to the Negroes.

## 5

France was now at war with England as well as Spain and an attack on the colony might be expected at any time. The French Government sent a military expert, General Galbaud, to help the Commissioners put the colony in a state of defense. Blanchelande having been deported by the Commissioners, Galbaud was given the title of Governor. The choice of Galbaud was unfortunate. He owned property in the colony and might have been expected to identify his interests with those of the planters, hostile to French policy. When he arrived in Le Cap, the Commissioners were in Port-au-Prince (renamed Port Républicain), and it was not long before news reached them that Galbaud was on the friendliest of terms with those among the planters whom they had most reason to distrust. Indeed, rumor had it that he intended to take things into his own hands and to deport the Commissioners. When Sonthonax and Polverel heard of this they returned to Le Cap to confront him, but took the precaution of having a large mulatto force accompany them.

Galbaud was taken unawares. When after a stormy interview the Commissioners informed him that they could dispense with his services and ordered him aboard a warship that was to take him back to France, he complied, but his submission was feigned. With the connivance of the squadron commander he visited the warships in the harbor and addressed the sailors, arousing them against the Commissioners and their mulatto allies. The principles of the Rights of Man had no more stanch supporters than the sailors, but the primitive instinct of race hatred Galbaud managed to arouse overcame the newly acquired ideas. On the twentieth of June, 1793, there were numerous clashes between sailors on leave and mulatto soldiers, and in the early morning of the twenty-first Galbaud landed with a force of three thousand men.

## 6

The garrison divided, some joining Galbaud, others supporting the Commissioners. The citizens joined in. Men fired at one another from behind barricades constructed of barrels, boxes and bales of cotton, from windows and roofs of houses. Galbaud pressed on towards the heart of the city. The arsenal was surrendered to him by the white commander and its mulatto defenders were massacred. When his artillery began shelling the Government Palace, the Commissioners retired to Haut-du-Cap, to that same Bréda plantation where Toussaint had been a slave.

The once peaceful plantation was now the key to the defensive system protecting Le Cap and its environs against the Negro rebels. A rebel force of some 15,000 men, under Macaya and Pierrot, was at that moment encamped a short distance from the city. When darkness fell and news reached the Commissioners that Galbaud was gaining steadily and would soon be in control of the city, they looked towards the bivouac fires of the Negroes and reached a momentous decision. They dispatched a horseman with an invitation to the two Negro commanders to come and see them immediately.

Macaya and Pierrot accepted the invitation. In a room of the plantation house – perhaps the same in which Toussaint had reached his agreement with the government party – with the crackle of musketry ringing in their ears, the Commissioners proposed to the Negroes that they enter the service of the Republic. If they agreed to do so, they and all their warriors would be declared freemen. "You will be the equals of all men, white or any other color; and will be granted all the rights and privileges enjoyed by French citizens."

Macaya and Pierrot knew that less than two years before the Colonial Assembly had refused to enfranchise a few score Negroes in order to obtain peace; now 15,000 were offered their liberty and the rights of French citizenship! They accepted.

That same night, in military formation, the Negroes crossed the breastworks that had so long kept them at bay.

## 7

Before the onrush of the Blacks, Galbaud's men were forced to yield. Then the inevitable happened. One house, then another burst into flames. Soon fires broke out all over the city, joined in a conflagration. The Commissioners have accused Galbaud's sailors of having set fire to the city to facilitate looting. Galbaud accused Macaya's and Pierrot's men. Still others have accused Negroes released from prison at Le Cap and destitute *Petits Blancs*. That the sailors looted is undeniable: the French consul in New York testified that they disposed of loot in that city.

In the streets lit up by the conflagration, amidst the crackling of flames and the crashing of falling timbers, the battle raged. Galbaud's men slowly retreated towards the harbor. Thousands of refugees packed the quay, carrying such belongings as they had been able to save. They were taken aboard the warships and merchant vessels as fast as circumstances would permit. Overcrowded boats upset and scores were drowned.

Galbaud ordered the cannon of the harbor fortifications spiked, so the fleet could not be fired on, and retired to the warships with the remnants of his force. On the night of the twenty-fourth, more than a hundred vessels, packed with ten thousand refugees, lifted anchor and set sail for the United States, leaving behind a city in ruins and streets strewn with corpses. Many of the refugees settled in the United States, where their descendants live to this day in New York, Massachusetts, Maryland, Virginia and some of the Southern states.

# 8

Galbaud's attempt to capture Le Cap had far-reaching consequences. Having freed 15,000 Negro warriors, the Commissioners were next obliged to free their wives and children. From this to the emancipation of all the slaves in the colony was only a step. On August 29, 1793, when Polverel was in Port-au-Prince, Sonthonax could no longer withstand the pressure and issued the emancipation proclamation. Polverel later approved it, but it was not the course he had meant to follow.

Robespierre wished political reform in France to be followed by economic reform. Polverel believed the situation in St. Domingo demanded that economic reform precede political reform. Thousands of Negroes were roaming the country and were acquiring habits of slothfulness and brigandage. No country could prosper or even exist under such circumstances. A measure was urgently needed that would induce the Negroes to return to work. Emancipation pure and simple would not only fail to accomplish this, but might have (and, indeed, did have) the opposite effect. The measure Polverel contemplated was immediate distribution of land to the Negroes. On September 3 of that year he wrote to Sonthonax: "Can you expect the Africans to resume work by giving them liberty, unless you have first given them land, and by doing so have created an incentive to labor they did not possess before?" Distribution of land would provide them with the further incentive to defend the country against invasion, "For," said Polverel, "it is not for the have-nots to sacrifice their lives in defense of the property of the haves." When order had been restored and the Negroes were at work on land owned by themselves, then, and only then, they should be given their freedom.

During his stay at Port-au-Prince, Polverel had made a beginning by confiscating land belonging to *émigrés* and either dividing it among the Negroes or turning it over to groups of

Negroes to cultivate in common. He felt bitter about the course events had taken and said in a proclamation: "Within six months you would have been property owners as well as free. But it was not to be. The hand of my colleague was forced by unfortunate circumstances. He has proclaimed universal freedom and himself was not free when he proclaimed it."

This points to a regrettable weakness in an otherwise remarkable man. While the emancipation proclamation made the realization of his program more difficult, it did not necessitate its abandonment. Peevishness is a poor substitute for adaptation. Polverel would probably have got over his fit of discouragement and have continued his noteworthy experiment, had not events made it necessary for him and Sonthonax to turn their attention to a matter that was even more pressing – the British invasion. But before we occupy ourselves with that invasion, let us see what effect the events in this chapter had upon Toussaint and his colleagues.

# CHAPTER V

## Toussaint and the Spaniards

AFTER the departure of Galbaud the Commissioners had taken counsel together. They realized that now they could no longer rely upon the whites to defend the colony. Nor could they rely upon the mulattoes. Mulatto slaveowners were no more pleased than the whites with the enfranchisement of thousands of slaves, and free mulattoes in general objected as strenuously to having Negroes become their equals as the whites objected to equality with the men of color. Of the army the Commissioners had brought with them, only shattered fragments remained. There was no one to turn to except the Negroes. The Commissioners sent forth an appeal to all Negro leaders and chieftains, in which they said: "Come and join us. We are enclosing a safe conduct. Become Frenchmen; be loyal to the French Republic. You will be free; you will be citizens, the same as we; you will receive high rank."

They had some success with the minor chieftains, but the really important leaders – Jean-François, Biassou and Toussaint – remained unmoved, and their attitude did not change even after emancipation had been proclaimed.

Why did Toussaint not rally to the Commissioners?

The negotiations with the previous set of Commissioners had convinced him that the authority of such officials was exceedingly doubtful. What guarantee existed that the French National Assembly would approve their promises? Had not Sonthonax himself said that the French National Assembly had no intention of freeing the Negroes? Moreover, it did not seem possible to him that the republican French Government would be able to withstand the assault of the European coalition. Royalist officers had assured him that the Allies were already in control of a large part of France. Was it not wiser to come to an understanding with the Spaniards, who undoubtedly would fall heir to the colony? Besides, his clerical friends had prejudiced him against the republicans – atheists, who had killed the King, the friend of the Negro.

He and Biassou were encamped in the Bois Caïman when an emissary from the Commissioners arrived to interview them. They gave their reply in writing. They found it impossible, they said, to negotiate with Commissioners whose authority they doubted. They had no intention of deserting their comrades in their struggle for the King's cause. Toussaint subscribed himself "General in the King's Army," and Biassou, "Governor-General for the King."

The Commissioners made a further attempt to convince Jean-François and Biassou. The two chiefs conferred together and sent this joint reply: "We cannot conform to the will of the Nation because from the beginning of the world we have executed the will of a King. We have lost the King of France, but we are esteemed by the King of Spain, who bestows rewards upon us and ceases not to give us succor. Consequently we are unable to acknowledge you, the Commissioners, before you have found a King."

Macaya, too, decided he preferred to fight on the side of the Spaniards and sent this curious epistle to explain why he had reconsidered: "I am the subject of three Kings: the King of the Congo, Lord of all the Blacks; the King of France, who represents his father; the King of Spain, who represents his mother. The three Kings are the descendants of those who, led by a star, went to adore the Man-God. I can therefore not serve the Republic, as I do not wish to be drawn into conflict with my brothers, who are the subjects of these three Kings."

## 2

The Spanish part of Haiti was twice as large as the French colony, yet had only 125,000 inhabitants, by far the greater part of whom were mulattoes. There were only 15,000 slaves. In all the vast territory there were but twenty-two sugar plantations, and barely enough coffee and tobacco was being produced to supply the population. Roads were few and so poor that outside Santo Domingo City vehicular traffic had fallen into disuse.

The inhabitants were cattle breeders, which meant that they allowed the cattle to breed unhindered, killing a cow or a calf now and then when they needed meat. A man might own thousands of heads of cattle and yet be miserably poor.

Clara St. Louis, a sister of Mary Hassall, an extract from whose letters to Aaron Burr has been previously quoted, gives, in a letter to her sister, this picture of a Spanish colonial household: –

About noon we saw a little hut. The guide, alighting, half opened the door, saying "May the holy Virgin bless this house!" This salutation brought out a tall sallow man, who gravely taking his segar from his mouth, bowed ceremoniously, and bid us enter. We followed him, and saw, sitting on an ox hide stretched on the ground, a woman whose ragged garments scarcely answered the first purposes of decency. She was suckling a squalid naked child, and two or three dirty children were lolling about, without being disturbed by the appearance of strangers. A hammock, suspended from the roof, was the only article of furniture in the house. Whilst the guide was unloading the mules to prepare our dinner, I went out to seek a seat beneath some trees; for the filth of the house, and the appearance of its inhabitants, filled me with disgust.

To my infinite astonishment, the plains which extended behind the house, as far as the eye could reach, were covered with innumerable herds of cattle, and on enquiring of the guide to whom they belonged, I learned, with no less surprise, that our host was their master. Incredible as it may appear, this miserable looking being, whose abode resembled the den of poverty, is the owner of countless multitudes of cattle, and yet it was with the greatest difficulty that we could procure a little milk.

A small piece of ground, where he raised tobacco enough for his own use, was the only vestige of cultivation we could discover. Nothing like vegetables or fruit could be seen. When they kill a beef, they skin it, and cutting the flesh into long pieces about the thickness of a finger, they hang it on poles to dry in the sun; and on this they live till it is gone, and then kill another.

Sometimes they collect a number of cattle and drive them to town in order to procure some of the most absolute necessaries of life. But this seldom happens, and never till urged by the most pressing want. As for bread, it was a luxury with which they are entirely unacquainted.

When such a colonist owned a few slaves, he did not overwork or ill-treat them. Raynal assures us that slaves in the Spanish colony were treated as members of the household and that their work mainly consisted of swinging hammocks. The misdirected energy of the Spaniards seems to have spent itself with the extermination of the Indians, giving place to inertia. About the only enterprising people in the colony were the slave traders, who stole Negroes in the French part of the island and exported them to Cuba and Puerto Rico.

The Negroes of St. Domingo, accustomed to the harsh treatment meted out to them by the French, felt attracted to the Spaniards and were ready to listen to the flattering offers made by Spanish officials. As soon as Spain found herself at war with France, the Spanish Colonial Minister, Don Pedro Acuna, wrote to the Governor of the colony, Don Joachim García, to try to persuade the Negro generals to ally themselves with the Spaniards. García was to make this offer: "Liberty, now and forever. The rights and prerogatives of Spanish citizenship. Valuable land concessions for all in the French or Spanish part of the island." In addition, the Negro leaders were to receive subsidies in money and supplies.

Obviously this offer applied only to the Negro leaders and to the men composing their armies – in other words, only to a fraction of the slave population of St. Domingo. Toussaint, however, chose to interpret it from the beginning as applying to all the slaves in the French colony. This deliberate disregard of the agreement necessarily had to lead to a speedy break between him and the Spaniards.

## 3

On August 25, 1793, four days before Sonthonax enfranchised the slaves, Toussaint issued this proclamation: –

> Having been the first to champion your cause, it is my duty to continue to labor for it. I cannot permit another to rob me of the initiative. Since I have begun, I will know how to conclude. Join me and you will enjoy the rights of freemen sooner than any other way. Neither whites, nor mulattoes have formulated my plans; it is to the Supreme Being alone that I owe my inspiration. We have begun, we have carried on, we will know how to reach the goal.

The meaning of this is clear. Toussaint, who kept well informed about what went on at Le Cap, knew that the emancipation proclamation was impending. He had reached an agreement with the Spaniards and feared the effect of the proclamation upon the Negroes. On the day of its appearance he sent forth this appeal from his headquarters at Turel: –

Brothers and Friends:

I am Toussaint L'Ouverture.* My name is perhaps known to you. I have undertaken to avenge you. I want liberty and equality to reign throughout St. Domingo. I am working towards that end. Come and join me, brothers, and combat by our side for the same cause.

TOUSSAINT L'OUVERTURE
*General of the Armies of the King*
*for the Public Good*

The two appeals are significant of Toussaint's determination not to permit a white man to claim the honor of having freed the slaves. He later always insisted that the Negroes did not owe their freedom to any white man, but had freed themselves.

## 4

It was about this time that Toussaint began using the name Louverture. Slaves were named after the plantation on which they were born, hence Toussaint's surname was Bréda. It has been claimed that he adopted the name Louverture on hearing that Polverel had exclaimed, "*Ce bougre-là se fait donc ouverture partout!*" – an exclamation which is said to have escaped the Commissioner after Toussaint had rebelled against the Spaniards and had cut his way through their lines. But Toussaint's proclamation of August 29, 1793, proves that he used the name long

* This is one of the rare documents in which Toussaint spells his name L'Ouverture, instead of Louverture.

before that time. Various other explanations are equally unsatisfactory. I shall hazard one of my own.

In adopting the name Louverture, Toussaint seems to have wished to impress upon the Negroes that by organizing the insurrection he had opened for them the gate to freedom. "Oh you Africans, my brothers," he says in one of his later proclamations, "have you forgotten that it is I who first raised the standard of insurrection against tyranny, against the despotism that kept you in chains?" The name, however, may have had a more subtle significance. The most beloved deity of the voodoo pantheon is the god Legba, affectionately called "Papa Legba" by the Haitian Negroes. Now, Legba is the keeper (hence the opener) of the Gate of Destiny. The Haitian Negroes to this day chant in Creole: "*Papa Legba, ouvri barrière pour moins!*" (Papa Legba, open the gate for me!) Does it not appear logical that in adopting the name Louverture, Toussaint should have thought of Legba? He was a loyal Catholic and later tried to suppress the voodoo religion, but he was a good politician and could not have helped realizing the advantage it would be to him to be associated in the minds of the Negroes with Papa Legba – the opener of the gate of destiny. When the Negroes called him Papa Louverture, as they often did, they seem to have made that association. "The cultivators," writes de Lacroix, "prostrated themselves before him as before a deity."

The adoption of the name Louverture thus appears as a stroke of genius on the part of Toussaint and undoubtedly contributed towards his success.

## 5

Toussaint's campaign against the army of the Commissioners does not give the measure of his military skill. The French army was now largely composed of Negroes and mulattoes, under the command of royalist officers. Often the men surrendered without fighting or after a minimum of resistance. Following a surrender most of the soldiers and many of the officers usually joined Toussaint's army. He began the campaign with 600 men, at its conclusion he had 5000!

He took in quick succession Gros-Morne, Marmelade, Plaisance, Acul, Limbé, Port-Magot, Le Petit Saint-Louis and Terre Neuve, thus becoming master of a large part of the North Province. The strict discipline he maintained and his reputation for humanity proved excellent assets. Towns that would have resisted Jean-François or Biassou to the bitter end, surrendered to him with little resistance, since it was known that he did not permit looting, did not make war on the civil population and treated prisoners of whatever color with humanity.

In this, as in all his campaigns, he gave evidence of physical courage that bordered on recklessness. He often led a charge against the enemy lines. In the course of his military career he was wounded seventeen times, but never seriously. He led a charmed life. Imagine a man being hit in the face by a spent cannon ball and escaping with the loss of a few teeth!

He had ways of endearing himself to his men. He shared their fatigues and hardships. He subsisted on the same fare as the soldiers and when food was scarce, as was often the case, their scanty ration sufficed him. When he would see artillerymen struggling to get a cannon into place, he would dismount and lend a hand, caring nothing about the consequences to his fine uniform. "The soldiers," says de Lacroix, "regarded him as an extraordinary being."

He achieved his greatest success against the army of the Commissioners at the beginning of the campaign, when with 600 men he captured Colonel Brandicourt's entire force of 1500. While clever maneuvering undoubtedly was partly responsible for the victory, unwillingness to fight on the part of the French officers was the chief reason for the success. The French colonel was taken prisoner during an ambush and Toussaint induced him to send a letter to his second in command, Pascaud, ordering him to surrender, which the latter seems to have done quite willingly. When the French force with flags flying and drums beating marched into Toussaint's camp, the vanquished appeared so much more formidable than the victors, that but for Toussaint's quick intervention, his men would have fled.

## 6

It has been said of the Southern planters of the United States that in the Civil War they fought not so much to preserve slavery as to preserve a mode of life, which, in its most favorable aspects, did not lack grace and beauty. Southern slavery was far from producing a civilization comparable to that of the ancient slave state of Athens. Such flowering as it had was certainly not worth the price that is still being paid. But it did produce something for which those privileged to enjoy it might well have formed an attachment without incurring the accusation of gross materialism.

Slavery in St. Domingo produced sugar, coffee, cotton, indigo, molasses, misery, corpses, deterioration of character and nothing else; yet the St. Domingo planters were as fierce in its defense, and as ready to renounce their country for daring to interfere with it, as were the planters of the United States. They formed a league, which adopted for its motto "Resistance against Oppression," and signed a treaty with England, transferring their allegiance to His Britannic Majesty in consideration of armed intervention to restore slavery. Less than a month after Sonthonax had issued the emancipation proclamation, British troops landed in Jérémie, in the South Province, and were greeted as deliverers.

One coast town after another was surrendered to the invaders by the royalist command. The frowning fortress of Môle St. Nicolas – "the Gibraltar of the Antilles" – with its two hundred cannon pointing out to sea, capitulated without a shot being fired. Bombarde, L'Arcahaye, Léogane, St. Marc, Verrette, Petite-Rivière welcomed the British. Port-au-Prince had to be surrendered the following year with its fleet of richly laden merchant vessels. Two-thirds of the entire colony was occupied by the British and the Spaniards.

General Laveaux, Commander in Chief of the French army and Provisional Governor, had entrenched himself at Port-de-Paix, in the North Province. His army, mainly composed of colonial troops, was ill-trained, ill-equipped and insubordinate. He was hemmed in by the British, the Spaniards and the Negro generals. His army stores had been destroyed in the conflagration at Le Cap, and the British blockade made it difficult to obtain fresh supplies from abroad. In the spring of 1794, he wrote to the Commissioners: "For more than six months we have been reduced to six ounces of bread a day, officers as well as men; but since the 13th of this month, we have none whatever, the sick only excepted. If we had powder, we should have been consoled. Our misery is truly great. Officers and soldiers experience the greatest privations. We have in our magazines neither shoes, nor shirts, nor clothes, nor soap, nor tobacco. The majority of the soldiers mount guard barefooted, like the Africans. We have not even a flint to give the men."

Colonel Whitelocke, the Commander of the British forces, did not believe in fighting if the same result could be achieved with less expenditure of energy. Thus far he had not encountered serious resistance. When a French commander showed an inclination to fight, Whitelocke held out a financial inducement which an already wavering loyalty found it difficult to resist. He held out an inducement of £5000 to General Laveaux, but received a challenge to a duel and the reply: "The fact that you are my enemy does not give you the right to call my honor into question." To his subordinates Laveaux wrote: "Answer any offer that is made you with lead. That sort of reply is never compromising."

But notwithstanding the loyalty and courage of Laveaux, the situation was desperate. So desperate that the emotional Sonthonax, weeping with rage, saw no other alternative except to set fire to such towns as the French were still holding and retire to the mountains. Polverel rebuked him. He had faith that their cause would still triumph. That faith proved justified, but it was neither the wisdom of the Commissioners nor the courage of Laveaux that brought about a reversal of the situation. "It must be acknowledged," writes de Lacroix, "that if the colors of France continued to wave over St. Domingo, it was due solely to an old Negro, who seemed to have received a mission from Heaven to cement the shattered fragments."

## 7

Toussaint was not satisfied with the bargain he had made with the Spaniards. He interpreted his agreement with them to mean that all the Negroes in the French colony were to be set free and acted accordingly. When he occupied a parish, his first act was to proclaim the freedom of the slaves. This was necessary, for the proclamation of Sonthonax had been ignored by the planters. Where the Negroes had not rebelled they remained slaves.

Toussaint's conduct was resented by Jean-François and Biassou even more than by the Spaniards. He had never been on good terms with Jean-François, now he also quarreled with Biassou. One reason for the quarrel was that they continued to sell Negroes to Spanish slave traders. Toussaint protested against this to the Spanish Governor, who, however, gave him no satisfaction. Biassou's mulatto secretary complained about Toussaint to Don Joachim García in these terms: –

> He raises and arms all the slaves, whom he tells that they are free. He gives orders for the re-establishment of posts Biassou has abolished, preaches disobedience and insurrection and declares himself chief of the rebels. We demand the head of the guilty man. In violation of the sacred orders of the King, he is promising liberty to all the slaves, including those who have resumed work and behave in an orderly fashion.

The issue was clear. The Spaniards were willing to grant liberty to the Negro leaders and to the few thousand Negroes who composed their armies. Jean-François and Biassou were satisfied with this. "In taking up arms I never meant to fight for general liberty, which I know to be a chimera," Gros quotes Jean-François as saying. Toussaint, however, wanted liberty for all the slaves and would take nothing less. The time when he would have been satisfied with a handful of enfranchisements was long since past.

The British invasion increased Toussaint's feeling of uneasiness. In all the territory the British had occupied they had restored slavery. Yet they were the allies of the Spaniards. When in February, 1794, the French National Assembly confirmed Sonthonax' emancipation proclamation, Toussaint became fully convinced that he had made a mistake. He did not belong with the Spaniards and their allies.

But to change sides now was to take a fearful risk. He would be fighting virtually unaided against the British, the Spaniards and the armies of Jean-François and Biassou. The French had nothing to offer him – neither military aid, nor subsidies, nor supplies. Yet he decided to take the risk.

## 8

Having made up his mind to change allegiance, Toussaint decided he owed it to his dignity to have General Laveaux make the first move. He called one of his officers, a certain Chevalier, and suggested that he join the French. Once in the French camp, he was to intimate discreetly to General Laveaux that if Toussaint received a letter from him asking him to place himself at the service of the Republic, he might consider doing so. Chevalier did as he was told, and it was not long before he was dispatched by Laveaux with a letter to Toussaint containing an urgent invitation.

So far, so good, but it was necessary for Toussaint to proceed with the utmost caution. He was surrounded by the armies of the Spaniards and their British and Negro allies. If they suspected him they would fall upon him and crush him. He had reason to believe that they were not wholly without suspicion and decided on a characteristic move: a journey to the Spanish colony. It was to be made supposedly to visit his family, whom he had not seen for many months – in reality to lull the Spaniards into a false security.

The Spaniards received him with great honors. Cabrera, the Commander in Chief, gave a banquet in his honor and a bullfight was staged for his entertainment. The Marquis d'Hermonas, Toussaint's immediate superior, presented him with a decoration in the name of His Catholic Majesty and notified him of his promotion to general. Toussaint managed to gain his confidence to such an extent that seeing him in church at his devotions, d'Hermonas exclaimed: "If God descended upon the earth He could inhabit no purer heart than that of Toussaint Louverture!"

The superiors of d'Hermonas evidently began to suspect that he was being taken in, for soon after he was relieved from his command. His successor showed himself decidedly cool towards Toussaint, who noticed that he and his family were being watched. Then Toussaint's nephew Moyse was arrested, and the black leader had some difficulty in getting him released. Finally Jean-François arrested several of his officers and removed them to Camp Barade. Toussaint, accompanied by his brother Jean-Pierre, hastened to the camp, to be received by a volley of musketry. Jean-Pierre fell dead from his horse. Toussaint gave his horse the spurs and escaped, but realized that unless he struck quickly his enemies might deliver a fatal blow.

# CHAPTER VI
## Toussaint Joins the French

BACK at his headquarters at Marmelade, Toussaint took counsel with his three principal subordinates – Moyse, Gabart and Paparel. He gave them his reasons for wishing to join the French and they assured him that the men would follow wherever he led. To Moyse was assigned the task of keeping Jean-François in check. Gabart was to defend Marmelade, and Paparel was to hold strategic Plaisance against the Spaniards. Toussaint himself was to undertake the offensive.

With the pick of his troops he marched swiftly upon Biassou's headquarters at Ennery, scattered a Spanish force on the way and fell upon the camp of his former chief like a thunderbolt. Biassou's men were thrown into confusion and he himself fled so hurriedly that he left behind his fine horses and carriage, a gold watch and a diamond-studded snuffbox. Toussaint had the instincts of a gentleman. He forwarded Biassou's personal belongings to him with his compliments.

He now wheeled about, attacked the Spaniards at Gonaïves, where there were large stores of supplies, and captured the town. Believing that he had sufficiently demonstrated the value of his services, he wrote to Laveaux and formally placed himself under his orders. He frankly acknowledged that he had made a mistake in joining the Spaniards. "It is true, General," he wrote, "that I have been deceived by the enemies of the Republic, but what man can boast of his ability to escape every pitfall? In truth, they caught me in their snares."

The French general replied most graciously and appointed him Commander of the Cordon of the West. This was the beginning of a friendship which did not even cease when Toussaint gently prodded Laveaux out of St. Domingo. He wrote Laveaux endearing letters, of which this is a sample: —

Undoubtedly there are ideal friendships, but I find it difficult to believe in the existence of a friendship more ideal and more sincere than the one I feel for you. Yes, General, Toussaint's affection for you is like that of a son for his father. Your grave will be his. He will gladly sacrifice his own life for your sake. His arm and his head will always be at your service. If I die, I will take with me into the grave the satisfaction of having defended a virtuous friend and father as well as the cause of liberty. The officers and soldiers of the army under my command assure you of their loyalty; as for me, I embrace you a million times.

Laveaux, more soberly, said of Toussaint, in an address he delivered in Paris, in 1797: "He fought against us until April 6, 1794. He fought for the freedom of the Blacks. He had been assured that only a King could grant that freedom. When I proved to him that the French Republic was sincere in its intentions, he ranged himself under the tricolor. He attacked the Spaniards at Gonaïves, which he captured, and brought with him more than 5000 armed Blacks, who fought under his orders."

## 2

A British admiral, wishing to give King George III a visual notion of the tortuous topography of Haiti, crumpled up a sheet of paper, threw it upon the table and said: "Sire, Haiti looks like that."

Through this labyrinthine maze Toussaint was weaving back and forth with his army, now attacking the British, now the Spaniards, now their Negro allies. Moyse had been forced to give way before the onslaught of Jean-François. Toussaint had quickly remedied the situation by falling upon Jean-François as unexpectedly as he had on Biassou. He reported to Laveaux: "I came very nearly capturing Jean-François himself. He owes his escape to the thickness of the underbrush, into which he dived, abandoning all his personal belongings. His baggage, letters and papers have fallen into my hands. He saved his shirt and breeches, nothing more. My men have done terrible execution among his soldiers and I have taken many prisoners."

Toussaint, like Bonaparte, owed much of his military success to the rapidity of his movements. The longest day's march credited to the Corsican is seventy-two kilometers; fifty-two in mountain country. Toussaint marched his army sixty-four kilometers in a single day through mountainous territory with only a trail to guide him. His soldiers, it is true, were unencumbered by baggage or even clothing. "They have neither coats, nor shirts, nor trousers, barely a few rags that do not cover a twentieth part of their bodies," he wrote to Laveaux.

With this tatterdemalion army he fought, in the space of a few months, over two hundred encounters, driving the enemy from the greater part of the North and West Provinces. He had to supply his army mainly by raids upon the enemy, but occasionally managed to purchase supplies from Spanish traders. In his memorandum to Napoleon he claims to have spent 648,000 francs of his own money in making the purchases. He refers to the money as savings made during his servitude and complains that it was never repaid. How it was possible for a slave to accumulate so large a sum he fails to explain. That the sum named was spent by him for arms and supplies appears probable, but it was undoubtedly money advanced to him by the Government Party and by the Spaniards at the beginning of the insurrection.

Although his men had to undergo many hardships their morale remained excellent. They had little to eat, but they were used to starving. The arduous marches were preferable to long hours of labor in the sugar field or at the mill, under the whips of the drivers. Strict disciplinarian though he was, Toussaint was a leader after their own heart. He would ride up and down the line during the march, encouraging his men, calling them his "children," mingling religious exhortations with coarse jokes, raising his voice in song together with the soldiers. When a river had to be crossed, he would stand up on the back of his horse, like a circus rider, and none laughed more heartily than he when he took a ducking.

His guerrilla tactics confounded the enemy. Says Métral: "He disappears – he has flown – as if by magic. Now he reappears again where he is least expected. He seems to be ubiquitous. One never knows where his army is, what it subsists on, how he manages to recruit it, in what mountain fastness he has hidden his supplies and his treasury. He, on the other hand, seems perfectly informed concerning everything that goes on in the enemy camp."

## 3

Toussaint defeated the British a number of times in the field, but lack of heavy artillery made it impossible for him to drive them from the coast towns. He laid siege to St. Marc and almost met with disaster as the result of the defection of a mulatto regiment.

Mulatto slaveowners had, with few exceptions, taken the side of the British. Other men of color were divided, and when a mulatto regiment from L'Arcahaye came to offer its services to Toussaint, he was overjoyed, for he ardently desired co-operation between Negroes and mulattoes. One day, during the siege, while helping to put a battery into place, he injured his hand so severely that he was forced to relinquish the command to a subordinate and retire to his tent. He was reclining upon a cot, when he heard confused noises and the sound of firing. He ran outside and saw the mulattoes attacking from all sides. Injured hand and all, he vaulted upon a horse, took command of his men, who had been thrown into confusion, and led an orderly retreat.

The incident was unfortunate, more from the political than the military viewpoint, for it still further increased ill-feeling between Negroes and mulattoes. "They will rue this some day!"

Toussaint exclaimed. To Laveaux he wrote: "From now on I'll deal differently with them. I have treated them like a father and they have repaid me by this dastardly attempt to turn me over to the enemy."

## 4

General Charles George Gordon – the famous "Chinese" Gordon, the story of whose life reads like a fantastic legend – exclaimed in one of his bitter moods: "There is nothing like a civil war to show what skunks men are!" What marks Toussaint Louverture as a historical figure akin to Lincoln is that in the midst of a civil war, complicated by the racial problem, he refused to be carried away by the forces of darkness, hate and vengeance. Not that his record is entirely unblemished. Under great provocation he sometimes forgot himself; but on the whole that record is one few leaders of men have been able to equal. This was due partly to mildness of temper, partly to the fact that during his years of bondage he had not been ill-treated, partly to religious influence and the reading of Epictetus, but also to the fact that he possessed the mentality of a statesman.

The statesman Toussaint realized that vengeance is a double-edged sword. "I will never cease to use what influence I possess and every means at my disposal to see to it that the blacks do not show themselves unworthy of liberty," he once wrote to General Hédouville. Could they do so by giving themselves over to demoralizing acts of vengeance, by imitating their former masters in acts of cruelty? "Vengeance is mine, I will repay, saith the Lord!" was written by a man who realized that we cannot exercise vengeance without injuring ourselves.

The statesman Toussaint realized that surrounded as were the Negroes of St. Domingo by slaveowning powers, they could not hope to maintain liberty without building an economically powerful state able to supply them with modern weapons of warfare. To do this the co-operation of the whites was indispensable. It could not be obtained on the basis of retribution for past wrongs.

So Toussaint set his face hard against any form of vengeance and ruthlessly suppressed every attempt at a renewal of the scenes that had marked the first phase of the insurrection. He deliberately tried, by acts of generosity that seem almost quixotic, to build up confidence and good will among the white population. For this he has been criticized by men of his own race, less far-sighted than he. The Haitian ruler Henri Christophe was to say of Toussaint: "He was favorable to the white colonists, and the care and partiality which he felt for them went so far that he was severely censured as being more attached to them than to the people of his color." In answer to criticism of this nature Toussaint replied: "Whoever the men are whose services I am forced to employ to aid me in my important projects, the day will come when I will prove that nobody less than I merits the reproach of having allowed himself to be dominated by them."

The co-operation of the white colonists enabled him to create an economy permitting the arming of practically the entire Negro population. It was this which, in the final analysis, was responsible for Haitian independence.

## 5

When in July, 1794, the news reached Toussaint that Jean-François had massacred some 800 white colonists at Fort-Dauphin, he trembled with rage and indignation. To Laveaux he wrote: "As for me, General, you may rely upon my sentiments of humanity. I have always had a horror of leaders who find satisfaction in the shedding of blood. My religion, whose precepts I mean to observe, forbids it."

When he learned that one of his most capable officers, Blanc-Cazenave, had shot forty white prisoners, he immediately ordered his arrest. The Negro commander was found dead in his prison cell a few days later and the accusation has been made against Toussaint of having had him strangled. He reported to Laveaux that the prisoner had died of apoplexy and added, with a touch of cynicism: "*Requiescat in pace.*"

He extended his protection even to French *émigrés*, who had come to St. Domingo in the hope of regaining their colonial possessions by aiding the British. This is all the more remarkable since the *émigrés* shot all Negro soldiers who fell into their hands and French law required him to execute all *émigrés* who aided the foreign enemy. He defied the French Government and refused to retaliate, being of the opinion that the *émigrés* should be conciliated and their abilities utilized to develop the colony. In his policy towards the *émigrés* he anticipated Napoleon by many years, but while in St. Domingo the *émigrés* proved useful, their main contribution in France was the White Terror after the Restoration.

## 6

Toussaint had invaded the West Province and defeated a combined Spanish and *émigré* army, under the Marquis d'Espinville, before Mirebalais. The Marquis, with some 800 *émigrés*, took refuge in the fortified town. Their situation soon became desperate and d'Espinville asked for an interview with the Negro general.

They met face to face, the scion of the old nobility and the representative of a race that, in the opinion of the colonists, was but a species of chimpanzee. One had received a classical education, the other had little book learning. One had outward grace and elegance, the other looked somewhat comical in his general's uniform and the yellow Madras handkerchief he habitually knotted over his crinkly hair. Yet, if evolution is spiritual as well as biological, there can be little doubt about who stood higher in the evolutionary scale.

The Marquis acknowledged that his position was extremely

difficult, but said that he and his followers might as well die fighting, since surrender meant death anyway. Toussaint meditated for a moment, then said: "I promise that nobody will be shot – more than that: those of you who wish to join my army may do so."

The Marquis looked at him incredulously. He suspected a trap. Toussaint, seeing that he was not believed, struck the scabbard of his sword and cried with a touch of temper: "I swear it upon my sword!"

He kept his word. The Colonial Committee of Public Safety, composed of white republicans and mulattoes, demanded that the prisoners be sent to Port-de-Paix to be court-martialed. Toussaint replied that he had given his word and refused to deliver them. Laveaux, who could not afford to quarrel with him, sustained him.

On the day of the surrender of Mirebalais another incident took place that shows the lengths to which Toussaint was prepared to go in order to conciliate the white population. A group of planters from the West Province, fearing that if Mirebalais fell escape would be cut off, had decided to seek refuge at Port-au-Prince. They loaded their most valuable belongings on some two hundred pack animals, and accompanied by their families and such of their household slaves as had remained loyal to them, departed for the coast city. But Mirebalais had already fallen and a detachment of Toussaint's army intercepted the caravan. The baggage was found to contain gold and silver bullion and many other objects of value – a rich prize for a general who had to supply his army with what he was able to capture from the enemy.

The dejected prisoners were brought to Toussaint's camp. Undoubtedly they expected to be retained as hostages and to see their belongings confiscated. The usages of warfare would have justified such a course. Toussaint, however, asked them if anything had been taken from them, and when they replied in the negative, said: "I'll give you an armed escort that will conduct you and your belongings safely to Port-au-Prince. As for the Negroes who are with you, those who of their own free will wish to accompany you, may do so."

The incident is vouched for by an *émigré* eyewitness, de Montfayou.

## 7

On July 22, 1795, Spain signed a peace treaty with the French Republic at Basle. Under the terms of the treaty His Catholic Majesty ceded to France the Spanish part of Haiti, with the understanding that Spanish troops were to continue to occupy it until a white French garrison could be sent. The Negro armies of Jean-François and Biassou were disbanded, most of their soldiers joining Toussaint's army.

Jean-François retired to Cádiz with the rank of lieutenant general. He had amassed great wealth and was received in the best social circles. Ebony-faced, but haughty in appearance, attired in a gold-braided uniform, his hands and the hilt of his sword flashing with jewels, possessing an eloquent tongue, he found favor with many white women, but the Negroes of Haiti ceased to interest him. He never returned to the island.

The far less prepossessing Biassou went to St. Augustine, in Florida, where he was killed in a brawl. Toussaint, considering that the Negro cause owed something to Biassou, and remembering no doubt that when Jean-François had imprisoned him Biassou had obtained his release, later granted his destitute widow a pension.

Toussaint was promoted to brigadier general by the French Directory and was now recognized as the foremost black man in Haiti and in the world.

# CHAPTER VII

## Toussaint and Laveaux

WHILE Toussaint's star had been rising in the northern part of the colony, that of a mulatto, André Rigaud, rose in the south.

Rigaud was the son of a French nobleman and a Haitian Negress. He was born in Les Cayes, in the South Province, had been educated in France, and before the Revolution had exercised the profession of goldsmith in his native town. He was of an adventurous disposition and had enlisted in the colored contingent that had fought with distinction at Savannah and Guadeloupe. When Sonthonax organized his mulatto legions, Rigaud formed the Legion of Equality in the South Province – by far the best trained body of mulattoes in the colony. He was not, like Toussaint, put to the test of fighting on several fronts, but made a good showing against the British, who in the South Province were unable to advance far beyond Jérémie, where they had first landed.

The capture of Port-au-Prince and Léogane by the British had isolated the South Province from the remainder of the colony, enabling Rigaud to rule without interference from anyone. He was opposed to slavery, but believed in the caste system and wished the mulattoes to be the dominant caste. He established in the South Province a mulatto dictatorship. White men were barred from holding public office; blacks serving in the army could not advance beyond the rank of captain.

Rigaud's views were shared by the majority of mulattoes and even by Negroes who had been freemen before the insurrection. Indeed, in St. Domingo an old free Negro was considered a mulatto, and a mulatto who had been a slave, a Negro. Governor Laveaux reported to the Minister of Marine: "The mulattoes are in despair at seeing Toussaint Louverture, a Negro, become brigadier general. Yes, Citizen, I must admit the fact: all the mulattoes and old free Negroes are the enemies of emancipation and of equality. They cannot conceive that a former Negro slave can be the equal of a white man, a mulatto or an old free Negro."

Thus was demonstrated the truth of Robespierre's saying: "Men would rather submit to masters themselves than see the number of their equals multiply."

## 2

Laveaux had established headquarters in Port-de-Paix, Le Cap being in ruins and difficult to defend. He had turned over the command of Le Cap to the mulatto general Villate. Rigaud, Villate and Toussaint were of equal rank, but Toussaint had by far the largest army.

Villate was vain and ambitious, but lacked Rigaud's ability. Nevertheless he had done at Le Cap what Rigaud had accomplished in the South Province – established a mulatto dictatorship, which, however, was principally distinguished for inefficiency and corruption. Laveaux received so many complaints that he decided to return to Le Cap and take up residence in the Government Palace, which the flames had spared. This was not to Villate's liking, and when Laveaux began inquiring into the city's finances, he stirred up a hornets' nest. Villate went so far as to threaten the Governor with armed force. Laveaux, who had no army devoted to him, was virtually helpless and appealed to Toussaint for protection. That the Governor of the colony should have come to such a pass shows the low ebb to which white prestige in St. Domingo had fallen.

Toussaint felt flattered by Laveaux's appeal and sent this hyperbolic reply: "What! They have dared to threaten you with armed force! What has got into them? Do they imagine they can do as they please? If necessary I'll die a thousand deaths to bring them to their senses. This very day I'm sending a delegation of four to them with a letter."

Toussaint knew he could speak with authority. Not only did he command a much larger force than Villate, but the greater part of Villate's army was composed of Negroes, who, in the event of a conflict, were certain to side with the black general. Indeed, one of Villate's principal subordinates, the Negro colonel Pierre Michel, commanding a force of four thousand men stationed at Haut-du-Cap, was in constant communication with Toussaint and kept him informed about all that happened in the city.

Toussaint's letter had a sobering effect, and for several months Laveaux was shown some of the consideration to which his rank entitled him.

## 3

Rigaud had watched with dismay the rise of Toussaint Louverture. He felt that not the Negroes, but the mulattoes, were entitled to inherit the power that had slipped from the hands of the white race. Since the Negroes were in the overwhelming majority, this could only be accomplished by means of a mulatto dictatorship, which Rigaud meant to extend to the entire colony. The first step towards this must be the removal of Laveaux, who favored Toussaint and the Negroes. He sent his friend Pinchinat to Le Cap to secure Villate's collaboration.

Villate, already resentful at the interference of Laveaux, did not need much persuading, especially since Pinchinat proposed that Villate should be the Governor's successor. Laveaux was to be arrested, placed aboard a ship and deported. Following the arrest, the Municipal Council, composed of mulattoes, was to name Villate Provisional Governor.

Toussaint was expected to accept the *fait accompli* rather than risk civil war; but the plot could not succeed unless the Negroes in the city could be convinced that Laveaux was their enemy. A campaign to discredit the Governor was set on foot. The rumor was spread that he had sold out to the British. The exact sum was mentioned – 5,000,000 francs – said to be on board a ship in the harbor, on which, it was claimed, he meant to flee as soon as the British fleet appeared in the offing. A warehouse on the quay was said to be filled with chains intended for the wrists and ankles of all former slaves. Many of the Negroes believed the story and an atmosphere was created favorable to the *coup d'état*.

Laveaux was aware of these machinations, but there was little he could do. In a letter to the Minister of Marine he wrote: "Villate is quite persuaded that he is going to be Governor, and in that mad notion all his partisans support him." Behind Villate's vacillating figure he discerned the capable and resolute Rigaud, "whose pride and ambition are such that he dreams of becoming dictator of the colony."

## 4

On the morning of March 20, 1796, there was a military parade on the Place d'Armes at Le Cap. Governor Laveaux reviewed the garrison and then returned to the Government Palace. Being an old man and liking his comfort, he put on his dressing-gown and slippers, and when the engineer Galley, who wished to discuss with him the strengthening of the city's fortifications, was announced, he received him in his bedroom. They were bending over blueprints when Villate called to report that the soldiers were back in their barracks and order prevailed throughout the city. The real purpose of the visit was to ascertain if the arrest of Laveaux was likely to encounter serious obstacles. What happened soon after the visit Laveaux thus recounts in a letter to Toussaint: –

On the morning of the 20th of March I was in my bedroom, seated at a table, conversing with the chief engineer. Suddenly the door of my work cabinet was thrown open and six or eight men entered. A crowd of about a hundred poured in at the same time through the door leading to the drawing-room. All were mulattoes – there was among them not a single Negro or white man. I thought they wished me to arbitrate a quarrel, and rising calmly from my chair, I asked: "Citizens, what is your pleasure?" Without replying they fell upon me. I fought back and managed to free myself. The engineer was seized. I called for help. My aide-de-camp Robert came running, but was unable to reach my side. They belabored me with fists and sticks. I was in my slippers and lost them during the scuffle. I was dragged into the street, by the arms, by the hair, barefoot, bareheaded. They threw me into prison, where medical assistance was denied me.

In the meantime the Municipality had met, Laveaux was declared to have forfeited the confidence of the people and Villate was named Provisional Governor. Thus far everything had gone smoothly. Mulatto soldiers patrolled the streets. A couple of Negro officers who attempted to arouse the Negroes were promptly arrested. The coup had succeeded admirably, except that Villate hesitated about placing Laveaux aboard a ship for deportation to France.

## 5

The Negro colonel Pierre Michel, encamped at Haut-du-Cap with his four thousand men, had no sooner heard of the happenings in the city than he sent a dispatch rider to Toussaint's headquarters at Gonaïves. Toussaint was prepared for just such an eventuality. Prominent mulattoes throughout the North Province were immediately taken into custody. A letter was sent to the Municipality of Le Cap demanding instant release of Laveaux. Generals Dessalines, Moyse and Belair were ordered to march to Haut-du-Cap with two battalions, totaling six thousand men, join forces with Colonel Michel and await further orders. At the same time (and this was a tactic Toussaint was to employ on several occasions) thousands of armed cultivators from the Plaine-du-Nord were sent into the city, but kept firmly in hand by Toussaint's agents. He himself remained at Gonaïves and awaited developments.

His plan was meant to accomplish two things: to restore Laveaux to power and to prevent armed conflict by making so formidable a show of force as to make its employment unnecessary. With ten thousand troops of the line massed at Haut-du-Cap and thousands of irregulars crowding the city, the conspirators realized that their situation was hopeless. The day following the arrest, the Municipal Council voted a resolution of loyalty to the Governor, then marched in a body to the prison to release Laveaux and tender its apologies. Immediately after his release Laveaux departed for Haut-du-Cap, where the black generals received him with military honors.

For an entire week Toussaint remained at Gonaïves and made no further move. He wished to give Villate and his fellow-conspirators ample time to seek safety. With the west coast occupied by the British, civil war must be avoided at any cost. It was not until the twenty-seventh that he appeared at Haut-du-Cap, where he and Laveaux fell into each other's arms.

The following day the Negro general, riding side by side with the Governor, made his entry into Le Cap at the head of ten thousand men. It was his first appearance in the city since he had been a slave. Through the streets where only five years before he had driven de Libertat's carriage – a graying, liveried coachman for whom life seemed to have little more in store – he now rode in general's uniform, at the head of long lines of infantry, cavalry and artillery, cheered by thousands of white men and Negroes. Mulatto historians, bitterly hostile to him, speak with admiration of the discipline of his army and the order he maintained among the thousands of irregulars, whom he controlled with a word, with a look.

## 6

On April 1, 1796, Le Cap was in a festive mood. Flags waved, bunting decorated the half-ruined houses. On the Place d'Armes, in solid array, the army stood massed. Laveaux and Toussaint, surrounded by their staffs, appeared to the cheering of the multitude. Commands rang out; the soldiers presented arms; the band played the Marseillaise. Then the Governor addressed the soldiers. His speech was a eulogy of Toussaint, whom he called the savior of the whites and the Negroes, the upholder of constituted authorities. Pointing to Toussaint, he shouted: "There stands this Spartacus, the Negro whose coming Raynal prophesied, whose destiny it is to avenge the outrages perpetrated against his race!"

Toussaint raised his sword and cried in a burst of enthusiasm: "After God – Laveaux!"

But this was not all. Laveaux announced Toussaint's appointment to the office of Lieutenant Governor and solemnly promised to undertake nothing of importance without consulting him. This virtually meant that he abdicated his power into the hands of Toussaint and would remain Governor and Commander in Chief in name only. "It must be acknowledged," comments de Lacroix, "that as soon as Toussaint officially became associated with the government, there was an immense improvement in the spirit of the Negroes. The voice of authority, no longer suspect, called them to order, to work, to submission. Toussaint's power became greater than ever. He changed the habits of the Negroes by his will alone."

The slave of the Bréda plantation had traveled far.

# CHAPTER VIII

## Toussaint Worries About a Friend

"It would be difficult to conceive of anything more calculated to dispel the prejudice against the Negro race than the conduct of Toussaint Louverture," declared the French National Assembly in a resolution. Nevertheless, the French Government felt uneasy about the Negro general's growing power. The war with England made it impossible to send a large army to St. Domingo, but the Government decided to dispatch a new set of Commissioners to curb the Negro leader. There was no intention of antagonizing him. He was to be promoted to division commander, thus becoming, after Laveaux, the highest-ranking officer in the colony – no longer the equal, but the superior, of Rigaud and Villate. He was furthermore to be presented with a magnificent sword and a brace of pistols of Versailles manufacture, as a token of esteem from the French Government. Still another honor was to be conferred upon him: he was to be invited to send two of his sons to France to be educated at the expense of the Republic. The members of the Directory must have winked at one another when they made this proposal, for it meant nothing else than that he was asked to give valuable hostages as a guarantee of good behavior.

The Commissioners selected were our old friend Sonthonax; the mulatto Raimond, who had so long represented the mulattoes in the French capital; Roume, a member of the first Commission; Giraud and Leblanc. Sonthonax was the only one upon whom some reliance could be placed to attempt to curb Toussaint. The mild Raimond was not of a caliber to grapple with a Toussaint Louverture. Roume was honest, but mediocre and was to occupy himself entirely with the former Spanish colony. Giraud and Leblanc were nonentities. To heighten their prestige the Commissioners were to be accompanied by a force of 1200 men, under Rochambeau and Desfourneau, and the squadron was to transport a large supply of gunpowder, 20,000 muskets and a dozen pieces of artillery. It was hardly an expedition calculated to overawe the Negro leader.

## 2

The Commissioners landed at Le Cap on May 11, 1796. Sonthonax immediately began an investigation of Villate's mutiny. The mulatto general was arrested and ordered deported. The Commissioner next sent a delegation to investigate Rigaud. The Dictator did not care to be investigated, and spread the rumor that the delegation had come to restore slavery. In the rioting that followed some two hundred whites were massacred. Rigaud, pretending to be greatly shocked, took the delegation under his protection and shipped it out of his domain, lest worse befall it. Sonthonax fumed and sent a report to France denouncing Rigaud, but there was little else he could do about it.

Toussaint had advised Sonthonax to leave Rigaud in peace, since it was impossible to deal firmly with him as long as the British barred the way to the South Province. He was angry with Sonthonax for his blundering move and with Rigaud for having resorted to a massacre.

Toussaint had been far from pleased with the arrival of the Commissioners. He had seen a vision. It was the vision of an independent Negro state, ruled by a Negro – Toussaint Louverture; a Negro state well governed and prosperous that could hold its head high in the family of nations; a Negro state able to challenge the right of the whites to consider the Negroes an inferior race and to keep them in slavery; a Negro state able to champion the cause of the Negroes throughout the West Indies.

He was too shrewd and too careful a man to resort to hasty and ill-considered measures to realize his ideal. He never forgot his favorite proverbs – "*Doucement allé loin,*" "*Patience bat la force.*" He had no intention to hurry matters, but had made up his mind to loosen the bond with France a little at a time, almost imperceptibly. He decided to make a beginning. Laveaux, Governor and nominal head of the army, and the interfering Sonthonax must leave.

## 3

The colony, whose provinces were now called "departments," was to elect representatives to the new French Chamber of Deputies (the Five Hundred) and to the Senate (the Council of the Elders). Toussaint decided to honor Laveaux and Sonthonax with two of the mandates. He did not trouble to consult the wishes of Sonthonax in the matter, but to Laveaux he sent this extraordinary epistle: –

My General, my Father, my Good Friend:
Foreseeing (as I do with sorrow) that great unpleasantness is in store for you in this unhappy land, for whose welfare you have sacrificed health and family, and wishing to be spared the pain of witnessing so painful a spectacle, I should like to see you elected to the office of Deputy. This will give you the satisfaction of seeing your fatherland and your wife and children again and will save you from becoming the plaything of factions constantly springing up in St. Domingo. At the same time my comrades-in-arms and myself will have gained the advantage of being represented by the most devoted of advocates. Yes, my General, my Father, my Benefactor, France has many excellent men, but where is the man who, like you, can be relied upon always to remain the true friend of the Blacks? No, your equal there will never be!

Laveaux understood perfectly and decided to accept the opportunity Toussaint offered him to make a dignified exit. He wrote to the Negro leader that he would be a candidate for the Senate and received this reply: –

I have not lost a single minute in sending confidential agents whose business it will be to impress upon all the electors how important it is for the welfare of the Blacks that you should be chosen to represent them. You will be! Everything it is in my power to do, will be done.

When in September of that year the Electoral Assembly met at Le Cap, two of Toussaint's "confidential agents" were on hand to offer advice. They were his nephew, General Moyse, and Colonel Pierre Michel. In order that their advice might have greater weight, they had provided themselves with a substantial military escort. Moyse stationed his men in front of the hall, while Michel, a pistol in one hand, a sword in the other and accompanied by a dozen soldiers, went inside and mounted the platform. He repeated the advice previously given, adding that failure to heed it might have unpleasant consequences. Thus forcibly reminded, the electors chose Toussaint's slate unanimously.

Soon after Laveaux left for France. Sonthonax, far from pleased with the honor conferred upon him, made no preparations to leave. He had plans of his own and believed himself sufficiently astute to make Toussaint his tool or to break his power.

# CHAPTER IX

## Toussaint and Sonthonax

SONTHONAX was justly popular with the Negroes of St. Domingo. They had not forgotten that it was he who had issued the emancipation proclamation. He had increased his popularity by distributing to the Negro cultivators the twenty thousand muskets he had brought with him. In handing out the muskets he had said: "This is the guarantee of liberty Sonthonax is giving you. Whoever tries to take it from you intends to reduce you to slavery again. Work, but remember that nobody has the right to make you work against your will."

He was almost equally popular with the mulattoes, notwithstanding his harsh treatment of Villate and his disagreement with Rigaud. The mulattoes remembered that it was he who had forced the whites to grant them civic rights, who had organized them into legions and had given them arms, who had repeatedly upheld mulatto officers when they were being snubbed by their white colleagues. He solidified his popularity with them by marrying a mulattress, Madame Villevaleix, a widow with several children and considerable property.

No white man, however, had ever been hated more bitterly by the white colonists of St. Domingo than Sonthonax. They considered him the author of all their woes. They hated him for all the things that had earned him the gratitude and devotion of the Negroes and the mulattoes. He had, moreover, dissolved the Colonial Assembly and had deported hundreds of colonists. They held him responsible for the burning and looting of Le Cap. Together with Polverel he had confiscated the land of scores of *émigrés*, until now two thirds of the land in the colony was the property of the State. They could forgive Toussaint Louverture – a Negro fighting for his own race, who moreover did all he could to protect the white population – but Sonthonax they could not forgive. He was a traitor to his race, the Devil incarnate.

Sonthonax returned their hatred with a vengeance. Hysterical by nature, he allowed his hatred to dominate him to an extent which might have had terrible consequences. Billaud-Varenne, a member of the Committee of Public Safety during the Terror, was to say later: "The greatest mistake you [the Negroes of St. Domingo] have made during the Revolution in your country is not to have exterminated all the colonists, to the last man." General Galbaud has charged that Sonthonax voiced a similar opinion, and Toussaint, in a report to the Directory, makes the startling accusation that Sonthonax made him a definite proposal to massacre the colonists.

It is not impossible that misguided altruism was principally responsible for this proposal by Sonthonax. Generous but ill-balanced natures can be aroused by the sight of injustice to a paroxysm of fury that may lead to the commission of unbelievable crimes. Marat, whose sympathy with the common people was as great as it was genuine, was largely responsible for the September massacres in Paris and advocated the beheading of 500,000 Frenchmen. In the complexity of the human soul altruism may, however, easily blend with egotism and ambition. Thus Marat advocated a dictatorship and undoubtedly aspired to be the dictator, while Sonthonax dreamed himself the white ruler of an independent Negro state. He believed that Toussaint would realize the absurdity of a half-educated Negro's being at the head of the government and would content himself with second place.

## 2

Sonthonax had begun courting Toussaint immediately on his arrival in the colony. When the Negro leader came to Le Cap to pay his respects, Sonthonax grasped his hand with great fervor and said he hoped Toussaint would be as loyal to him as he had been to Laveaux. Then he added, with an air of mystery, that he had plans which concerned Toussaint as well as him, which he intended to communicate to him shortly.

His unsolicited election to the Five Hundred had disconcerted him somewhat (it was so obviously an invitation to leave), but he soon recovered from the shock, and in December 1796, when Toussaint made a visit to Le Cap, invited him to his work cabinet and laid his cards on the table. He proposed that Toussaint declare his independence, and that together they found a Negro Republic in conformity with the principles of the French Revolution. As for the whites – they must be exterminated. There could be neither safety nor security for the Negroes as long as a single former slaveowner remained in the colony.

Toussaint listened without interrupting him. He believed the Commissioner suspected him of harboring thoughts of independence and was making a clumsy attempt to get him to commit himself. When Sonthonax finished speaking, Toussaint said with a grin: "And when I have declared my independence of France and have massacred the whites, what would the Commissioner advise me to do with him?"

Further attempts to draw him out being answered in the same bantering fashion, Sonthonax changed the subject, but at every succeeding meeting managed to bring the conversation around to the proposal. One day Toussaint became irritated and told him he wanted to hear no more of it.

The Negro leader had by this time acquired the conviction that Sonthonax meant what he said, but he had no intention of going into partnership with the Commissioner. He disagreed with Sonthonax's policy towards the Negroes as well as that towards the whites.

Sonthonax did not idealize the Negroes. He had at one time written in a report: "To speak of laws to the Negroes is to burden them with things too metaphysical for their understanding. To these people the man is everything: at his voice they are quite carried away, and his name is to them what the fatherland is to genuine freemen. The régime we found established upon our arrival at St. Domingo was exactly similar to the feudal system of the 8th century. Law and liberty were but idle names: the cultivators and the soldiers passively obeyed their military chiefs and fought for them alone while crying 'Long live the Republic!' "

If Sonthonax believed this, then his indiscriminate distribution of muskets to the Negro cultivators was ill-advised. Toussaint later armed the Negro population on a far larger scale than Sonthonax had ever dreamed of doing, but not until he had established order and had organized the cultivators into a militia. The Negroes had not yet learned to combine work with freedom. A cultivator put in possession of a musket usually took to the mountains and became a bandit. Work was necessary to save St. Domingo, and Toussaint felt that by arming the Negro population prematurely and without preparatory organization, Sonthonax was making confusion worse confounded. He did not argue with the Commissioner; but as fast as Sonthonax handed out the muskets, Toussaint gathered them in.

Toussaint considered the policy of Sonthonax towards the

whites shortsighted as well as cruel. Their co-operation was indispensable to restore the economy of St. Domingo, and they were valuable hostages. With military power in the hands of the Negroes twenty-five or thirty thousand white colonists were not a menace but a guarantee against attack. Far from wishing to massacre or to banish them Toussaint encouraged those who had fled to return. While their presence did not save St. Domingo from invasion it greatly hindered the movements of the invading army.

## 3

Sonthonax did not give up hope of converting Toussaint to his point of view and waited for a favorable opportunity to resume his blandishments. In the spring of 1797 Toussaint made a brilliant attack on the British lines, capturing several outposts, prisoners and cannon. Sonthonax took this opportunity to appoint him Commander in Chief of the army. An impressive ceremony took place on the Place d'Armes at Le Cap, during which Toussaint and Sonthonax made patriotic speeches. Then followed a banquet at the Palace, after which Sonthonax, feeling that Toussaint must now be in a receptive mood, invited him into his work cabinet and laid before him a modified plan for the establishment of an independent Negro commonwealth. It would not be necessary, he said, to massacre the whites, banishment would suffice. He felt that by making this concession he had made the plan acceptable to Toussaint. The Negro leader, however, got up angrily and said: –

"Commissioner, I am displeased with you. I thought it was understood that we should not talk of this again. Today you tell me that the whites should be banished; yesterday you said that they should be massacred. I am leaving."

He went towards the door. Sonthonax, alarmed, ran after him and caught him by the arm. "It is finished!" he cried. "I thought we should be able to agree, but since we can't, let's not talk any more about it. Promise me that you will not tell anybody what has passed between us."

Toussaint promised, on condition that the matter was irrevocably settled.

## 4

Having become convinced that it was useless to count on Toussaint, Sonthonax set out to consolidate his position and to undermine that of the Negro leader. He gathered all the power of the Commission into his own hands. Giraud was induced to depart for France. Leblanc died under circumstances many considered suspicious. Roume, who was in Santo Domingo City, was not in a position to interfere, so was left in peace. There remained the mulatto Raimond, to whom Sonthonax suggested Paris as a more suitable field for his activities, but who stuck to his post. When Sonthonax discovered that Raimond was a *protégé* of Toussaint, he contented himself with ignoring him.

No man can climb to power without making numerous enemies. Toussaint was no exception. Men as ambitious, but less capable or less daring than he, had been elbowed aside by him. Others considered that they had been slighted or not rewarded according to their merits. Still others were consumed by jealousy. Some, fanatical by nature and lacking his vision, considered his policy towards the white colonists a betrayal. All such men grouped themselves about Sonthonax. He artfully caressed their vanity, fed their hopes, sharpened their suspicions. Thus the Government Palace at Le Cap became the center of a cabal against the Negro leader. Leveillé, the Negro commander of the Le Cap garrison, became entirely devoted to the Commissioner. So was the Negro adjutant general, Mentor, whom Toussaint had likewise honored with a Deputy's mandate, but who preferred to remain.

Power in St. Domingo meant control of the army. To break Toussaint's power it was necessary to depopularize him with the officers and soldiers. This was no easy matter, but Sonthonax succeeded fairly well by the following maneuver: he increased the pay of the Le Cap garrison, leaving it to the Commander in Chief to do as he pleased concerning the army in the field. Now, although since the arrival of the Commission Toussaint was no longer officially connected with the civil government, he continued to think in terms of the colony rather than of the army. Knowing that the finances of St. Domingo were in a deplorable state, he was incensed at Sonthonax's move, which he knew to be political, and refused to imitate him. This was as the Commissioner had expected. He thus increased his own popularity with the army and injured Toussaint's. To heighten the dissatisfaction of the army in the field, he withheld supplies. At the same time Adjutant General Mentor made several trips to various parts of the front and held conferences with the officers. The upshot of it all was that a serious mutiny broke out. But Sonthonax had underestimated his man. Toussaint was prepared. He arrested sixty-seven officers and suppressed the mutiny.

He knew, however, that the real seat of the trouble was the Government Palace at Le Cap. As long as Sonthonax could continue his machinations the situation would remain dangerous. To take action against so important a representative of the French Government was, however, a serious matter. With the west coast still occupied by the British, the Spanish garrisons still in the former Spanish colony, Rigaud in control of the Department of the South, he had no desire to pick a quarrel with France. French ships were running the gantlet of the British blockade and bringing him supplies. Yet he realized that unless Sonthonax left the island nothing was solved. He decided to force the issue.

## 5

On August 16, 1797, Toussaint marched with a large force to Petite-Anse, a short distance from Le Cap, made camp and the following morning rode into the city accompanied by a few officers. He called on Raimond and asked him to inform his fellow Commissioner that he must leave for France to fill the mandate conferred upon him nearly a year before. If he refused, he would be expelled.

Raimond was startled. Did Toussaint realize what he was doing? The Directory could not help regarding the expulsion of its chief Commissioner as rebellion against the Republic. Toussaint replied that he had weighed the matter carefully, but that his mind was made up. Raimond tried to dissuade him, but finally agreed to deliver the message.

When Sonthonax received Toussaint's ultimatum he flew into a towering passion. He paced the room like a caged animal, pounded the table with his fist, wrung his hands, wept with impotent rage. Finally he demanded to see Toussaint. The Negro leader agreed, but suggested that Raimond be present at the interview. Sonthonax insisted that it be private.

The Commissioner never made public what passed between him and the Negro leader, but we have Toussaint's detailed account in his report to the Directory. He reproached Sonthonax for having deliberately stirred up mutiny in the army, for having incited him to break with France and to massacre the colonists, for having corrupted Negro officers to further his plans. "Whenever some scoundrel, be he white, mulatto or black, has some dirty work he wants done, he incites the Negroes to do it for him!" he shouted.

Sonthonax denied the charges. He threw the blame for the withholding of supplies upon subordinates. He claimed that Toussaint had misunderstood him regarding independence and the proposed massacre. "How can you do this to me? How can you treat the founder of liberty in such a manner? Is it not I who proclaimed liberty in the colony? Is it not I who defended your cause? Is it not due to me that you are now Commander in Chief?"

Toussaint remained obdurate. The Commissioner must leave.

He could preserve appearances and depart apparently voluntarily, or force would be used.

Sonthonax resolved to gain time. Very well, he would leave, but he needed three days to put his affairs in order, and must have a letter, signed by Toussaint and his principal Negro commanders, expressing gratitude for all he had done for the Negroes and petitioning him to go to France, so his voice might be raised in the French Parliament on behalf of the Blacks.

Toussaint granted the delay. As for the letter – the Commissioner could compose it himself; he and his staff would sign it. "I do not wish it to be known that I am forcing you to leave. You are my superior in rank. The effect on discipline might be bad."

Then he returned to Petite-Anse and waited.

## 6

The delay of three days had long expired before the letter Sonthonax himself had composed was delivered to Toussaint. It was excessively laudatory of the Commissioner, and its supposed authors appeared excessively humble, but Toussaint and his staff signed it and returned it without comment. Then came another letter in which Sonthonax said that he had read the touching communication with emotion and had decided to grant the request of his Negro friends. But Toussaint, who kept informed about all that happened at Le Cap, knew that Sonthonax was making feverish preparations to resist. A meeting of the officers of the garrison had been held at the Palace and the Commissioner had made an impassioned speech. Artillery was being shifted from the coast defenses to those on the land side. There was unwonted activity at the arsenal and there were constant troop movements. Toussaint wrote to Sonthonax: "It grieves me to receive the information that you have assembled the officers of the garrison and have prevailed upon them to oppose your departure, while informing me of the satisfaction it will give you to fulfill the honorable mission to which the people of St. Domingo have elected you." At the same time he notified the Municipality that he would hold them responsible for any bloodshed that might result from the military preparations they allowed to be made. Then again he waited.

But his patience was not inexhaustible.

On August 27, at four o'clock in the morning, when it was still dark and Le Cap asleep, Toussaint's white chief of staff, General Agé, arrived before the Palace with an armed escort. He dismounted and ordered the guards to awaken the Commissioner, for whom he had an urgent message. He was admitted to the work cabinet and waited by candlelight while Sonthonax made a hasty toilet. Finally the Commissioner entered and Agé delivered the message: If at sunrise Sonthonax was not aboard the frigate *L'Indien*, ready to depart, Toussaint would enter the city with an armed force and deport him. If there was resistance, he would break it.

Sonthonax wilted. He begged for a delay of a few hours. Toussaint had foreseen this and had authorized Agé to give him until eight o'clock. At sunrise the Negro leader rode into the city at the head of a large force of dragoons. He encountered no resistance.

The Commissioner's baggage had already been taken aboard the vessel, and a little before eight Sonthonax himself appeared, with his mulatto wife and stepchildren, and followed by Adjutant General Mentor, Colonel Leveillé and several other Negro and mulatto officers who considered it expedient to share his exile. The rumor of his departure had spread throughout the city and hundreds of Negroes and mulattoes crowded the streets leading to the quay. Whatever his faults, Sonthonax had been a good friend to them. A mournful silence reigned and hats were removed as he and his family passed.

Appearances were well preserved. The dragoons lined up on the quay raised their swords in salute. Toussaint, who had dismounted, bade respectful farewell to the Commissioner and handed him a letter in which he expressed his personal gratitude and the hope that Sonthonax would continue to champion the cause of the Negroes. Then the Commissioner, his family and his retinue were rowed to the frigate. The guns of the fort fired a salute, the ship dipped its flag and slowly moved out of the harbor.

## 7

Sonthonax later denied the allegations made by Toussaint in his report to the Directory. Commenting on that document (which is too detailed to be wholly accurate), he said: "Up to this time no one ever accused me of stupidity. Nevertheless, this ridiculous conversation makes me appear a schoolboy under a rod, stammering absurdities and called to order by this pedagogue. Certes, if anyone should be suspected of having harbored designs of independence, it is he whose political career has been one long revolt against France. Toussaint has fooled two kings; he may well end by betraying the Republic."

Nevertheless, Toussaint's story is corroborated by Galbaud's statement, while the fact that Billaud-Varenne, whose temperament was remarkably like that of the Commissioner, expressed such views openly removes Toussaint's accusation from the realm of the incredible. In truth, the only thing that distinguishes the Sonthonax proposal from other proposals of the same nature is that he favored the extermination of people of his own race. A proposal to exterminate the Negroes was made by Napoleon's brother-in-law, Leclerc, in an official document and by several planters in private correspondence. From the contemplation of such an act to its performance is, however, a long step, and Sonthonax had already relented when he made his final proposal to Toussaint. In justice to him it should also be said that he seldom employed capital punishment. Banishment and sequestration of property were his methods of dealing with rebellious colonists. Charges of terrorism brought against him and Polverel by the planters had a hearing shortly after Thermidor, when terrorists fared badly, and were found to be baseless.

## 8

Toussaint felt uneasy about the effect the expulsion of Sonthonax might have on the French Government. To reassure the Directory he resolved to make a great sacrifice. He had thus far managed to avoid sending his sons to France on the pretext that he did not wish to run the risk of their capture by the British. He now allowed them to depart. This decision created great rejoicing among the colonists. They imagined that with two such valuable hostages in the hands of the French Government, Toussaint would be a pawn in their hands. They expressed their satisfaction so openly that the report of this reached Toussaint, who, on November 5, 1797, sent this significant communication to the Directory: –

> They [the colonists] seem to think that fear for my children's fate will make me agree to their perfidious designs. It is not surprising that men willing to sacrifice their country to their personal interests should be unable to conceive what sacrifices a man (a better father than they) may be capable of for the sake of his country. I will never hesitate between St. Domingo and my personal interests, but I feel I have nothing to fear. It is to the French Government that I have entrusted my children. I should tremble indeed had I given them as hostages to the colonists. But let them take notice that even if such proved to be the case, and they were to punish my children for their father's loyalty to his country, they merely would have added one more barbarous action to their many barbarities without making me depart one iota from what I consider my duty.

What he considered his duty he made plain when he learned that the wave of reaction sweeping over France made it appear probable that the French attitude towards slavery might change radically. Vaublanc had made a speech in the French Chamber of Deputies which was practically a plea for the restoration of slavery. Toussaint wrote to the Directory: –

> My attachment to France, the gratitude of the blacks, make it incumbent upon me to inform you that we are fully aware of what is being plotted and of the oath we have taken (which we hereby renew) to be buried under the ruins of a country revivified by liberty rather than to suffer a return to slavery.

# CHAPTER X

## Toussaint and the British

THE French Republic was piling victory upon victory in Europe and was at the same time departing further and further from the generous humanitarianism that had characterized the first years of the French Revolution. As Toussaint's letter to the Directory proves, he suspected as early as 1797 that the last word concerning slavery in St. Domingo had not yet been spoken. This, more than personal ambition, made him resolve to make St. Domingo an independent state. But before independence could be thought of, two things had to be accomplished: the British invaders must be expelled and the entire island placed under a single command. Having reorganized his army and freed himself from the interference of Sonthonax, Toussaint now turned his attention to the British.

He had been harassing them incessantly, making it impossible for them to gain a permanent foothold in the interior, but his attempts to retake the coast towns had been abortive. At the beginning of 1798 the British held a narrow strip of land along the west coast, with the city of Port-au-Prince (Port Républicain), the important harbor towns Jérémie, L'Arcahaye, St. Marc and Môle St. Nicolas, the inland towns Mirebalais and

Croix-des-Bouquets and numerous villages. This territory was protected by a line of well-constructed forts, considered impregnable by an army such as Toussaint commanded. In the course of five years the British had lost 40,000 men, many dying of yellow fever, but their army had been repeatedly reinforced and now numbered 20,400 men. Of these 5000 were English, 8000 were Negroes (purchased to serve as soldiers and carefully trained), the remainder were Welsh, Irish, French *émigrés*, white colonists and mulattoes. Brigadier General John Whyte was in command, but was eventually to be replaced by Brigadier General Thomas Maitland.

Toussaint's army was inferior in numbers and equipment, consisting of ten demi-brigades of 1600 men each. His chief of staff was the white General Agé, whose appointment by Toussaint was political and whose part in determining the course of the operations was negligible. His principal commanding officers were the Negro generals Moyse, Dessalines, Belair, Paul Louverture (Toussaint's brother), Morney and the mulatto generals Laplume and Bauvais.

## 2

The exigencies of white prestige seem to have weighed more heavily with white historians than historical accuracy in their accounts of Toussaint's military successes. If we are to believe them the climate and yellow fever were principally responsible for the defeat first of the British and then of the French. That both contributed to his success is undeniable. Toussaint's strategy was often based upon them. He would keep his army intact, fighting delaying actions until the rainy season had made the enemy's position difficult, when he would attack in full force. But if the British and French commanders allowed themselves to be caught in such climatic traps, they erred in military strategy as much as if they had failed to take into account the topography of the country. It should be remarked, however, that many of the losses ascribed to yellow fever were in reality sustained in battle. Thus General de Lacroix says in his memoirs that nearly 2000 Frenchmen fell before Crête-à-Pierrot, but that the French Commander in Chief, Leclerc, reported the loss as only 500 and asked his subordinates to do the same in private correspondence. The remaining 1500 were reported as having died of yellow fever! It is probably no exaggeration to say that at least half of the supposed victims of yellow fever during the British and French invasions were killed in combat.

The same fatuous underestimation of a foe not belonging to the Caucasian race, which in our own day has been responsible for disaster after disaster in warfare against the Japanese, was at the bottom of many of the British and French reverses in St. Domingo. Then, as now, supposed military experts and individuals claiming special knowledge misled their governments. Thus the French general Becker, after an inspection of Toussaint's army, reported to his government that the Negro soldiers were "without regular discipline and instruction." Concerning the commanding officers he said that "the best of them are hardly equal to poor European officers." Colonel Malenfant says in his memoirs that on the eve of the French invasion the Commander in Chief of the expeditionary force, General Leclerc, said to him: –

"When the Negroes see the army they will lay down their arms. They will be only too glad to receive amnesty."

"People who told you that have misled you," retorted Malenfant.

General Leclerc: One of the colonists here told me he was ready to go into the interior of the country with sixty grenadiers and arrest Toussaint.

Colonel Malenfant: I know there are coxcombs everywhere. He has more hardihood than I. I should not care to undertake it with less than 60,000.

Less than a year later the disillusioned Leclerc wrote to Napoleon: "There prevails in Europe an entirely false notion of the kind of men we have to combat."

His successor Rochambeau tried to explain his own failure by saying that "a superior race of blacks inhabits St. Domingo."

Toussaint's soldiers were often ragged, but so were the *sans-culottes* who drove the armies of the European coalition out of France. General de Lacroix, who came to grips with Toussaint's army, had, as we have seen in a passage already quoted, an altogether different notion regarding "the discipline and instruction" of the Negro soldiers than the fatuous Becker. He repeatedly speaks with admiration of the tactics employed by the men who were "hardly equal to poor European officers." * Colonel Lemonnier-Delafosse exclaims concerning Toussaint's own tactics: "All strategical combinations, all military science are unavailing against that Negro!"

The showing made by Toussaint, his generals and his soldiers, against the British and the French proves conclusively that the Negro is not inferior to the white man either as a fighting man or as a commanding officer. Indeed, when one considers that Toussaint and his generals had received no military instruction – in fact, hardly any instruction whatever – one would more naturally arrive at the conclusion that the Negro possesses special aptitude for military leadership.

## 3

Toussaint ordered the assault on the British lines on February 3, 1798. Wishing to hold the west coast from Jérémie in the south to Môle St. Nicolas in the north, the British had been compelled to string out their forces in a long, tenuous line. Toussaint's strategy consisted in massing his army against only a part of that line, thus depriving the British of their numerical advantage. In doing so he exposed himself to a flanking movement, relying on his mobility to cut the enemy from his base

* As, for example, when speaking of Magny's and Lamartinière's withdrawal from Crête-à-Pierrot, which he calls "a remarkable feat of arms." The full quotation appears later in this volume.

if such an operation were attempted. The British failed to make the maneuver. They had faith in the strength of their defensive position and grossly underrated the Negro army and its commander. Toussaint might be an excellent guerrilla leader, but they did not consider him capable of carrying out successfully such a major military operation. His offensive would probably spend itself after the capture of a few outposts, as had happened in the past. When they realized their mistake the situation had deteriorated too far to permit further hazards.

After a month of persistent and brilliantly managed assault Toussaint was in possession of the greater part of the fortified line. Port-au-Prince, Croix-des-Bouquets, L'Arcahaye and St. Marc were exposed to direct attack and it was evident that they could not be held. In a little over a month the fruits of five years' effort, of the sacrifice of 40,000 men and the expenditure of £20,000,000, were snatched from the British.

Before we accompany Toussaint on his triumphal entry into the colonial capital, let us examine some of the proclamations and letters he sent out from his headquarters during the campaign.

## 4

In a proclamation to the army, on the eve of the assault, Toussaint says: –

Do not disappoint me. Prove yourselves men who know how to value liberty and how to defend it. Do not permit the desire for booty to turn you aside from the performance of your duty. It is not for booty we are fighting. It will be time enough to think of material things when we have driven the enemy from our shores. We are fighting that liberty – the most precious of all earthly possessions – may not perish. We are fighting to preserve it for ourselves, for our children, for our brothers, for our fellow citizens.

To the commanding officers: –

I call your attention to the strict orders given by me not to burn plantations, to treat all prisoners humanely and to receive deserters from the enemy ranks as friends and brothers. I will hold you personally responsible for any act contrary to these orders that remains unpunished. Communicate these instructions to your men and impress upon them to conduct themselves accordingly.

To the inhabitants of L'Arcahaye, who had called in the British: –

I promise you that the moment you have restored to the Republic the territory you surrendered to the British, you will receive full pardon and enjoy the advantages of the Constitution. The veil of forgetfulness will be drawn over your past acts. This applies even to the most culpable among you. Your lives will be protected and your property respected.

To Brigadier General John Whyte, to assure him that he need have no uneasiness concerning British officers captured by the Negroes: –

The fortunes of war have delivered into my hands a number of British officers, among whom is Major Hally. The mutual consideration civilized men owe one another and the dictates of humanity, have prompted me to take all necessary measures to insure their entire safety.

(The officers were paroled and allowed to go to Port-au-Prince to arrange personal affairs.)

To Brigadier General John Whyte, regarding an order found upon a captured British officer: –

You have demeaned yourself in the eyes of this and future generations in allowing one of your commanders (the cowardly Lepointe) to issue this order, which could not have been issued without your knowledge: "No quarter for the brigands! Take no prisoners!" And that in spite of the fact that I have given instructions to my commanders to treat all prisoners with humanity.

I am only a black man. I have not had the advantage of the fine education the officers of His Britannic Majesty are said to receive;

but were I to be guilty of so infamous an act, I should feel I had sullied the honor of my country.

He assures General Whyte, however, that there will be no reprisals: –

Whatever the circumstances, nothing will induce me to depart from a code imposed upon me by the laws of humanity and by republican principles.*

To Commissioner Roume, at Santo Domingo City, concerning the inhabitants of Mirebalais, who three times had taken the oath of fealty to the Republic and three times recalled the British to restore slavery: –

I have sent the inhabitants of Mirebalais to Port-de-Paix, to remain there until further orders. Please give me your opinion what to do with them. I do not like to punish them.

To Brigadier General Thomas Maitland, who has asked for an armistice and has offered to evacuate the threatened territory, on condition that the inhabitants who had sided with the British be granted amnesty: –

If you had not made that demand, I myself would have insisted that it be embodied in the terms.

To General Hédouville, after Toussaint's entry into St. Marc, whose inhabitants had likewise called in the British: –

What has given me greatest satisfaction is that I have not found it necessary to punish a single person.

Notwithstanding this and other evidence of Toussaint's humanity and inherent culture, the learned Theodore Lothrop Stoddard, champion of white supremacy, expresses this opinion of the Negro leader: –

* It is interesting to compare this letter with one written by Thomas Jefferson, who, as Governor of Virginia, wrote to the British colonel George Mathews, during the Revolutionary War: "Iron will be retaliated by iron, prison ships, by prison ships, and like for like in general."

Judged by white standards Toussaint is in many ways a sinister and repulsive figure; yet he should be measured, not with Europeans, but with the great men of his own race – the Zulu Chaka and with Macandal.

One cannot help recalling the words of Henry Thomas Buckle concerning learned men afflicted with "ancient prejudices" – "men whose erudition ministers to their ignorance and who, the more they read, the less they know." *

## 5

The British were facing disaster. A large part of their army was in imminent danger of annihilation or capture. Brigadier General Whyte was recalled and Brigadier General Thomas Maitland appointed in his place, with instructions to evacuate the threatened territory and hold only Jérémie in the south and Môle St. Nicolas in the north. Immediately on his arrival General Maitland wrote to Toussaint, asking for an armistice and offering to evacuate Port-au-Prince, Croix-des-Bouquets, L'Arcahaye and St. Marc. Toussaint has been criticized for agreeing to an armistice and allowing the British to depart, when he could have crushed them, but it was not in his nature to seek military glory at the cost of wanton destruction of life and property. However, it was on his terms, not their own, that the British departed. Maitland demanded amnesty for the inhabitants who had sided with the British and the right to carry off all the artillery of the forts. Toussaint replied that amnesty was a matter of course, but that the forts must be turned over to him in the condition in which the British had found them. Maitland was obliged to agree.

When the British had departed, Toussaint's troops occupied the evacuated territory, but he himself remained at his headquarters. This caused some uneasiness at Port-au-Prince, where

* "A scholar who is a blockhead, must be the worst of all blockheads, because he is without excuse." – James Boswell

the ragged Negro army recalled Macaya's hordes, whom the colonists blamed for the burning of Le Cap. But the fear subsided when it became clear that Toussaint's men made up in discipline what they lacked in sartorial appearance. As days went by and there was no disorder, no political arrests were made and even the *émigrés* from France remained unmolested, a feeling of gratitude and admiration began to spread among the inhabitants. Letters and petitions rained in on Toussaint, begging him to visit the occupied territory.

At the beginning of April, Toussaint, accompanied by his staff and a detachment of his bodyguard, left his headquarters and visited St. Marc. Then he traveled southward, through L'Arcahaye and Croix-des-Bouquets, towards Port-au-Prince. Everywhere he was received with enthusiasm. Officials and leading citizens made addresses of welcome and expressed their gratitude to him and his generals for the consideration shown the inhabitants. At L'Arcahaye, however, Toussaint saw much destruction and learned that the mulatto general Lepointe had wrought as much damage as he could after receiving the evacuation order. This added another to the long list of grievances that envenomed the relationship between Negroes and mulattoes.

## 6

In the afternoon of April 14, 1798, Toussaint made his entry into Port-au-Prince, the colonial capital. It was raining, but this did not prevent practically the entire population from turning out to welcome him. A procession was formed and went up the road to meet him. First came two acolytes, carrying the cross and the banner; then choirboys holding censers; then the clergy of the district; then leading citizens and planters from the Plaine du Cul-de-Sac, headed by Mayor Borgella; then Creole ladies in carriages; then a guard of honor on horseback, composed of planters' sons; finally, the populace—whites, mulattoes and Negroes, the last but recently freed by Toussaint's victory. White girls carrying baskets of flowers ranged themselves on either side of the road, and as Toussaint and his following rode up, showered them with the contents.

Toussaint dismounted and genuflected before the cross. He was wearing a general's uniform and had his famous yellow Madras handkerchief knotted about his head. Borgella and the leading ecclesiastic made addresses of welcome. Then a baldachin, carried by four of the wealthiest planters, was raised over his head, while choirboys swung their censers. He quickly stepped aside and said with a frown: "It belongs to God to walk under a baldachin and have incense wafted towards Him." It was explained to him that this was the traditional manner in which Governors making their entry into the city were received, but he persisted in his refusal and walked uncovered in the procession, which conducted him to the doors of the Government Palace, where cavalry stood at attention.

That evening there was a banquet followed by a ball. The following morning a solemn *Te Deum* was sung. Then came another ceremony at the Palace. A delegation of twelve planters, headed by the Mayor, came to present the victor with a gold medal bearing his effigy and this astonishing inscription: "After God – He." Toussaint, in a burst of enthusiasm for Laveaux, had uttered these words at a ceremony at Le Cap. Their appearance upon the medal may have been a cynical jest on the part of the planters, but more than likely it was an insincere attempt to please.

## 7

Toussaint was to prove on a number of occasions that he was not particularly susceptible to flattery. In his reply to Borgella's presentation address he did not allude to the gift, but read the planters a lecture on slavery as an economic fallacy. "The appearance of the country through which I passed on my way over here," he declared, "has filled me with dismay. This [the indifferent cultivation] alone should have convinced you long ago that in calling in the British you were deluding yourselves. You expected to profit, but you have only harmed yourselves. Men from whose wrists the shackles of slavery have been struck – who have the opportunity to enjoy liberty without license and to reap the fruits of their toil – will till these fields much better than they have been tilled hitherto."

Thus, after having given a British general a lesson in the usages of civilized warfare, the former slave gave instruction to the planters in economics.

When the welcoming ceremonies were concluded, Toussaint devoted himself to the reorganization of the administration of the department. Finding that Borgella – who was a wealthy planter as well as a merchant – seemed sincerely desirous to co-operate with him, Toussaint made him his counselor. It should be said of Bernard Borgella that his attitude was not feigned. He had reached the conclusion that Toussaint was an extraordinary man and that the colonists could do no better than to forget old scores, accept the new order of things and give him their whole-hearted support. He was one of the few white men who remained loyal to him until the end.

During his stay at Port-au-Prince Toussaint was besieged by officeseekers. There were few Negroes who possessed the education and training required for administrative functions, and the attitude of the mulattoes made it more hazardous to trust them than to trust the whites; hence most of Toussaint's appointees were white men. By keeping military power in the hands of the Negroes he hoped to overcome the danger this implied.

Among those who came to solicit an appointment was a colonist who coveted the post of Custodian of Government Supplies. Toussaint denied him the appointment "either because he did not know him, or knew him too well," says Malenfant. A few days later the colonist's wife, who had recently given birth to a boy, came to ask Toussaint to do her and her husband the honor to be the child's godfather. Malenfant quotes their conversation verbatim, communicated to him by the woman herself.

TOUSSAINT: Why do you wish me to be your son's godfather? Tell the truth, Madam, is it not because you hope that it will result in your husband's appointment to the post he is seeking?

THE WOMAN: How can you think so, General? My husband loves you. All the whites are attached to you.

TOUSSAINT: Madam, I know the whites. If I had the color of their skin it would be another matter. But I am a Negro, and know but too well that at bottom the whites detest us. Have you given due consideration to what you are asking? If I were to accept, might it not be that when your son grows up he will reproach you for having given him a black man for godfather?

THE WOMAN: But General . . .

TOUSSAINT: Madam, God alone is immortal. When I am dead, who knows if my people will not again have to pass under the yoke of slavery? Who knows if they will not be dying again under the white men's whips? Man's work does not endure. I know but too well that the whites are the enemies of the blacks. You wish me to appoint your husband? So be it! Let him be an honest man and remember that even if I can't see everything, wrong does not remain unpunished. As for becoming your son's godfather, I can't grant that request. The whites would blame you, and the time might come when your son would blame you too.

## 8

The British made an attempt to retain a foothold in St. Domingo by holding Jérémie and Môle St. Nicolas, but Toussaint had no intention of permitting them to do so. The mulatto general Rigaud recognized him as his superior only grudgingly and some risk was involved in sending him reinforcements and supplies to enable him to attack Jérémie. Toussaint boldly accepted the risk. At the same time he notified Maitland that unless the British completed the evacuation he would storm

Môle St. Nicolas. The possibility of successful resistance did not seem favorable to the British, who, moreover, had reached the conclusion that Toussaint was virtually independent ruler of St. Domingo and might be induced to sign a treaty which would be of more value than a precarious foothold on the island. So General Maitland wrote to Toussaint that he would like to meet him and talk over things which it was inadvisable to treat by correspondence.

The meeting took place on August 31, 1798, at British headquarters at Pointe-Bourgeoise, a short distance from Môle St. Nicolas. Toussaint and the officers accompanying him were received with military honors. British troops marched in review before him and luncheon was served in a marquee. Maitland drank Toussaint's health and presented him with an exquisitely wrought bronze cannon and two double-barreled carbines of expert workmanship "as a token of my personal esteem and in appreciation of the humanity with which British prisoners have been treated." Then the officers withdrew and the two generals commenced their intimate discussion.

The proposals made by Maitland were later committed to paper by one of Toussaint's white secretaries. The document, which has since disappeared, found its way to the archives at Port-au-Prince, where, in 1802, General de Lacroix read it. In his memoirs he sums up the contents. The British offered to evacuate the two ports they were still occupying, to recognize Toussaint as King of Haiti and to protect him against attack by the French. In return he was to sign a commercial treaty with Great Britain.

The reason Toussaint frowned on the proposal that he assume the title of King should not be ascribed to devotion to republican institutions. A monarchical form of government, with most of the power concentrated in the hands of the monarch, was the only kind possible in Haiti at that time. The dictatorial government he established a short time later differed in no essential from an absolute monarchy. Nor could it have been loyalty to France that made him forego the prospect of immediate independence under the protection of the guns of the British fleet. The lip service he continued to give to the French Government was only a ruse. The reason he rejected the proposal was that he doubted the ability of the British to prevent an invasion by the French. In May of that same year the French general Bonaparte had managed to elude the British fleet in the Mediterranean and to land in Egypt. Two years previously Sonthonax had landed at Le Cap with twelve hundred men in spite of the British blockade. It was evident therefore that the protection of the British fleet was not an absolute guarantee against invasion. Moreover, the island was still far from united. A French invading force would have the support of Rigaud and of the Spaniards. Toussaint preferred to preserve an appearance of loyalty towards France and to feel his way towards independence gradually. The French Republic, whose armies were victorious in Europe and Africa, was too powerful a nation to provoke for the sake of a title. Unlike most Negroes, who took a childish delight in titles, Toussaint was indifferent to them. He had never adopted a grandiose title such as those that delighted Jean-François or Biassou. When he had joined the French he had told Laveaux that the rank of colonel would suffice him.

But a commercial treaty with England – especially if it could be kept secret – was another matter. Haiti was languishing as a result of the British blockade. There was no outlet for its agricultural products; trade and industry were at a standstill. He had no objection to trading with England if it could be done discreetly. Not only would the economic advantages be enormous, but he would then be able to obtain large quantities of arms and supplies and thus prepare for the day when France could no longer be placated. So a preliminary draft of the treaty was made. Maitland was to depart for London, submit the draft to the British Cabinet and then return for final discussion and the affixing of signatures. In the meantime the British army was to evacuate Jérémie and Môle St. Nicolas and specified Haitian ports were to be thrown open to British commerce.

But when the details of the evacuation were discussed Toussaint raised a serious objection. The British had purchased some 16,000 Negroes whom they had trained as soldiers. Some six thousand were still living. Toussaint said he would not permit them to be taken from Haitian soil and sold into slavery. Maitland was obliged to yield, and Toussaint obtained the further concession of six months' pay for the black contingent.

## 9

On October 5, 1798, Toussaint made another triumphal entry, this time into "the Gibraltar of the Antilles" – Môle St. Nicolas. Maitland and the British troops had departed, except for a detachment under Colonel Spencer, who turned the stronghold over to Toussaint and in the name of the British Government presented him with the fine mansion the British had erected for use as General Headquarters.

The growing friendship between Toussaint and the British came, however, near suffering shipwreck as a result of the indiscretion of London newspapers, who got wind of the impending treaty and could not refrain from expressing their satisfaction. Thus the fact that a treaty was about to be concluded became known in the French capital. Edward Stevens, American Consul-General in St. Domingo, wrote to Timothy Pickering, Secretary of State: "He [Toussaint] is so much displeased at this want of secrecy in the British Cabinet that his confidence in it is much diminished."

Toussaint's annoyance was, indeed, so great that he wished to break off negotiations with the British and sign a treaty with the United States. The British, however, notified him that while they had no objection to the United States being made a party to the treaty, they must insist on equal privileges for themselves, or the blockade would be maintained.

When Maitland returned from London, Roume, the French Commissioner in Santo Domingo City, learned of his debarkation and ordered Toussaint to arrest him. The British general heard of this while on his way to Toussaint's headquarters and wondered if he was walking into a trap. Having faith in Toussaint he continued on his way. When he reached the headquarters he was kept waiting so long that he became uneasy. He had just about come to the conclusion that Toussaint had played him false, when the Negro leader entered and handed him two letters with the words: "There, General, read these two letters. One is from Roume, the other is my answer. I would not come to you before I had written my answer to him, so you may know how safe you are with me and how incapable I am of treachery."

The treaty was signed on June 13, 1799. Although it is tripartite – the United States being granted equal privileges with Great Britain – the document bears only two signatures, Toussaint's and Maitland's. The ports of call for British and American ships are specified. Great Britain and the United States were to maintain consular agents in Haiti and Toussaint was to have an agent in Jamaica. The Negro leader further promised that he would indulge in no expedition against British possessions in the Caribbean or the territory of the United States of America.

All this, of course, was highly irregular. Great Britain was at war with France and an undeclared war was in progress between the French Republic and the United States. Toussaint was a French general, not empowered by his government to negotiate treaties, least of all with powers with whom France was at war. As a general of the French Republic he was obviously guilty of a reprehensible act; as *de facto* ruler of the Negro State of Haiti he served his country well.

# CHAPTER XI
## Toussaint and Hédouville

On March 27, 1798, shortly before Toussaint's triumphal entry into Port-au-Prince, three French warships dropped anchor in the harbor of Santo Domingo City. They had brought to the island the successor of Sonthonax, "Special Agent" General Hédouville (erstwhile Count d'Hédouville) and his party of administrative and military experts.

General Hédouville was forty-two – a man of outstanding ability who had earned the sobriquet of the Pacifier of the Vendée. To pacify that turbulent province of France had required diplomatic, administrative and military talents of a high order, hence he was believed to be exceptionally well fitted to deal with Toussaint Louverture and the complicated situation in the colony. He did not underestimate the difficulties confronting him. Before his departure he had had a long conference with Sonthonax and with Laveaux and it was upon his suggestion that the squadron put in at Santo Domingo City, so he might confer with Commissioner Roume. He had likewise asked the planter Gironet, who was acquainted with most of the personalities in the colony, to draw up a memorandum giving the principal characteristics of each. Concerning Toussaint, Gironet had written: "Very reserved. Possesses the faculty of reading the secret thoughts of those with whom he deals."

The men accompanying Hédouville took a less serious view of the situation than their experienced chief. Most of them were a little immature – few had passed the age of thirty. The military men among them had participated in victorious campaigns against the greatest captains of Europe and considered this to-do about an old darky and his army of Negroes slightly ridiculous. They had seen pictures of Toussaint with the Madras handkerchief knotted about his head and opined that he looked like "a monkey in a linen headdress" and that, were he to become really obstreperous, four intrepid men should suffice to place him under arrest. When on their arrival in Santo Domingo City they learned that the old darky had just routed one of the largest colonial armies Great Britain had ever assembled, they were somewhat surprised, but not sufficiently impressed to alter their opinion.

We do not know the nature of the conversations between Hédouville and Roume, but in a letter the Commissioner later wrote to the Special Agent he says concerning the Negro leader: "General Toussaint Louverture is a man possessing extraordinary qualities. He has self-control, prudence, clarity of vision, but the enormous power he has been allowed to acquire might easily be abused were he not the most virtuous of men."

Hédouville remained three weeks in Santo Domingo City, sufficiently long to discover that the colonial treasury was empty and the pay of government functionaries greatly in arrears. Then he journeyed by land to Le Cap, and at San-Yago had an interview with a veteran colonial campaigner, General Kerverseau, who expressed this view of Toussaint: "He is a man with a great deal of common sense, whose attachment to France cannot be doubted. Men of every color have faith in him, and his influence upon people of his own race is extraordinary. With him you can do everything, without him, nothing."

Kerverseau's faith in Toussaint's loyalty to France proves that the Negro leader was at least as expert in hiding his own secret thoughts as in divining those of others.

## 2

Toussaint made use of duplicity to abolish injustice, his enemies employed the same tactics in order to maintain it. General Hédouville had come to St. Domingo prepared to essay a particularly perfidious policy. Since war with England made it impossible to send a large army, he had arrived at the conclusion that the best way to hold the colony for France was to aggravate the ill-feeling between Negroes and mulattoes and to create as much dissension as possible among the Negroes. In the meantime, however, he sent a copy of his credentials to Toussaint, together with a friendly letter in which he assured him that it was his intention to consult him concerning all important appointments and solicited his collaboration. Toussaint replied: "I will aid you to the best of my ability, which, however, is not like that of people who have had the advantage of a brilliant education, but consists of such qualities as it has pleased the Supreme Being to bestow upon me. They are founded upon love of country, unshakable loyalty to France, respect and obedience to her laws and gratitude for the blessings she has conferred upon us."

Hédouville gave high praise to Toussaint for his negotiations with the British concerning the first phase of the evacuation and wrote: "Come as soon as possible. Nothing can equal my impatience to make your acquaintance." Toussaint, not to be outdone, wrote: "I burn with desire to know you." In the meantime, however, Hédouville was likewise corresponding with the mulatto general Rigaud, whom he encouraged to report directly to him instead of to the Commander in Chief.

## 3

The first meeting between Toussaint and Hédouville took place in May, 1798, when the Special Agent had been in the colony nearly two months. Toussaint journeyed to Le Cap and was received by Hédouville with suitable courtesy. In the course of the conversation the Agent suggested that since access to the Department of the South was now open, it might be advisable to arrest Rigaud, whom Sonthonax had outlawed. There can be no doubt that he made the suggestion only to probe Toussaint, for Rigaud was his most important trump. He received the reply: "Arrest Rigaud! I would as soon think of arresting myself. Surely you know that he is one of the most zealous defenders of the cause for which we are fighting. I regard him as a worthy son."

Toussaint's reply indicates that he had not relinquished the hope of cementing relations between Negroes and mulattoes and is proof of his determination not to allow white men to meddle in the intraracial quarrel. He was a firm believer in Napoleon's dictum: "*Il faut laver son linge sale en famille.*"

Toussaint's visit to Hédouville enhanced rather than diminished mutual suspicion. The young swashbucklers surrounding the Special Agent injected a touch of mockery into their intercourse with the visitor which did not escape the astute black man. Hédouville's aide-de-camp and Admiral Fabre – the commander of the squadron, which had circumnavigated the island and now lay anchored at Le Cap – were likewise guilty of indiscretions. When during a conversation with Fabre, Toussaint spoke of the arduousness of his task and expressed his longing for rest, the Admiral purred: "How flattered I should be if after having had the honor of bringing General Hédouville over here, I could take back Toussaint Louverture, who would find in France recognition of his services, honors and a well-earned rest."

Toussaint shot him an angry look and replied: "Your vessel is not big enough for a man like me."

Hédouville's aide-de-camp extolled the beauties of France and suggested that Toussaint could do no better than to retire to the mother country. The Negro leader pointed to a sapling in the garden and said: "I'll go when this has grown big enough to make a ship."

All this so clearly pointed to a desire on the part of the French to remove him from the scene that he thought it prudent to decline Fabre's invitation to dine aboard the flagship.

## 4

A Negro state of Haiti that failed to take the mulattoes into account was inconceivable. Toussaint realized this and did his best to minimize differences between the two castes. Once when rioting had broken out between them at Port-de-Paix, he had addressed the crowd, and holding up a bottle in which red and white wine had been mixed, cried: "You should become like this – one substance! Love one another."

But it was not easy to get the mulattoes – especially those who had been freemen before the insurrection – to accept equality with the Negroes. They refused to identify themselves with the Negro race and feared domination by the blacks even more than by the whites. They lived in a racial no man's land in which they were unhappy, but which they would not abandon for the camp willing to receive them.

The Negroes, on their part, found it difficult to forget the betrayal of the "Swiss" and the fact that in the Department of the West the mulattoes had made common cause with the British to restore slavery. Since the siege of St. Marc, when the mulattoes had attempted to deliver him over to the British, even Toussaint had not found it easy to overcome his distrust. He preferred white men to mulattoes in positions of trust. His principal aide-de-camp, Case, was a white man, as was his confidential secretary, Guybre. Nevertheless he tried to remain on a friendly footing with the mulatto leader Rigaud. He had advised Sonthonax against interfering with him, had sent him reinforcements and supplies, had spoken well of him to Hédouville. But when he learned that Rigaud was reporting directly to the Special Agent, he felt seriously alarmed. It was not so much that his authority as Commander in Chief was being flouted, but that it indicated a tendency towards separatism and its recognition by the French.

One day he learned that Rigaud had been summoned to Le

Cap and would pass through Port-au-Prince, where was Toussaint's headquarters. His staff advised him to place the mulatto leader under arrest. A white planter who was present relates that Toussaint meditated for a moment, then said: "No. Let him go and get his instructions from the Agent of the Directory. Don't be alarmed." Then he added: "I wish to be alone."

The officers saluted and withdrew. The civilian was about to follow when Toussaint said: "You may remain. Your presence does not disturb me." Then, pacing the floor and speaking to himself more than to the planter, he said: "I could stop him, but God forbid! I need Monsieur Rigaud. He is violent. He suits me as an opponent. If I were to take away their Rigaud the mulattoes might find a better man. I know Monsieur Rigaud. He lets go the bridle when he gallops. He shows his hand when about to strike. I gallop too, but I know how to curb. And when I strike people feel the blow, but do not see it coming. Monsieur Rigaud's method of provoking a crisis is bloodshed, massacre. There are better ways of arousing the populace. I hate violence. Where I show myself there must be order."

In his decision not to arrest Rigaud, Toussaint followed Alexander Hamilton's line of reasoning when advising Washington against the proposed kidnaping of the British Commander in Chief, Sir Henry Clinton: "Why, General, we shall rather lose than gain by removing Sir Henry from the command of the British army, because we so perfectly understand his character; and by taking him off we only make way for some other, perhaps an abler officer, whose character and disposition we have yet to learn."

## 5

On his arrival at Port-au-Prince Rigaud paid a visit to his chief. The two leaders had never met. Toussaint saw a dark-complexioned man, small of stature, polished of manner and wearing a straight-haired wig. The mulatto told Toussaint the reason for his journey, and the Negro blandly replied that he had heard about the appointment and had written to Hédouville that he would come at the same time. Far from betraying his annoyance, Rigaud expressed his satisfaction and offered Toussaint a place in his commodious carriage. Toussaint accepted and they departed together.

Sometime during the journey Toussaint committed an indiscretion which must be attributed to his desire to see Negroes and mulattoes make common cause against any attempt to restore slavery. He told Rigaud of his misgivings, his consequent determination to gain virtual independence, and asked him to cooperate. Rigaud, however, had different plans, of which equality with the Negro caste was not a part. He remained noncommittal and Toussaint realized too late that he had made a mistake in taking him into his confidence.

On their arrival at Le Cap, Rigaud hastened to the Government Palace. He was received by Hédouville, who found him far more sympathetic than the black Commander in Chief and listened with interest to the account Rigaud gave him of Toussaint's proposal. A statement made by two employees of the Palace reveals that while Hédouville and Rigaud were in conference, Toussaint called and was shown into a room separated only by a thin partition from Hédouville's work cabinet. He was thus able to overhear what was said, but there can be no doubt that he had already determined upon a course.

When it was his turn to be admitted, Toussaint immediately brought up the subject of his conversation with Rigaud, saying that in order to probe him he had made certain proposals. He was happy to be able to report that Rigaud's loyalty could not be doubted. Hédouville might or might not have believed him, but Toussaint's move deprived him of a powerful weapon.

## 6

Slowly, but surely, relations between Hédouville and Toussaint deteriorated. Since Toussaint wished to gain his independence, but was unwilling to deprive his country of the services of white men, the most desirable colonists from his point of view were French *émigrés*, whom the Republic had outlawed. Hédouville pointed out to him that by protecting them he was breaking French law, to which Toussaint replied that the *émigrés* were "more unfortunate than guilty." Hédouville realized that Toussaint's motives were not purely humanitarian and wrote: "Toussaint Louverture now receives the *émigrés* with open arms; yet at the same time never ceases to fill the cultivators with suspicion against all white men, so they might never succeed in destroying his despotism."

The problem of how to keep the Negro cultivators at work likewise became a bone of contention. Hédouville issued an edict, known as "the edict of the 6th of Thermidor," obliging the cultivators to make three-year work contracts. Toussaint took exception to the edict and wrote to the Directory: "The dissatisfaction of the cultivators has greatly increased as a result of the compulsion imposed upon them by the edict of the 6th of Thermidor to contract their services for three years. They see in this a partial return to slavery. Far from encouraging them to work, the edict fills them with misgivings." *

It was during the negotiations for the surrender of Môle St. Nicolas by the British that the disagreement between the Special Agent and the Negro leader became acute. Hédouville, anxious to push Toussaint into the background, had no sooner learned of the British decision to evacuate the stronghold than he sent Brigadier General Dalton to arrange terms with Colonel Spencer, Commander of the British garrison. Toussaint, however, had already reached a complete understanding with Spencer's superior, General Maitland, who nullified the Spencer-Dalton

* According to General de Lacroix, Toussaint himself issued an edict in which he says: "In truth, the blacks are free, but they must continue to work for five years on the plantations of their former masters." No trace of such an edict is to be found among Toussaint's state papers and his letter to the Directory is in direct contradiction to it. De Lacroix's error has been copied by the historian Madiou and by Toussaint's biographers, some of whom indulge in an elaborate defense of the nonexisting edict.

agreement and apologized to Toussaint. The Negro leader wrote Hédouville a sharp letter and got as good in return.

Hédouville suspected that there were secret clauses in the Toussaint-Maitland agreement, for when the Negro leader wrote him concerning the honors shown him by the British, he replied: "I should have been more pleased if I did not have the conviction that Maitland has duped you." Later Hédouville was to reverse this opinion and write that Toussaint had duped both the British and the Americans. In the meantime, however, Toussaint felt touched to the quick and sent in his resignation with the words: "Your constant reminders that it is in your power to dismiss me lead me to believe that you should very much like to do so." The resignation was only a bluff. He knew that as long as the Negro army remained intact Hédouville did not dare to accept the resignation: the army would have revolted. To get rid of Toussaint it was first necessary greatly to diminish the power of the army.

## 7

Hédouville and the Directory now made a bold attempt to rid themselves of Toussaint and the Negro army at the same time. As is well known, Napoleon's Egyptian adventure had been proposed to him by the Directory not so much for the military advantage to be derived from the expedition, but to eliminate a general whose presence was becoming embarrassing. The youthful Bonaparte had swallowed the bait, and it was thought that Toussaint might likewise be persuaded to seek military laurels away from St. Domingo. A French officer who had served with the British, a certain Debuisson, was dispatched from France with the proposal that Toussaint should invade Jamaica and the Southern States of the United States of America. He was to receive the aid of the French fleet and all foreign ships in Haitian ports were to be seized to transport his men.

In France the Girondists had set out to liberate the world

while liberty was still far from secure in their own country; Toussaint, however, was too much of a realist to fall into the trap. The philanthropic project of liberating the slaves of Jamaica and the United States only to give the French the opportunity to restore slavery in St. Domingo did not appeal to him. When the proposal was later renewed he notified the American Consul-General Edward Stevens and asked him to communicate it to Maitland. Stevens wrote to the British general on May 23, 1799,* and on September 30 of that same year wrote concerning the proposed invasion of Jamaica to Timothy Pickering, Secretary of State: "Success would forever separate from Great Britain one of her most valuable colonies and diminish her resources. Should they [Toussaint and his army] fail, they will fall victims to their rashness and presumption or like Buonaparte and his army cease to be objects of dread and jealousy to the Government of France. The old system might then be restored in St. Domingo and slavery re-established."

This method of ridding St. Domingo of the defender of Negro freedom and of his army having failed, Hédouville prepared a plan of his own and had it approved by the Directory. It called for the virtual disbanding of the Negro army and the elimination of Toussaint as a factor in the affairs of St. Domingo. The evacuation of the island by the British was to be used as a pretext for reducing the army to three small contingents, dispersed over the three departments. The commander of each contingent was to be directly responsible to the Special Agent and the post of Commander in Chief was to be abolished.

Hédouville decided to make a beginning by dispersing the 5th Negro Regiment, commanded by Toussaint's nephew Moyse. That regiment was chosen because it was garrisoned at Fort-Dauphin (renamed Fort-Liberté) where there were white and mulatto troops superior in number. In order that the move might not be interpreted as an attack upon the Negroes, Hédouville appointed as his Special Deputy at Fort-Dauphin a Negro justice

* Stevens' letter to Maitland is quoted in the Foreword.

of the peace, a certain Manigat, a bold and resolute man. A pretext was to be furnished him to arrest Moyse and disarm and scatter the regiment. Toussaint, who was at Gonaïves, was to be lulled into inactivity by special emissaries, while emissaries already dispatched to Rigaud were to urge the mulatto general to march to the Department of the North with all possible speed. While Toussaint was hesitating, Rigaud would arrive and the white and mulatto troops from Fort-Dauphin would form a junction with those at Le Cap. If Toussaint showed an inclination to resist he would find formidable forces confronting him.

The plan had its merits, except that Hédouville's calculation went wrong on two points: Toussaint did not hesitate; Rigaud did.

## 8

The first part of Hédouville's plan was carried out successfully. Moyse saved himself by flight, but the 5th Negro Regiment was disarmed and scattered. The emissaries sent to paralyze Toussaint's action had, however, little opportunity to exercise their talents. Toussaint placed them under arrest immediately on their arrival. Confronted with the crisis the Negro leader acted with greater decision and precision than Napoleon displayed on the famous 18th Brumaire. With his own hand he penned an order to Dessalines to isolate Fort-Dauphin, march upon Le Cap and seize the forts. At the same time his agents, like so many Paul Reveres, galloped through the Plaine-du-Nord, rousing the cultivators with the cry: "Hédouville wants to restore slavery! He made a beginning with the law of 6 Thermidor, now he is disbanding the Negro army! On to Le Cap!"

By thousands and tens of thousands the cultivators heeded the cry. They armed themselves as best they could and marched upon the city. The commander of the white troops at Fort-Dauphin, speeding to Le Cap to confer with Hédouville, was arrested. Three white officers returning from their mission to Rigaud were stopped, tried to cut their way through and were slain. Dessalines was storming the forts. Le Cap was in a panic. The Pacifier of the Vendée and his young swashbucklers, who had thought four men as intrepid as they should suffice to arrest "the old darky," found the situation too much for them and took refuge aboard a warship.

Then Toussaint appeared on the scene. Soberly arrayed in the undress uniform of a French general, the yellow Madras handkerchief knotted about his head, astride his favorite horse Bel-Argent, he rode into the midst of the excited cultivators. They received him with cries of "Papa Toussaint! Papa Toussaint! Save us!" He called them his children, calmed their fears, but forbade them to enter the city. Accompanied by only a few officers he rode into Le Cap, where white, mulatto and black, seeing in his presence a guarantee against disaster, received him with frantic enthusiasm. White men lifted him from his horse and carried him in triumph to the Palace. He sent a message to Hédouville informing him that he had nothing to fear and could return to his post. But the Special Agent had had enough of St. Domingo and gave the order to sail.

## 9

The following morning, a solemn *Te Deum* in the parish church . . . Toussaint mounted the pulpit. He condemned Hédouville's conduct. He deplored the lives lost during the storming of the forts. He affirmed his unswerving loyalty to France. When he left the church and mounted his horse the crowd massed outside raised a loud cheer. He held up his hand for silence. In a voice that seemed to tremble with emotion he said: "I have learned too much of the human heart not to be convinced that it is only in the bosom of my family that I can find happiness." He was old and weary, he said, and had decided to lay down the burden. He intended to retire and turn the command over to General Rigaud – a worthy citizen and an excellent soldier.

Consternation. Then a full-throated cry – "No! No! No!" White men ran up and seized his hands. Negroes fell on their knees and implored him not to abandon them. Mothers held up their babies towards him, while the multitude cried: "Papa Toussaint! Papa Toussaint! Don't leave us!" He quietly surveyed the scene of his histrionic triumph, then said: "So be it. Since you demand it, I will make the sacrifice. God preserve you and St. Domingo."

## 10

Toussaint arrived at Fort-Dauphin on the night of October 25, 1799. Order had been restored. His troops were occupying the town. Moyse had returned. The 5th Regiment was back in its barracks. Manigat and his Negro confederates were meditating in prison on the consequences of their act.

The following morning the garrison and the populace were assembled on the public square to hear Toussaint speak. He had ordered that Manigat and his fellow prisoners be placed in the front row. He mounted a cart and made this speech, reported by Delatte, Moyse's white secretary: –

"Just as I had driven the British from the colony, just as I was about to enjoy the fruits of so much struggle and labor, Hédouville found a Manigat. Yes, a Manigat. Are you Manigat? Well, you're an expert plotter.* Hédouville chose a Negro to destroy the brave General Moyse and the 5th regiment, who have contributed so much towards clearing the colony of our enemies. You wanted to kill them. Did you not realize that behind them stood a mass of blacks who would have avenged their death? Did you not realize that you were endangering the lives of all the European troops and of your own wives and children? The insult you offered to the 5th regiment is an insult to the entire army. As head of the army I have, however,

* Toussaint makes a play on words which it is impossible to translate. He says: "*Vous êtes bien Manigat? Et vous manigassez fort bien.*" *Manigasser* means to scheme or plot.

not forgotten the words: Forgive us our trespasses as we forgive those who trespass against us. Mindful of this injunction, I forgive you. Remember henceforth that neither a Manigat, nor a Hédouville has a right to suspend a general and that he who draws the sword shall perish by the sword.

"Hédouville would have you believe that I am an enemy of liberty, that I have sold myself to the English, that I am striving for independence. Who is likely to value liberty more – Toussaint Louverture, the slave of the Bréda plantation, or General Hédouville, former Marquis and Chevalier of the Order of St. Louis? If I had wished to hand the colony over to the English I would not have driven them out. It is Hédouville who is an enemy of liberty. It is he who made use of a Negro – a Manigat – to destroy the defenders of liberty.

"There is good reason for the saying: Give a drink of rum to a Negro and he will do whatever you tell him; show a piece of ham to a mulatto and he will trot all about the colony for you. Remember that there is only one Toussaint Louverture in St. Domingo and that his name should make you tremble."

That same evening, at dinner at the house of Moyse, he was more than usually communicative and Delatte reports him as saying: "Hédouville has spread the rumor that he was going to France to raise an army and that he will return. He thinks he can frighten me. I've been making war for a long time, and if it is necessary for me to go on, I'm ready. I've been at grips with three nations and have got the best of all three. I'm at ease. My soldiers will always be ready to defend their hard-won liberty. France had better keep her soldiers to fight the English; she has none too many for that. She has already lost 22,000 men in our country and those whom she sends over now might meet the same fate. I don't want to fight France. Until now I've preserved this country for her; but if she attacks me I'll defend myself."

A few days later he was back at Le Cap, where with the assistance of his white aide-de-camp Case and his white secretaries he concocted a long report to the Directory. The document, like most of his reports, is diffuse and full of sophistical reasoning. His object in maintaining the fiction of loyalty to France is somewhat obscure. He could hardly have expected the Directory to believe him. One is reminded of William of Orange, who never ceased to proclaim his loyalty to the King of Spain while engaged in a life-and-death struggle with the King's armies.

# CHAPTER XII

## Toussaint and Rigaud

BEFORE taking refuge aboard a warship Hédouville had sent a messenger to Rigaud with this letter: –

> As a result of the ambition and perfidy of General Toussaint Louverture, who has sold himself to the British, the *émigrés* and the Americans and has violated the most solemn agreements, I find myself obliged to leave the colony. I hereby relieve you, Citizen General, of the obligation to recognize him as your Commander in Chief and instruct you to assume command of the Department of the South, as delineated by the Law of 4 Brumaire.

The Law of 4 Brumaire enlarged the Department of the South at the expense of that of the West, placing the important garrison towns Jacmel and Léogane and the towns of Petit-Goâve and Grand-Goâve under Rigaud's jurisdiction. The edict had been issued for the express purpose of weakening Toussaint's authority and had already strained relations between him and Rigaud. Toussaint had written to the mulatto general: "It appears to me that the Agent means to make use of you to keep down the blacks."

Rigaud was well pleased with Hédouville's letter, but refrained from making it public. He wrote to Toussaint, however, that he disapproved of his treatment of the Special Agent: "The Directory will consider its authority violated. All France will think it is our intention to gain independence."

Toussaint himself was somewhat concerned about the impression Hédouville's forced departure would make in France and looked about for a means of placating the Directory. He thought of Commissioner Roume, in Santo Domingo City, and asked him to transfer his headquarters to Le Cap and take charge of the government.

Roume was a mild-mannered man of advanced middle age, honest and possessing moral courage, but not particularly distinguished for ability or judgment. He had received secret instructions from the Directory to take up the reins of government in case Hédouville found it necessary to depart, hence was quite willing to accede to Toussaint's request. After his first meeting with the General he wrote to the Directory: "The high opinion of his heart and mind I had already formed, was still further enhanced by the reality. He is a philosopher, a legislator, a good general and a good citizen. The merit of Toussaint is so transcendent that I have difficulty in conceiving why some people do not find qualities in him to praise, but only to criticize and malign."

Toussaint could hardly have found fault with so ardent an admirer.

## 2

Roume disapproved of Hédouville's policy of embroiling the Negroes with the mulattoes and characterized it as "Machiavellian and unrepublican." Wishing to undo the damage that had been done, he called a conference at Port-au-Prince to iron out the differences resulting from the Law of 4 Brumaire. He invited Toussaint, Rigaud and the commanders of the two disputed garrison towns. Bauvais, Commander of Jacmel, was a mulatto whose sympathies were with Toussaint, but whose mulatto troops were enthusiastic Rigaud partisans. Laplume, Commander of Léogane, was a Negro, outspoken in his sympathy for the Commander in Chief.

The conference settled nothing, but while it was in progress an incident occurred that greatly aggravated the situation. After a riot in a small town in Rigaud's territory twenty-nine Negroes and a white man had been imprisoned in a windowless shed by the mulatto authorities. It was the story of the Black Hole of Calcutta upon a smaller scale. When the door was opened the jailers found a heap of corpses. A wave of indignation swept through the ranks of the Negroes. The explanation that the building had been recently whitewashed and poisonous emanations from the whitewash had killed the prisoners did not satisfy Toussaint, who wrote to Rigaud: "It is always the blacks who pay the penalty of these deliberately provoked disorders."

Rigaud, who expected Hédouville to return with an army and did not fear a conflict, replied in an insolent fashion. Toussaint, convinced that a clash was inevitable, abandoned his usual moderation. He denounced Rigaud in a proclamation, saying that the mulatto general would kill his own father and mother to gain a little higher rank. Rigaud struck back, accusing Toussaint of having made a secret treaty with the British and the Americans. Toussaint boldly replied: "Rigaud says I have made a treaty with General Maitland and with the President of the United States of America in which there are secret clauses. I do not deny it. They were put there in the interest of the colony. I owe no accounting of my actions to Rigaud. That sanguinary and barbarous subaltern does not merit to be taken into the confidence of his chief. Yes, there are secret clauses; the well-being of St. Domingo required them."

Rigaud's reply was the publication of Hédouville's letter and the repudiation of Toussaint as his chief.

## 3

It was now merely a question of who would strike first. Hundreds of mulatto officers and soldiers deserted from Toussaint's army and went to join Rigaud. Numerous mulattoes and old free Negroes packed their belongings and moved to the Department of the South. White men and Negroes from the South came to seek Toussaint's protection.

The situation at Port-au-Prince, where the mulattoes were in the majority and had a powerful militia, was menacing in the extreme. Toussaint was advised to transfer his headquarters. He refused, but announced that he would address the people in the parish church. The building filled quickly. Toussaint arrived on horseback and mounted the pulpit holding several sheets of paper in his hand. He shook them at the crowd, saying they were documents proving that the mulattoes had meant to massacre the white inhabitants and turn the city over to Rigaud. In a voice trembling with indignation he thus addressed the mulattoes: –

"You, who from the beginning of the Revolution have been betraying the blacks, what is it you want? Everybody knows what you want. You want to rule the colony. You want to exterminate the whites and subjugate the blacks. Consider well before you take the fatal step – you who have dishonored yourselves by your complicity in the deportation and massacre of the Swiss, who fought for you. Why did you sacrifice them to the passion of the *Petits Blancs?* Because they were black. Why does Rigaud refuse to obey my orders? Because I am black. As for Rigaud, he is lost. I can see him in my mind's eye at the bottom of the abyss. The hosts of liberty will crush him, the rebel and traitor! Mulattoes, I can see to the very bottom of your souls. You meant to revolt, but remember that even if my entire army were to depart from the Department of the West, my eye and my arm will remain here – my eye to watch you, my arm to reach out for you."

This harangue, reported by de Lacroix,* did not have the desired effect. It was even whispered that Christophe-Mornet, the Negro commander of the garrison, was a Rigaud partisan and might revolt at any time. Rumblings of dissatisfaction came from various parts of the country. The political horizon was black with portent.

## 4

Rigaud struck. His troops were concentrated on the frontier, while Toussaint's were scattered over the Departments of the West and the North. The mulatto leader attacked Petit-Goâve with four thousand men. Laplume, who defended the town with seven hundred Negro soldiers, was forced to retreat and barely escaped capture. The mulattoes massacred eighteen white men whom they accused of complicity with Toussaint. In a letter to Timothy Pickering, dated June 24, 1799, Edward Stevens thus sums up the situation: –

> The uninterrupted trade he [Rigaud] has carried on from the South with St. Thomas, the Continent of America and the island of Jamaica, has supplied him with plenty of provisions, clothing and ammunition. Toussaint's army, on the contrary, is in want of everything. He has but little ammunition and few military stores. All these circumstances have induced him hitherto to remain on the defensive, and have enabled Rigaud to gain ground. He is only waiting for the supplies he momentarily expects from Jamaica, to put his forces into motion and strike a vigorous blow. When he commences his operations the contest will be short. Toussaint has on his side most of the Blacks and all the Whites of the colony. His humane and mild conduct has rendered him respectable to the latter and they now look up to him as their only shield against the tyranny of Rigaud. When the latter had got possession of Petit-Goâve, all the Whites in Port-au-Prince rose in a mass, and desired

* Kerverseau gives a somewhat different version, which seems, however, to be another portion of the same speech.

permission to march against him, but Toussaint objected to it, observing that they had already suffered misfortunes enough by the Revolution, and that he had men enough to finish the contest and protect them, without subjecting them again to the horrors of war.

The worthy Consul-General was somewhat too sanguine. The situation was far more menacing than he supposed. The worst menace did not come from the South, but from Toussaint's own territory, where there were numerous discontented elements. Among these were the mulattoes scattered throughout the colony, Negro generals to whom Rigaud had made lavish promises, Maroon Negroes and Negro cultivators who did not like Toussaint's gospel of work. All these, encouraged by Rigaud's victories (he had taken Grand-Goâve as well as Petit-Goâve), now rose in revolt.

## 5

Christophe-Mornet, Negro commander of Port-au-Prince, revealed himself a Rigaud partisan. So did Pierre Michel, who commanded a part of the garrison at Le Cap. At St. Michel the mulattoes raised Rigaud's standard. The garrison of Môle St. Nicolas declared for Rigaud and occupied near-by Jean-Rabel. There was unrest at Fort-Dauphin. Maroon Negroes, led by Lubin Golard, besieged Port-de-Paix. Maroons in the mountains east of Port-au-Prince were advancing to aid Rigaud in capturing the capital.

Had Toussaint shown any hesitation, had he given any sign of weakness, he would have been lost. His remaining generals would have deserted him. Flight into the mountains would have been his only resource. But the fifty-five-year-old Negro leader was equal to the emergency. Danger acted as a spur upon him. Whatever his private thoughts, he gave no sign that he doubted the outcome even for a moment. He ordered Dessalines to march south with his army, disarm the mulattoes at Port-au-

Prince and attack the Maroons east of the capital. Laplume was told to keep Rigaud in check. He himself hastened north, gathered an army on the way, appeared suddenly at St. Marc and put down the rebellion in that important harbor town. Then, falling in the rear of Lubin Golard, he completely routed his forces and relieved Port-de-Paix. Moyse and the mulatto general Clervaux, who had remained loyal to him, were ordered to recapture Môle St. Nicolas and Jean-Rabel at any cost. Henri Christophe was told to attack Pierre Michel and purge the Le Cap garrison.

Fired by the energy of the Commander in Chief the generals responded. The mulattoes at Port-au-Prince were disarmed; the Maroons east of the city driven back to their mountain strongholds; Rigaud was kept in check. Christophe-Mornet and Pierre Michel faced firing squads. Fort-Dauphin was pacified; Môle St. Nicolas and Jean-Rabel surrendered after a terrific bombardment. In an unbelievably short time the rebellion in Toussaint's own territory was crushed.

Leaving his army behind the Negro leader now hastened south to direct operations against Rigaud. He was crossing the mountains, riding side by side with his white physician, when shots rang out and the white man tumbled dead from his horse. Several Negro officers were killed and the panache on Toussaint's hat was carried off by a bullet. He himself was unharmed and continued his journey in a carriage. After a while, however, he left the carriage and mounted his horse, the vehicle remaining some distance ahead of him. As the carriage rounded a bend in the winding mountain road there was another burst of musketry and the coachman fell dead from the box. When Toussaint rode up the attackers had fled.

News of the double ambush and Toussaint's miraculous escape spread through the country and greatly heightened his prestige. Cultivators who had always believed him to be more than a man considered their faith confirmed. Others were ready to acknowledge that the gods were obviously on his side. Toussaint returned to Port-au-Prince clothed with new authority and ready to carry the war into Rigaud's territory.

## 6

To invade the Department of the South without knowing what attitude Bauvais, the Commander of Jacmel, meant to take, would have been foolhardy. With his garrison of 4500 men, composed largely of mulattoes, he would have been in a position to cut Toussaint's line of communications and attack the rear of the invading army. So Toussaint asked him to declare himself. Bauvais was in a quandary. He had no faith in Rigaud, but did not wish to fight the mulatto caste. Toussaint would not tolerate neutrality and it is doubtful if Bauvais's officers – rabid Rigaud partisans – would have tolerated it. He declared reluctantly for Rigaud and Toussaint laid siege to the town.

To capture Jacmel with the means at Toussaint's disposal would have tasked the genius of any of the great captains of history. The place was a natural stronghold. A half-circle of mountains protected it on the land side. Blockhouses, redoubts and hidden batteries made capture by assault impossible. From the sea the town was more vulnerable, but Toussaint possessed no fleet. Nothing remained except to starve out the defenders.

Unless a siege has a Homer to sing it, it derives its fame from its historical importance. Had Haiti preserved the rank among nations it possessed in the days of Toussaint, the Siege of Jacmel would be famed as one of the memorable sieges of history. It lasted five months and was replete with deeds of valor and with dramatic incident. Edward Stevens had a map made of the field of operations and sent it to Timothy Pickering with the comment: "It will give you a pretty accurate idea of the regularity with which military operations are conducted in this country."

It was not Bauvais, however, who was responsible for the stubborn defense. On a moonless night he slipped out of the harbor in a small boat in the company of a few officers. His successor, Fontaine, becoming convinced that resistance was futile, followed his example. Notwithstanding this double desertion the garrison fought on. Its heroism was rewarded by the arrival of Pétion, an exceedingly capable mulatto general, who managed to steal into the stronghold in the manner his predecessors had left it and assume command. When Toussaint had said that if he took away Rigaud the mulattoes might find a better man, he must have had Pétion in mind.

To isolate the town and the Department from the sea, Toussaint invoked the aid of the United States by writing to President John Adams. His request was supported by Stevens, who had written to Pickering: "I beg leave to report what I have already hinted in my letter, that it might be prudent to direct some of the American ships of War to cruise in the South of the island, and about Jérémie, in order that they might co-operate with the British in cutting off all supplies of provision and ammunition."

It cannot be said, however, that the British proved co-operative. In fact, Stevens was to write later that he suspected the British, as well as the French, of hoping that Toussaint and Rigaud might exhaust each other.

## 7

The changed attitude of the British was due to fear of what might happen once Toussaint had his hands free. For these misgivings Commissioner Roume was responsible. He had renewed the proposal for an atttack upon Jamaica, and when Toussaint turned a deaf ear, had sent two agents – Debuisson and Sasportas – to the British island to provoke rebellion among the slaves. Debuisson was denounced by a Negro and arrested. He was condemned to be hanged, but the Governor offered him a pardon if he would give the name of at least one accomplice. He saved himself by denouncing Sasportas.

Sasportas, who was a Jew, spurned a pardon offered on the same terms. The offer was renewed when the noose was about to be placed around his neck. He replied contemptuously: "Do you take me for a Debuisson? Accomplices? Of course I had accomplices. I see many of them in the crowd, even among the officials. But you will not get their names from me. Some day the seed I have sown will sprout and there will be an explosion." Then, running quickly up the ladder, he shouted: "Negroes and mulattoes of Jamaica! When will you imitate your brothers of St. Domingo? Kill your masters and gain your freedom!"

The Governor, who was present, ordered the executioner to hurry.

Sasportas died the death of John Brown and for the same cause.

## 8

Men like John Brown and Sasportas are the conscience of mankind and the despair of realistic leadership. The heroic Jew had thrown such a scare into the British that they looked askance at Toussaint's military operations. He had decided to bombard Jacmel with heavy siege guns and had them loaded on six vessels at Port-au-Prince, for transportation to the south coast. The British admiral, Sir Hyde Parker, thought the ships were part of an invasion fleet and had them stopped. They were taken to Jamaica where they were condemned and sold by the prize court.

Toussaint swore he would have nothing more to do with the British and refused to see the two British agents assigned to him – Wigglesworth and Colonel Grant – who wished to explain matters. Finally he calmed down and the affair was settled for 1,500,000 francs, but the siege of Jacmel had been greatly prolonged.

The Negro general managed to have siege guns dragged across the mountain barrier and the besieged now had to withstand a constant bombardment besides the pangs of hunger and the ravages of disease. Horses, dogs and cats had all been eaten; rats and lizards were considered a delicacy; leaves and grass were the principal articles of diet. When lead and cannon ball gave out the besieged fired rocks and pebbles at the besiegers, but as long as they had gunpowder they would not hear of surrender.

Finally Pétion decided that noncombatants must leave. He counted on Toussaint's humanity to allow them to pass through his lines. He was not mistaken as far as Toussaint was concerned. The starved women, children and old men who had the good fortune to go out at the gate opposite which Toussaint himself commanded were allowed to pass, were fed and sent into the interior. But on another part of the long front a terrible tragedy took place. There the besieged saw their wives and children mowed down by the fire of Henri Christophe, future King of Haiti.

On a moonless night Pétion decided to cut his way through with the remnants of the garrison, but Toussaint got wind of the maneuver and only a few managed to escape death or capture.

## 9

"Love," says Bulwer-Lytton, "is the idleness of the busy and the business of the idle." Rigaud would have done well to have adopted some such motto to guide him. He did not lack military talent, but was known to turn the command over to a subordinate during a battle and go in pursuit of a pretty wench he happened to espy. While the heroic defenders of Jacmel were counting on him to relieve them, he spent his time carousing with women friends. It was only after the town had fallen that he came to his senses, suddenly realizing the gravity of the situation. His first reaction was a blast of words. He issued a proclamation in which he called Toussaint "a monster thirsting for human blood, an ungrateful wretch, a traitor to the Republic, a devastator of St. Domingo, the executioner of Jacmel, the persecutor of French Agents and the slave of the English. – If he is mad enough to undertake the invasion of the Department of the South, I swear to you, fellow citizens, that he and his army will find themselves under the sod before they have advanced two miles."

Toussaint replied with a proclamation of which this is a part: –

"I am merciful. I am humane. I stretch forth fatherly arms towards you. Come, all of you come! I will receive you all – you from the South as well as you from the West and the North, who seduced by Rigaud have left your wives and children to join him. If Rigaud, who bears the responsibility for all this disorder, were to come to me and acknowledge his mistake straightforwardly, I would receive even him. But if he remains stubborn and fails to take advantage of my offer, it should not prevent you, fathers and mothers of families, from coming to me. I will welcome you with open arms. When the prodigal son repented he was welcomed by his father."

The effect of the proclamation was immediate and profound. The inhabitants were tired of Rigaud's antics. They longed for peace. There was murmuring. The mulatto general met the new danger by concentrating all power in his own hands. He ordered resistance unto death.

No quarrel is so bitter as one between relatives. Of all the wars that ravaged St. Domingo none was more terrible than the war between Negroes and mulattoes. It is known as "the war of knives." The combatants were known to discard their muskets so they might fight breast to breast, cut each other's throats, tear each other with their teeth. Rigaud's soldiers, realizing that the population was against them, massacred the people they were supposed to defend. The terrified cultivators fled the plantations and sought refuge in the towns. Crops were not tended and famine made itself felt. In the midst of this fratricidal struggle a new Commission arrived from France, sent not by the Directory, which had ceased to exist, but by the Republic's new ruler, the First Consul.

## 10

Toussaint and Rigaud had each sent a representative to France. Toussaint's emissary, the white general Vincent, arrived in Paris in time to witness the seizure of power by Bonaparte.

At the commencement of his political career Napoleon asked his advisers what colonial system had given the best financial results. He was told that it was the system prevailing before the Revolution. "Then," said the former Jacobin, "the sooner we return to it the better."

As the initial step towards the restoration of slavery Napoleon decreed that laws governing the mother country no longer applied to the colonies, which were henceforth to be ruled by special decree. He appointed a Commission of three – of which General Vincent was made a member – to acquaint the people of St. Domingo with his decision. He assured the Negroes in a proclamation that "the sacred principles of liberty and equality for the blacks will not be infringed upon or modified," bade them remember that "the people of France alone recognize the liberty of the blacks" and ordered these words emblazoned upon the tricolor displayed in the colony. Since he was not yet in position to make his power felt in St. Domingo, he took care not to offend Toussaint. The Commission was to inform the Negro general that the First Consul confirmed him as Commander in Chief. Roume was to be maintained as Special Agent. As for Rigaud, his situation being considered hopeless, he was ignored, but the Commissioners were to make an attempt to put an end to the hostilities.

Toussaint was not deceived. The astute black man kept informed about all that went on in the French capital. There are letters in existence, written to him from Paris by two white men, Huin and d'Hébecourt, who served as his secret agents.

They made frequent trips to Haiti and managed to receive advance information concerning any decision affecting the colony. Toussaint's first intention appears to have been to deport the Commissioners immediately upon their arrival. The fact that Vincent, whom he trusted and who proved worthy of that trust, was a member of the Commission probably decided him to adopt a more conciliatory attitude. Nevertheless he received the French general somewhat morosely and when Vincent had given him Napoleon's assurances, replied: –

"It is not a fortuitous concession of liberty, made to us alone, that we want, but a recognition of the principle that whether a man be red, black or white, he cannot be the property of any other man. We are free to-day because we are strong. The First Consul maintains slavery in Martinique, which means that he will make us slaves when he feels he is strong enough to do so."

He refused to place the inscription upon his banner, saying: "The Negroes do not owe their emancipation to France, but to their own valor." He at first rejected, but later accepted, Vincent's proposal to act as mediator between him and Rigaud. He appointed a Negro and a mulatto to accompany him and offered these terms: –

Rigaud was to reside abroad until the situation in St. Domingo had become stabilized. He could, if he wished, leave his family behind. "I will treat them as I would want my own family to be treated under like circumstances," Toussaint wrote. The mulatto's property would not be confiscated. General amnesty was to be proclaimed, from which only four general officers – deserters from Toussaint's army – were to be excluded. In the interest of discipline they were to serve a short prison term.

## 11

The delegation arrived by boat at Les Cayes. The mulatto dictator was not in his capital and the officials received Toussaint's emissaries with obvious relief. As soon as Rigaud heard of their arrival he hastened back, lest peace be concluded without him. Vincent describes him as small of stature, with shifty eyes that had a ferocious gleam. He wore a green uniform without insignia of rank, had a huge sword strapped to his side, pistols in his belt, and held an unsheathed dagger in his hand, the blade hidden within his sleeve. He railed against Toussaint, browbeat and threatened the delegates. When Vincent handed him a letter from his (Rigaud's) young son, who was in school in France and who wrote to his father that General Vincent had visited him and had been very kind, his mood changed. He was seized by a fit of despondency, talked of suicide and nervously chewed a corner of his handkerchief.

It was impossible to reach an agreement with him and the delegates departed. Toussaint ordered Dessalines to advance. All resistance collapsed and the Negro army marched swiftly towards Les Cayes.

Rigaud ordered the houses smeared with tar preparatory to giving them over to the flames. He ran to the arsenal with the apparent intention of blowing it up, but was persuaded to desist. It is doubtful if his intention had been serious, for at near-by Tiburon three ships, laden with valuables, were waiting for him. He now assembled his officers and his bodyguard and bade them a touching farewell. Then he hastened to Tiburon, where his family had preceded him, and set sail for France.

In Paris he was received by Napoleon, who listened gravely to his tale of woe and then said: "General, I have but one fault to find with you – you have lost."

## 12

Toussaint made his entry into Les Cayes and was received with rejoicing by the populace. Rigaud's stanchest supporters vied with one another to do him honor. One pointed to his long beard and assured him that he had taken an oath not to cut the hirsute adornment until he had had the opportunity of welcoming Toussaint in Rigaud's capital. The Negro leader snapped: "You've said enough. Get out!"

Toussaint remembered that many years ago, when he was still a child, his sister Geneviève had been sold to a planter near Les Cayes. Inquiry revealed that she was the widow of a mulatto named Chancy and lived in a suburb with her three children. A messenger was sent to tell her that Toussaint was her brother and wished to see her. "It isn't possible," she said, "that that little boy is now the ruler of the colony." She asked if one of his fingers curved upward and having received assurance on this point, hastened with her children to meet her brother. Toussaint received her affectionately. He was pleased with the appearance of his nephew, Bernard Chancy, and attached him to his staff. He gave his sister a pension of 1800 francs and sent his two nieces to his plantation at Ennery, where they became part of his household. The younger, Louise, later married his son Isaac.

The Negro leader reorganized the civil and military administration of the department, placing Dessalines, Commander of the Department of the West, in command. He addressed the people in the parish church and, turning to the newly-appointed officials, said that all should be forgiven and forgotten and that no distinction should be made between Rigaud's partisans and others. His failure to enforce this injunction is the most serious blot on his career.

## 13

Dessalines, whom Toussaint had appointed Commander of the Department of the South, was a Congo Negro whose military ability was second only to Toussaint's, but he was cruel and tyrannical, devoid of public or private morals. In violation of Toussaint's amnesty decree he began a purge of the two departments under his jurisdiction. No record exists of the number of his victims, but estimates vary from 1000 to as high as 10,000. Even the lowest estimate should be viewed with caution. Partisanship is apt to exaggerate such matters to a fantastic degree. Royalist writers have placed the number of victims of the Jacobin priest Schneider during the revolutionary Reign of Terror in Alsace at as high as 40,000. In the case of Schneider reliable records exist. The number of his victims was – thirty! If such exaggeration is indulged in when the truth can be easily ascertained, how much reliance can be placed on estimates when imagination and partisanship can allow themselves free scope?

A number of prisoners (some say 300) were massacred at Léogane. Some fifty mulatto officers in prison at Port-au-Prince were taken to a point now marked with a cross and known as Croix-des-Martyrs, and there bayoneted to death. Prominent mulattoes were executed throughout both departments.

Toussaint was at Port-au-Prince when the massacre of the officers took place, but was ignorant of what was happening. The mulatto historian Madiou, who censures him severely for failing to keep faith with the mulattoes, tells this story: –

One of the officers, who was only wounded, managed to drag himself at night to the cabin of a Negress and begged her assistance. She took him in, bound up his wounds, and the following morning went to the Palace at Port-au-Prince. She threw herself at Toussaint's feet and implored him to pardon the officer. Toussaint raised her up and asked: "Pardon him? What has he done?"

"He is mortally wounded."

"How did it happen? Have the assassins been arrested?"

She then realized that he knew nothing of the massacre and told him. He covered his face with his hands and wept. Then he ordered the officer brought to the Palace and had his personal physician look after him. The man recovered.

Later, Toussaint made a tour of the Department of the South, and whenever he came to a place where some prominent mulatto resided, would ask to see him. In most cases he received evasive answers which made him fear the worst. Once he cried out: "I did not want this! I told him to prune the tree, not to uproot it!"

## 14

To what extent must Toussaint be held responsible for Dessalines's purge? Knowing Dessalines as he must have known him, it was imprudent, to say the least, to have told him "to prune the tree," besides being a violation of his promise of general amnesty. He may have discovered that the mulattoes were yet far from subdued and were ready to revolt a second time, and his hand may have been forced. It is likewise a question to what extent he was able to control Dessalines. De Lacroix has said: "His generals trembled before him. Dessalines hardly dared look him in the face." This opinion, however, is not shared by Sonthonax and Rochambeau, who claim that Toussaint's principal generals were difficult to control. During a battle, under his personal command, they would obey orders, but at other times (says Rochambeau) they were like so many caciques, doing very much as they pleased. It is certain that Toussaint, who had to keep the ultimate aim in view and could not dispense with their services, was often obliged to close his eyes to their misdeeds. Southern historians have compared Sherman with Attila, but only the most fanatical blame Lincoln for not having called Sherman to account. He who during a civil war writes in the account book of history cannot hope to write only on the credit side.

Toussaint hated excesses, not only because he was humane by nature, but because he considered them demoralizing. He once wrote to Hédouville: "I watch over the liberty of my brothers. I consider that excesses are more likely to result in a loss of liberty than all the perfidious machinations of their enemies." To Roume he wrote: "I have pardoned those whose guilt was secondary, as I hope God will pardon me. But notwithstanding my endeavor to obey the Divine Commandment, they have made me out the executioner of the mulatto caste of St. Domingo."

When he came to Le Cap, where many mulattoes had been imprisoned, he had the prisoners assembled in a church, had money and clothing distributed, and sent them home with the words: "You are free. I forgive you. Be of good cheer and return to your families."

He wrote a letter to Dessalines telling him to exercise moderation, but the letter lacks the note of authority. It recommends when it should have commanded.

# CHAPTER XIII
## Toussaint and Roume

It is not pleasant to discover that one has been led by the nose. Commissioner Roume, at one time so vehement in his defense of Toussaint, had made the unpleasant discovery that he had been a dupe. The Negro leader's relations with the enemies of the Republic were such that it was impossible not to suspect his loyalty to France. Roume had been forced to adopt the view that Hédouville had been right, that Toussaint was striving for independence. He no longer criticized his predecessor's policy of embroiling the Negroes with the mulattoes and was, in fact, beginning to imitate it. On June 24, 1799, Edward Stevens had written to Timothy Pickering: –

I hinted to you, some time ago, my suspicion that Rigaud was privately supported by the French government, from the cruel policy of weakening both Mulattoes and Negroes, by fomenting and keeping up a contest between them. Every day confirms me more in this opinion and I have no doubt that the Agent is the secret and diabolical instrument employed by them for this purpose. He certainly is privately in the interest of Rigaud, and Toussaint seems well acquainted with this fact. Policy, however, induces him to temporise. A few days ago he wrote him a very severe letter, which he read to me. He concludes with calling to his recollection that he has requested him several times to publish a Proclamation of Outlawry against Rigaud, that he repeats the request for the last time, and that nothing but his prompt obedience will convince him that the government stands in any further need of his services. I can readily anticipate the result of this mandate. Roume will publish the proclamation, tho reluctantly, and will then be suffered quietly to strut about the Government House in the costume of the Agency, until something else is required of him.

## 2

Something else *was* required of Roume after the fall of Jacmel. Feeling that the pacifying of the South could now be left to Dessalines, Toussaint turned his eyes towards the east – towards the Spanish part of the island. It had been ceded to France in 1795, but was still garrisoned by the Spaniards. It was Toussaint's ambition to unify the entire island under his command. Needless to say the French Government did not desire a further extension of his power and was perfectly willing to allow the Spaniards to remain in possession until white forces of occupation could be sent.

What Toussaint now required of Roume was a decree authorizing him to occupy the former Spanish colony. He was able to give excellent reasons. Not only was slavery maintained in San Domingo, but the Spaniards did a thriving business kidnaping Negroes in the French part of the island and shipping them to Cuba or Puerto Rico. Boume refused to issue the decree and wrote to the mulatto general Chanlatte – French Commissioner in Santo Domingo City – that he would allow himself to be cut to pieces before doing what Toussaint demanded.

With his usual perseverance Toussaint set to work to obtain the decree. From one end of the colony to another indignation meetings were held. Angry crowds clamored against Roume and called upon Toussaint to take over the reins of government and put a stop to the slave traffic. Stevens reported to Pickering: "It is not difficult to discover that all those Assemblies in the different parts of the colony have been planned and regulated by the leading chiefs, and that, far from being tumultuous or dangerous, they have been perfectly under control."

But Roume remained obdurate. Nothing remained except to force the issue. Toussaint transferred his headquarters to Gonaïves, twenty miles from Le Cap, and unleashed one of his famous popular uprisings. As on previous occasions, thousands of cultivators, apparently carried away by their emotions, set out for Le Cap. The harassed citizens prevailed upon Roume and the municipal officers to meet the marchers some distance from the city and try to reason with them. Roume and his companions soon found themselves in the midst of an angry, gesticulating crowd clamoring for the decree. He would not yield. When a sword was held over his head he cried: "Strike! France will avenge me!" Orders were strict. Nothing must happen to Roume. The Agent and the municipal officers were locked in an empty chicken coop and the crowd made camp, awaiting further orders.

In the meantime Toussaint remained at Gonaïves, apparently ignorant of the indignity inflicted upon the representative of the French Republic. His ignorance lasted nine days, then he allowed himself to be informed and professed to be greatly shocked. He hastened to the scene of the disorder, remonstrated with the crowd, freed the prisoners and accompanied them to Le Cap. He assured Roume that it would be impossible for him to restrain the mob from invading the city and departed with the decree in his pocket.

## 3

Toussaint's white chief of staff, General Agé, was sent to Santo Domingo City to arrange for the transfer of authority. He met with a cool reception. The Spanish Governor – the same Don Joachim García in whose service Toussaint had been – informed him that he could not give up his office without an order from the authorities in Madrid, who of course would have to consult the French Government. The French Commissioner, General Chanlatte, agreed that this was the proper procedure.

In the meantime the populace had got wind of the purpose of Agé's visit. What! San Domingo was to be occupied by a Negro army! A former slave was to rule the ancient city of Columbus! Never! When Agé showed himself on the street he was insulted. A crowd formed. Toussaint's envoy was forced to take refuge in the Convent of Santa Clara. The street in front filled with an angry mob. Stones went flying. García arrived in his carriage with a cavalry escort. Agé was hustled into the carriage, which drove off at breakneck speed. Later the General was escorted to the frontier.

Roume was not in the least unhappy that his decree had been flouted. The British, too, were not displeased. The Negro general was becoming too ambitious for the safety of British possessions in the West Indies. Toussaint had sent an armed schooner, filled with white soldiers from Le Cap, to back up Agé, but His Britannic Majesty's appropriately named frigate *The Alarm* had intercepted the vessel. Roume announced that García's suggestion of leaving the matter to the decision of the authorities in Paris and Madrid was reasonable and revoked his decree. Napoleon mixed in and had his Minister of Marine, Forfait, write to Toussaint that "the man who stains himself with the blood of his fellow citizens will bring down upon his head the malediction of men and heaven. He [the First Consul] expects, therefore, to be informed by the first dispatches that you have made your peace with Roume and restored order."

Toussaint appeared to be foiled.

4

One morning General Moyse arrived at the Government Palace at Le Cap with two traveling coaches and a company of dragoons. Admitted to Roume's presence, he politely informed him that he had orders to escort him and his family to the Dupuy plantation at Dondon, where everything had been got ready for their comfort. The indignant Roume threatened and pleaded. All in vain. With his mulatto wife and daughter he was forced to mount into the first coach, while members of his suite mounted into the second. The dragoons surrounded the vehicles and Moyse gave the order to start.

In this peremptory fashion Toussaint disposed of still another French Agent. Whenever the Negro leader happened to be in the vicinity of Dondon he would write to the Commissioner, inquire about his health and deplore the fact that the press of business made it impossible for him to visit him. He wrote to the First Consul, explaining why he had found it necessary "to invite Citizen Roume to cease his functions and retire to Dondon. He is at your disposal. When you want him I will send him to you."

Napoleon did not deign to reply and Toussaint finally packed Roume off to France, explaining that Roume's health was delicate and that he did not wish to run the risk of having calumny attribute the Commissioner's death to him.

# CHAPTER XIV

## Toussaint Conquers the Spanish Colony

Edward Stevens did not believe Toussaint possessed either the power or the audacity to carry out his project of conquering the Spanish part of the island. He wrote to Secretary Pickering: "It will be impossible for the General in Chief to take possession by force, even though he should wish to do so. The Spaniards are too numerous and too much opposed to the Domination of the blacks to render such a measure practicable."

The excellent Consul-General of the United States proved himself a poor prognosticator. Immediately after the forced retirement of Commissioner Roume, Toussaint wrote a polite letter to the Spanish Governor in which he informed him that he was sending his nephew, General Moyse, to San Domingo to take over the government. To guard against a repetition of incidents such as had marred Agé's mission, Moyse would be accompanied by a force sufficient to maintain order.

Don Joachim replied: "I protest one thousand and one times against this threat to a dependency of the Republic without your Government's consent. The preservation of order in this territory has been entrusted to me. Not until the proper authorities have reached a decision in the matter can I surrender the trust."

Toussaint, who did not lack a sense of humor, wrote: "Your thousand and one protestations are futile. It is my intention to occupy the territory purely and simply in the name of the Republic. I will hold you responsible one thousand and one times for any untoward incident that may result from your intransigence."

Moyse crossed the frontier at Ounamenthe with 10,000 men. He scattered the Spanish militia that sought to oppose him and at El Porteguelo clashed with the main Spanish force under Don Domingo Perez Guerra, whose martial surname did not save him from defeat. In the meantime Toussaint, with 4000 men, advanced along the southern coast towards Santo Domingo City. Herrera, Commander in Chief of the Spanish army, was giving a ball celebrating his daughter's marriage when news of Toussaint's advance reached the Spanish capital. The tocsin sounded. The young men of the city flew to arms. Their volunteer battalion, commanded by the Spanish general Nunez and the French general Kerverseau, sallied forth to teach the insolent Negro a lesson. Alas for Spanish pride! After the first brush with Toussaint's seasoned veterans the Spaniards fled, leaving a number of prisoners in Toussaint's hands. The Negro general released the prisoners and gave them this message to their fellow citizens: If the Spaniards wished to be reasonable, he could promise that order would be maintained, life and property protected and divine worship not interfered with. Soon after he made a junction with Moyse and established headquarters at Boca Nigua, where a chastened delegation of Spaniards came to discuss terms of surrender.

## 2

Toussaint entered Santo Domingo City on January 26, 1801. The Governor and other Spanish grandees received him at the Government House. Antonio Delmonte Y Tajada, an eyewitness, gives these details about the appearance of Toussaint and his following: "He was dressed in a blue uniform with gold-embroidered cuffs and large gold epaulettes. Over this he worc a flesh-colored cloak. His boots, equipped with spurs, were of the finest leather. His hat was adorned with a tricolor cockade and a panache in the colors of the Republic. A sword completed his costume. His aides-de-camp and other officers were elegantly attired."

When Toussaint entered the *Sala Capitular* he saw the officials standing stiffly behind a table, covered with green baize, on which the keys of the city had been neatly placed in a row. Custom demanded that the retiring Governor hand the keys over to his successor. But handing over the keys would imply recognition of Toussaint's right to receive them. Don Joachim wished to oblige Toussaint to complete his act of force by taking possession of the keys without his intervention. If he supposed that the former slave lacked the acumen to grasp the significance of the gesture he was mistaken. Toussaint looked at the row of keys and said: "I did not come to San Domingo as your enemy, but as the representative of a friendly and allied nation to receive fulfillment of a treaty solemnly entered into. To take the keys myself would be the act of a usurper. I therefore ask Your Lordship to be good enough to hand them to me."

The Governor hesitated and asked if Toussaint would swear by the Holy Trinity that he would govern with justice and righteousness. Toussaint replied: "Such an oath would be appropriate for an official of His Catholic Majesty. I am the servant of the Republic. I solemnly swear, however, to forget the past and to endeavor to make the inhabitants, who are now French citizens, happy and contented."

Don Joachim then gathered up the keys and handed them to him. Delmonte Y Tajada pays this tribute to the Negro leader's attitude: "Toussaint's graciousness and courtesy contributed much towards easing the situation. His bearing was martial, his aspect noble and imposing, his expression benevolent. His manner was friendly and unconstrained, yet dignified. When addressed by an officer of lower rank, he would incline towards him and listen affably. He graciously acknowledged the marks of respect shown to him, but seemed to wish to avoid special recognition."

The ceremony at the Government House was followed by a *Te Deum* at the cathedral, which Toussaint and his following attended. This made an excellent impression upon the Spaniards, to whom republicanism was synonymous with atheism.

General Guillermin, who was in Santo Domingo City at that time, has recorded this conversation between Toussaint and Don Joachim García: –

TOUSSAINT: Your Lordship undoubtedly has known Count d'Hermonas intimately.

GARCÍA: Yes, an excellent officer.

TOUSSAINT: Few can testify to that better than I, who served under him. He defended the interests of his sovereign with courage and ability. His Majesty is to be congratulated if he has many servitors like him.

García: I agree with you entirely.

Toussaint: Perhaps Your Lordship remembers a plan of campaign for the conquest of the French part of the island he submitted to you. I flatter myself on having contributed a little towards that plan.

García: I remember it very well.

Toussaint: If at that time Your Lordship had evaluated the Count at his true worth and had allowed him to carry out the plan, I might still be in the service of His Catholic Majesty. The island would belong to Spain and Your Lordship would have been spared the painful necessity of handing over the keys of the colony.

While conversing with the Mayor, Toussaint asked information concerning a run on the bank of the Ozana. Before the *cabilde* could reply another official put in: –

"It is the palace of Christopher Columbus, who was sent to Spain in chains for wishing to make himself independent."

There was an awkward silence, then Toussaint quietly said: "In answering my question you have alluded to a matter that has no bearing upon it. I doubt if in doing so you have correctly interpreted His Honor's intentions. I know as well as you that Columbus was rewarded with ingratitude by Spain. Such is the lot of most men who serve their country. They have powerful enemies who sooner or later manage to undermine them. No doubt the same fate is reserved for me."

Guillermin has expressed this opinion of Toussaint: "While he lacked the facility of expression and the analytical faculty conferred by education, there can be no doubt of the loftiness of his conceptions. He would form a plan and with keen insight watch over its execution. The men who served under him were but the passive tools of his will."

## 3

Toussaint treated the Spaniards to an exhibition of energy such as the colony had never witnessed. The restless energy of the conquistadors had been devoted to conquest and acquisition. It brought riches to the conquerors, but despoiled the country and made slaves of the inhabitants. It remained for a Negro to administer the country in the interest of the entire population.

Toussaint proclaimed the abolition of slavery in the Spanish territory. Slave ships about to depart when he entered Santo Domingo City were stopped and forced to unload their human cargo. But he did not wish a repetition of what had occurred in the French colony, when thousands of liberated Negroes had left the plantations and had lived in idleness or had turned brigands. He issued this proclamation: –

> I have never considered that liberty is synonymous with license, that when men have gained their liberty they have the right to live in idleness and create disorder. It is my firm intention to see to it that the cultivators remain at their work, that they be given one fourth of the revenue of the plantations and that no one can treat them unjustly without suffering for it. But at the same time it is my wish that they work harder than heretofore,* that they obey orders and be strict in the performance of their duty.

He reorganized the administrative and judicial systems, injecting new life into both. He decreed that landowners must plant export crops – sugar, coffee, cotton, cocoa, ginger, indigo – and organized a rural police to enforce the decree. He offered land concessions and government subsidies to those planting such crops and to new settlers. He promoted the creation of

* It should not be forgotten that Raynal has said that the hardest work performed by the slaves in the Spanish colony was swinging hammocks. While this is obviously an exaggeration many others have testified that the indolence of the Spaniards extended to their slaves.

new industries. He abolished the custom barrier between the French and Spanish colonies and threw the ports open to British and American commerce. He undertook an extensive road-building campaign, with the result that for the first time in centuries travel and transport by means of four-wheeled vehicles became possible. He cleared the coast of pirates and the mountains of brigands. He made a journey through the Spanish territory and preached the gospel of work to the somnolent inhabitants. To quiet their fears lest a purge would follow after his departure, he assumed personal responsibility for the security of life and property and appointed his brother commander of the most important part of the territory. He demanded an accounting from the former Governor and decreed that all who did not wish to become French citizens must leave. He gave every facility to those who wished to depart, allowing them to take their movable property with them. A young officer, however, was stopped at the last moment, Toussaint giving this explanation to Don Joachim García: –

He promised to wed Doña Ursula Guerrero, yet is preparing to depart for Porto Rico without fulfilling his obligation. I have always been of the opinion that a wise government should watch over the morals of its citizens, and believe that you, who are the head of a family, will be shocked to learn that an officer of His Catholic Majesty was preparing to leave without fulfilling a solemn promise and a sacred obligation.

# *PART THREE*
## *Toussaint Rules*

# CHAPTER I
## Toussaint's Statesmanship

Toussaint had defeated the British and the Spaniards and had forced them to withdraw from the island. He had suppressed rebellion, stopped French interference, unified the country. He now had an opportunity to prove that he could rule with justice and wisdom. Opinion is practically unanimous that he acquitted himself well. He did not create an earthly paradise. He did not settle all problems. Many abuses continued to exist and fresh abuses crept in. He made mistakes. But there can be no doubt that he ruled more wisely and more justly than any man had yet ruled on the island.

Edward Stevens thus reported to Timothy Pickering the result of Toussaint's rule in the Department of the South: –

> Since I had the honor of addressing you last the most perfect tranquility has been restored to this colony. The cultivators of the South have been recalled to their respective plantations, the various civil administrations re-organized and the most effective measures adopted for the future peace and good order of the department. Agriculture and commerce are beginning to revive.

The French historian Thiers pays this grudging tribute: –

> This black slave, who became dictator, had established in St. Domingo a tolerable state of society. He accomplished things which might almost be called great had the stage been ampler and had they proved less ephemeral.

General de Lacroix is more enthusiastic: –

The colony was regaining all its old-time splendor, as if by magic. Agriculture prospered. Every day there was progress. In Le Cap and throughout the North buildings sprang up like toadstools after a rain.

During the rule of the planters maintenance of the "old-time splendor" had exacted a yearly toll of one ninth of the Negro population. This, according to Malouet, former Minister of Marine and plantation owner, was no longer the case: –

All accounts agree that there is a decrease in mortality among Negro infants. This is ascribed to absolute rest enjoyed by pregnant women and to better working conditions.

Malouet's statement is confirmed by another contemporary writer, the Englishman James Stephens, who says that there was "a large increase in the rising generation of Negroes, instead of that dreadful falling off which is always found in a colony of slaves." He goes on to say: –

So rapid was the progress of agriculture, that it was a fact, though not believed at the time in England, that the island already produced, or promised to yield in the next crop, one third part at least of as large return of sugar and coffee as it had ever given in its most prosperous days. This, considering all the ravages of a ten years' war, and the great scarcity of all necessary supplies from abroad, is very surprising, yet has since clearly appeared to be true.*

Thus, while greatly improving the condition of the laborers, Toussaint nevertheless made good his boast: "I'll know as well as the planters how to make the colony pay."

Colonel Poyen, French military historian, writes: –

* Stephens, as is the habit of Englishmen, is given to understatement. In 1800 the crop appears to have been more than two thirds of what it had been in St. Domingo's richest pre-Revolution year. In 1801 it was still larger. Figures given by Idlinger, Comptroller of Customs, are even more startling, but are in conflict with those of Vollée, Administrator-General.

He [Toussaint] was responsible for the most extraordinary activity in all departments of the administration. He busied himself with the building of fortifications, the stocking of arsenals, the acquisition of supplies, the instruction and discipline of the army. He spurred the agricultural inspectors to intense activity. He restored and embellished the cities and built bridges. He administered justice, kept an eye on the exercise of religion, visited schools and distributed prizes to the best scholars. He frequently visited hospitals and barracks. It is difficult to sum up the amazing activity of this extraordinary Negro, who slept only two hours out of twenty-four. His body, accustomed to privations, was entirely under the control of his will.

The mulatto historian Madiou, who has overlooked no opportunity to criticize Toussaint and speaks well of him only when the evidence in the Negro leader's favor is overwhelming, pays this tribute to his short reign: –

After the occupation of the eastern part of the island, the prosperity of the colony grew by leaps and bounds. Agriculture and industry flourished. The Reign of Terror disappeared. Political executions ceased. Mulattoes could go wherever they liked and received equal consideration with Negroes and whites. Bickerings among the castes came to an end. Vagabondage was suppressed. The children of the poor were reared at the expense of the State, were taught a trade, reading, writing and the principles of religion. It must be said, however, that the power of the government had become absolute. Work was obligatory for the cultivators. The whites, supported by Toussaint's formidable authority, remained leaders of colonial society. Laws were strictly enforced. Toussaint appeared before the world as the regenerator of St. Domingo.

## 2

The war between France and England could not last forever. The chances were that as soon as it was over Napoleon would strike. Toussaint realized this and prepared. His method of doing so has been criticized by men of his own race. Henri Christophe has written that the measures taken by Toussaint "were responsible for the weak resistance the French met with in Haiti." His opinion is not shared by Generals de Lacroix and Leclerc, who had to overcome that resistance. They describe it as exceedingly formidable, especially on the part of the cultivators. If Toussaint's plans went awry it was not due to lukewarmness on the part of the cultivators, but to treason on the part of the generals, of whom Christophe was one of the most guilty.

That Toussaint's first duty was to put the country in a state of defense cannot be gainsaid. All else he could have accomplished would have been futile if the Negroes were fated again to be reduced to slavery. What purpose would it have served to have divided the land if both land and people were doomed to become again the property of the planters? That this and nothing else was the French Government's intention is evident from the correspondence between the First Consul, the Minister of Marine (Decrès) and General Leclerc.

On June 14, 1802, Decrès wrote to Leclerc: –

> When they [the Negroes of St. Domingo] have learned the difference between the yoke of a tyrant and usurper and that of their legitimate masters, interested in their welfare, then the time will have arrived to bring them back to their former state, from which they never should have been allowed to depart. As for the slave traffic, it is more necessary than ever, since the gaps caused by ten years of disorder and non-replacement must be filled.

On August 7, 1802, Napoleon wrote to Decrès: –

> Everything must be prepared for the restoration of slavery. This is not only the opinion of the metropolis, but is also the view of England and other European powers.

On August 25, 1802, Leclerc wrote in cipher to Decrès: –

> Don't count on re-establishing slavery here for the present. I hope to have everything in readiness so that my successor will be able to put the government decree into effect. However, in view of the

endless proclamations I have issued guaranteeing liberty to the blacks, I don't want to contradict myself. But you can assure the First Consul that my successor will find everything prepared.

On October 7, 1802, Leclerc wrote to Napoleon: –

With the troops I am asking for Nivôse I can establish order and complete the disarmament [of the blacks]. With the troops that are to arrive the 12th year of the Republic, my successor can carry out your design. To attempt to do so sooner would be a mistake.

There is furthermore the testimony of Fouché and of Thibeaudeau, members of Bonaparte's Council of State. Fouché says in his memoirs that a definite decision was reached in the Council to restore slavery in St. Domingo. The Abbé Grégoire, also a member and a friend of the Negroes, remarked on that occasion that if the gentlemen were suddenly to turn black they would sing a different tune. Thibaudeau quotes Napoleon as saying: "I am for the whites because I am white. I have no other reason. That one suffices. Do you believe that if the majority in the Convention had known what it was doing and had had any acquaintance with the colonies it would have freed the blacks? To maintain that policy now is hypocritical."

It has already been remarked that Toussaint had means of knowing what went on behind the scenes in the French capital. The war between France and England was a golden opportunity to prepare against an invasion aimed at the enslavement of his people.

## 3

The French Commissioner Polverel had planned to prepare St. Domingo to meet a combined British and Spanish invasion by distributing land to the Negroes. He rightly reasoned that they would fight unto death to keep what had been given them. But this presupposed that France would supply them with arms.

The French, however, could hardly have been expected to supply arms to Toussaint to defend the country against themselves. He had to purchase arms and supplies in the United States. For this much money was required, which could be obtained only by producing export crops – sugar, coffee, cotton, indigo, ginger, etc. The question confronting Toussaint was to choose the best method of producing such crops.

He had experimented with the small farm system by allowing individual Negroes and groups of Negroes to acquire land at very low cost. The experiment had not been a success. It should be remembered that two thirds of the Haitian Negroes were African-born. Their tradition – in which slavery had been but a hateful interlude – was against hard, sustained labor. The excesses of the slavery period had given them a loathing for such labor. The climate permitted a return to ancestral habits. A makeshift dwelling they themselves were able to construct, a minimum of clothing, a few potatoes and bananas could be obtained without much effort if one owned a few acres of land. Diogenes and Thoreau would undoubtedly have said that, in preferring to loaf and to dance the *chica*, the Negroes showed true wisdom. But could Toussaint adopt this view with the shadow of Napoleon lying over the land? And even if this immediate danger had not existed, what reason was there to believe that the slaveowning powers surrounding them would leave the Haitian Negroes in peace once they had reverted to ancestral ways? To remain free, they must be strong. To be strong they must have vast quantities of war supplies. To purchase war supplies they must produce export crops in abundance. The small-farm system gave no promise of such crops and deprived the large plantations of badly needed labor. Toussaint risked his popularity by deciding against the small-farm system.

## 4

On February 7, 1801, Toussaint issued a decree forbidding the sale or purchase of land without a special permit. A permit could not be obtained for the acquisition of less than fifty acres, and then only if the prospective purchaser was able to prove that he had sufficient funds to develop the land. Toussaint invited the planters to return and operate their holdings under strict government supervision. Since many planters had died or failed to return, more than two thirds of the land was operated by the State, under the supervision of the military commanders. Abuses crept in. The military commanders waxed rich. They became *nègres dorés*. Some, especially Dessalines, drove the laborers excessively. That they drove them as hard as had the planters in slavery days is denied by so important a witness as Malouet. The fact that the output per laborer greatly increased (according to de Lacroix it more than doubled) must be ascribed to better food, greater incentive and better working conditions.

Drastic measures were taken to oblige the Negroes to remain at their work. Liberty and ten years of war and civil war had made them restless. They moved from plantation to plantation, in search of the ideal employer. When they had money they often stopped work altogether, went to town and remained there until it was spent. On October 12, 1800, Toussaint had issued this drastic decree, later supplemented by measures that made it virtually impossible for the cultivators to absent themselves from their work: –

Civil and military authorities, here is the plan that must be adopted. Here is the goal that must be reached. The maintenance of liberty imperiously demands it:

Managers, foremen and cultivators must conduct themselves as if they were officers, non-commissioned officers and soldiers. A soldier cannot leave his company, battalion or demi-brigade to join another group without the permission of his superiors. So also the cultivators must be forbidden to leave their plantations and go elsewhere without a legal permit. At present they come and go and work is neglected.

I command most emphatically that all managers, foremen and cultivators attend to their duties exactly as if they were members of the armed forces.

Toussaint's early biographer, the mulatto Saint-Rémy, has said of this measure that it proves Toussaint to have been "in league with the planters to restore slavery in the form of peonage." It is only necessary to point out that the most advanced democratic leadership would not have hesitated to adopt forced labor during a crisis involving freedom or slavery for the inhabitants.

The compulsory labor decree was followed by this proclamation: —

I have been informed that the useful measures I have taken are misrepresented by many ill-intentioned persons of all colors, but especially by old-time plantation owners. They say to the cultivators: "You claim you are free. All the same you must remain on my plantation, whether you like it or not. I will treat you as I did of old, and show you that you are not free."

Military men of all grades and police officers are hereby instructed to arrest any person guilty of such utterances and to hold him at the disposal of the Commander in Chief. If the guilty party is a civilian, he or she shall not be released except on payment of two thousand francs; if a member of the armed forces, he will be reduced to a soldier's rank.

## 5

Cultivators were entitled to one fourth of the plantation revenue. Elaborate measures were taken to prevent their being cheated. Settlement had to be made every trimester before a justice of the peace. The military commander of the parish had to be present with his secretary. The secretary made an affidavit in duplicate of each case separately. The affidavit had to specify whether payment was made in specie or in kind. If the latter, the nature, quantity and quality had to be stated. The duplicates were sent to the Communal Administrator, whose duty it was to compare the sums paid to the laborers with the total revenue of the plantation. He sent his findings to the District Administrator, who approved or disapproved them and forwarded the affidavits with his recommendations to the Chief Administrator, a white man named Idlinger. The dislike of Idlinger expressed by many of the planters warrants the belief that he attended to his duties conscientiously.

The workday was from dawn until sunset and was interrupted by a three hours' rest, beginning at eleven o'clock. The use of the whip was prohibited, but there is evidence that a stick, called *cocomacaque*, was often used. While there are some well-authenticated cases of cruelty to laborers, especially on the part of Dessalines, it may be taken for granted that the vast majority was treated far more humanely than in slavery days. It should not be forgotten that the crisis confronting Toussaint forced him to regard every citizen as a soldier and that the use of the stick was common in European armies. Writers like Castonnet des Fosses and Lothrop Stoddard who claim that forced labor under Toussaint was at least as bad as slavery are contradicted by no less a contemporary authority than Malouet. They fail to explain why the cultivators rose like one man when they became convinced that slavery was to be restored, and why Toussaint was able to arm virtually the entire population, when a similar action on the part of the planters would have immediately resulted in their overthrow.

## 6

If Toussaint forced the Negro cultivators to work, he did not spare the planters. Heavy taxes were necessary to finance the purchases of arms and supplies and for his social program, which included the creation of a school system and support by the State of indigent children. One fourth the revenue of the privately owned plantations was collected by the State, but when this proved insufficient Toussaint contemplated a land tax that would balance his budget. The threat of further taxes was partly responsible for the growing coolness of the planters towards him.

To keep the French Government in ignorance concerning his warlike preparations Toussaint found it necessary to take liberties with his financial accounts. In the budget of 1801 the sum of 16,500,000 francs is allocated for army pay. In reality the sum expended for that purpose was 4,500,000 francs. But there is no appropriation covering the purchase of large quantities of muskets, gunpowder, saddles, swords, pistols, etc. acquired in the United States through the good offices of Secretary of State Pickering himself. The Secretary corresponded with Stephen Higginson and other suppliers and made arrangements with the Secretary of the Navy so the armament would reach Toussaint. Leclerc later complained to Napoleon: "It is the United States that has brought here the muskets, the cannon, the gunpowder and all the munitions of war. It is they who have instigated Toussaint to defend himself."

To pay for the supplies Toussaint secretly transferred money from the Haitian treasury to banks in Philadelphia. At the time of his death there was still over 6,000,000 francs on deposit in his name in Philadelphia banking institutions. His son Isaac, eager to obtain this money, claimed that it represented revenue from Toussaint's plantations and that the deposits had never been used to acquire war supplies. He wrote to General Vincent, who had been his father's friend, and asked him to support his claim. He received this rebuke from the French general: "Your father loved the freedom of his people more than he loved France. You are not honoring his memory by trying to prove that he took no measures for the defense of the country he governed, when possessing definite information that a powerful expeditionary force was being prepared, the avowed object of which was the restoration of slavery."

## 7

Toussaint was a man of order, even excessively so. He had no great faith in man's ability to keep out of mischief without the aid of the policeman. "Man is unjust, more inclined towards evil than towards good," he said in a speech at Les Cayes, and warned the local authorities that they must "suppress men's perverted instincts." He was inclined towards Puritanism, at least as far as other people's morals were concerned. He forbade divorce. He once ordered his nephew, Bernard Chancy, imprisoned for an affair with a married woman. Public officials who allowed themselves the luxury of a concubine risked dismissal. When a citizen of Le Cap, whose housekeeper had been his concubine for many years, deserted her, he was given the choice of marrying the woman or going to prison. Toussaint closed gambling houses at Le Cap and Port-au-Prince far more effectively than such places are usually closed. He established a censorship of books and papers arriving from France lest they contain material injurious to morals. When a white girl attended a ball at his palace in a gown that was excessively low-cut, he modestly covered the offending flesh with his handkerchief and asked the girl's mother to conduct her daughter home.

De Lacroix informs us, however, that when the French army entered Port-au-Prince and a search was made of the Palace, a chest was found which proved to be equipped with a double bottom. The secret compartment contained "locks of hair of all colors, rings, arrow-pierced hearts, little keys, vanity cases and an infinite number of love letters, which left no doubt concerning the success the old Toussaint Louverture had with the fair sex." A similar statement has been made by Leclerc's secretary, the French historian de Norvins, who writes: "The letters were all signed and nothing, not even jealousy, was lacking." Three white women – Madame Valabrègue, Madame Lartigne and the latter's daughter – were commonly named as his mistresses. In discussing similar inconsistencies in the character of Englishmen Santayana says: "These alternations are phases of the inner man, not masks put on in turn by some insidious and calculating knave." The reader may decide for himself if Toussaint merits the indulgence of some such interpretation.

His preoccupation with other people's morals was no doubt due to his constant association with the cloth. Father Lantheaume, his confessor, Father Martini, his almoner, and Father Molière were his intimate friends and advisers. He wrote to the ecclesiastical authorities in Paris asking that more priests be sent. A dozen came, led by Father Mainvielle. Toussaint received them with great honors and named Mainvielle bishop of the colony. The episcopal residence was at Santo Domingo City.

Toussaint's request for additional priests was part of his campaign to destroy the voodoo cult and establish the Catholic religion as the State religion. He had already decreed that officers and soldiers must attend matins and vesper service. He ordered his commanders to destroy the voodoo altars and take into custody any *huñgan* or *mambu* who continued to hold voodoo rites. The worshipers, if caught, were soundly caned. Dessalines, who did nothing by halves, had his soldiers attack a voodoo assembly with the bayonet, some fifty being killed during the operation. Voodooism, however, having adopted some of the Catholic symbols and ritual, is still the favorite religion of the Haitian Negroes.

# CHAPTER II

## Toussaint and the Racial Problem

In his handling of the racial problem Toussaint showed tolerance and comprehension. If the collaboration of the whites was to be secured they must have no feeling of humiliation. The rise to power of the despised Negro caste required a somewhat painful readjustment on their part. Toussaint appears to have been anxious to make the transition as little onerous as possible. He insisted that whites should be treated with respect and set the example by addressing white men and women as "Monsieur" and "Madame," all others as "Citoyen" and "Citoyenne."

For reasons that have been explained his chief administrators were white men. He experienced a certain satisfaction in surrounding himself with white satellites. This may have been partly due to vanity, but was undoubtedly also due to the fact that he found among them more intellectual compeers. While the Creoles were hardly models of culture and learning, yet there were men among them whose conversation he found instructive and profitable. He admired the manners and social graces of men who had been educated in France. Once when a white man made a courteous gesture in his presence, he turned to the Negroes surrounding him and said: "Now, that is the way to behave. You Negroes should acquire such manners. See what it means to have been educated in France. My sons will be like that."

Toussaint entertained the hope that the white minority would become an integral part of the Haitian nation and that racial barriers would eventually be obliterated. Was this hope justified? Jefferson and Lincoln have expressed a contrary opinion. Said Jefferson: "Nothing is more certainly written in the book of fate than that these people are to be free. Nor is it less certain that the two races, equally free, cannot live in the same government. Nature, habit, opinion have drawn indelible lines of distinction between them." And Lincoln: "I yield to all which follows from necessity. What I would desire would be a separation of the white and black races."

## 2

We have seen that in spite of the existence of slavery racial lines were not sharply drawn in the early days of St. Domingo. When the influx of white women created a stronger barrier, there was still constant complaint that white men preferred mulattresses. Now that power had passed into the hands of Negroes, white men and women gave every indication that they would be able to adapt themselves to the changed circumstances. The number of white women cohabiting with Negroes became so great that General Leclerc found it quite impossible to carry out Napoleon's order to have such women deported. The whites, who had at one time discussed whether Negroes belonged to the human race, now appeared convinced that Toussaint was a superman whom few white men had ever equaled. When he entered Le Cap after the conquest of the Spanish colony, they chose the most beautiful Creole woman in the city to place a laurel wreath upon his brow and to welcome him with verses in which he was compared with Hercules and Alexander the Great. When Toussaint rewarded her with a kiss, they led the applause. At Port-au-Prince the Apostolic Vicar, Lacune, received him with a speech in which he lauded his humanity, piety, sense of justice and wisdom. The baldachin under which he was asked to seat himself in the church bore the inscription: "God has given him to us, He will preserve him for us." The publications of the whites usually referred to him as "the Bonaparte of the Antilles." Their fear of the First Consul probably restrained them from calling the latter "the Toussaint Louverture of Europe."

Their flattery gave Toussaint a somewhat exaggerated sense of his own importance. When Bayon de Libertat, the manager of the Bréda plantation, had received permission from Toussaint to return to the colony, he rushed immediately upon his arrival to the Palace to embrace his former slave. Toussaint eluded the embrace and said haughtily: "Not so fast, not so fast, Mr. Manager! Remember that the distance between me and you is now far greater than it was once between you and me. Go to your plantation. Be just, but firm. See to it that the cultivators work well, so the State as well as you and your employer may be benefited."

## 3

The etiolating and deodorizing qualities of wealth and power are, indeed, extraordinary. In the first part of this volume a document has been quoted in which the colonial administrators expressed the fear that the growing prosperity of the mulatto caste would break down the racial barrier between whites and mulattoes. It is likewise interesting to note that wealthy free Negroes were considered as belonging to the mulatto caste.

Racialism, like nationalism, has of recent years received a new lease of life, but there was a time when even the Anglo-Saxons, who more than any other branch of the white race discriminate against the colored races, were nothing loath to forget their prejudices for the sake of economic advantage. There is no better historian of the manners, modes, habits, customs and prejudices of his countrymen than the author of *Vanity Fair*. In his famous novel Thackeray tells us of a certain Miss Swartz, "a rich, woolly-haired mulatto from St. Kitts" – the daughter of a German Jew and a West Indian mulattress or Negress. Miss Swartz's complexion is described as "mahogany" and she is called a "Hottentot Venus." She is, however, an heiress, "reported to have I don't know how many plantations in the West Indies; a deal of money in the funds; and three stars to her name in the East India stockholders' list. She had a mansion in Surrey and a house in Portland Place. The name of the West India heiress had been mentioned with applause in the *Morning Post*." These things being so, she was received in the best London society. A wealthy merchant, Mr. Osborne, threatens to disinherit his son George for refusing to marry her. He is thus advised by the banker, Fred Bullock: "Let George cut in directly and win her. Strike while the iron is hot, you know – while she's fresh to the town: in a few weeks some damned fellow from the West End will come with a rotten rent-roll and cut all us City men out."

Indeed, Miss Swartz, after contemptuously refusing Osborne senior, is finally wedded to the Honorable James McMull, "a young sprig of Scotch nobility." She is presented at Court and shines at all social functions "as elegantly decorated as a she chimney-sweep on May-Day."

It is hardly likely that Thackeray – who prides himself on having introduced nothing into his novel that might offend British taste – would have made use of the incident if it had not been characteristic. He says in his Preface to *Pendennis:* "I ask you to believe that this person writing strives to tell the truth. If there is not that, there is nothing."

Toussaint's hope that a judicial handling of the racial and economic problems might eventually result in the disappearance of the racial barrier does not, therefore, appear to have been an idle one. That barrier, far from being "natural," is artificial and is crumbling slowly, but surely, in spite of the efforts of demagogues and snobs to keep it intact. The snobs, who are worshipers of power, would undoubtedly be among the first to cross the color line openly (as many of them now do clandestinely) if they were citizens of a nation where power was in the hands of Negroes. The behavior of the St. Domingo planters, who at one time drew the color line even more sharply than the British,* clearly points to this.

As a result of Toussaint's moderate policy the racial barrier was crumbling so fast in St. Domingo as to lead General Vincent to exclaim in a communication to Napoleon: "Races melt beneath his hand!"

* In Jamaica third generation mulattoes enjoyed the same rights as white men; in St. Domingo, before the Revolution, no person of color was ever admitted to equality with the whites.

# CHAPTER III
## Panoply of Power

TOUSSAINT divided his time between Le Cap, Port-au-Prince, his plantations at Ennery and tours of inspection. De Lacroix writes: "Nobody knew what he intended doing, whether it was his intention to stay or go, whence he came, where he was going. Often he would announce that he was at Le Cap when he was at Port-au-Prince. When everybody imagined him to be at Port-au-Prince, he would be at Les Cayes, at Môle St. Nicolas, at St. Marc. He would depart on a journey in a carriage, but a few miles from the starting point would mount his horse and order the vehicle and the guards to proceed, while he would appear where he was least expected accompanied only by a few officers."

With such constant supervision by the head of the government, public employees who neglected their duty stood little chance of remaining undetected, and it would have been a bold planter who would have risked returning to practices common in slavery days.

Toussaint had the Government Palace at Le Cap remodeled to his taste, which was far from vulgar. In the reception rooms, walls and floors were of white marble and white marble columns lent dignity to the vestibule. The furnishings were in the style of Louis XVI. A feature of the decoration was the large number of portraits of beautiful white women. The palace at Port-au-Prince underwent similar transformation.

Toussaint's bodyguard equaled that of many a European monarch. It was composed of two regiments of one thousand men each, one of infantry, the other of cavalry. The men were chosen for their appearance, courage and loyalty and wore the elegant sky-blue uniform of the famous Swiss guard of Louis XVI. The sons of the wealthiest planters considered it an honor to serve as officers of the guard and did not appear to mind receiving orders from Negro superiors. The regimental band was German.

Toussaint further sought to impress by appearing on state occasions preceded by two heralds, mounted on white horses and wearing red-plumed silver helmets.

The receptions he gave were of two kinds, and were known as the *Petit Cercle* and the *Grand Cercle*. The *Petit Cercle* was an exclusive affair. The élite of the colony thronged the marble hall. There were diplomats, planters with their wives and grown sons and daughters, wealthy merchants, Negro generals, white and mulatto officeholders. One might see a planter listen politely to a Negro who a decade before had been his slave; a planter's son, in the uniform of Toussaint's bodyguard, pay compliments to an ebony or mulatto beauty. The lion and the lamb were lying down together, but only after it had been discovered that the lamb was not really a lamb, but had teeth as sharp as the lion's.

Suddenly there would be a fanfare of trumpets. The great double door swung open and Toussaint entered, followed by his staff. His following was brilliantly attired, but he himself wore a plain uniform with few adornments. The guests had ranged themselves on both sides of the hall, and as he appeared, officers saluted, gentlemen bowed, ladies curtsied. Toussaint bowed to both sides of the hall, then slowly walked up one side and down the other, exchanging a few polite words with each guest. When he reached the door he bowed again and withdrew, not to be seen again throughout the evening.

The *Grand Cercle* was democratic. No invitation was necessary. Planters, shopkeepers, handicraftsmen, even cultivators who had received permission to go to the city filled the hall and the garden. Toussaint, dressed in white and wearing a broad-brimmed straw hat, mingled freely with the crowd. He listened to complaints, gained valuable information, gave advice, exchanged badinage with former comrades in arms, pinched girls' cheeks, received the solicitations of officeseekers. Once a Negro asked him for an appointment to a judicial post. "I'll gladly do so," said Toussaint, "for of course you know Latin. . . . What! You don't! How the devil do you expect to be a judge without knowing Latin? *Vade retro!*"

He liked nothing better than to approach a group of Negro officers and cry out by way of greeting: "*Dominus tecum, salve Domino, tibi gratias!*" When they looked at him with puzzled faces, he would shake his head and say: "You don't know Latin? Too bad! Too bad! You will never amount to much."

The *Grand Cercle* was always followed by a private gathering in his study to which a few chosen guests were invited. The conversation would be about France, travel, religion, agriculture, but never about politics. He always conducted the guests to the door himself and if some woman had particularly impressed him, she might be the recipient of a floral offering the following morning.

When the guests had departed he would call his secretaries, of whom there were five, and plunge into his correspondence. He read and answered an average of two hundred letters a day. "Nothing in the world," says de Lacroix, "would have induced him to sign a letter of which he had not weighed every word carefully. If a secretary used a term the meaning of which escaped him, he would have the letter rewritten by different secretaries until a mode of expression had been found that exactly reflected his thought." He once wrote to Hédouville: "The statement that I would sign a letter or order that I had not read or dictated is an insult to me. To believe this is to impute a weakness to me foreign to my nature. I have the honor to repeat: I never sign anything that I have not either read or personally dictated."

There was a hotel at Le Cap known as *L'Hôtel de la République*, which, according to Rainsford, compared favorably with the best European hostelries. Americans, Englishmen and other foreigners who came on business to the island were enthusiastic about its table d'hôte. Americans were then rapidly displacing Frenchmen in the business life of Haiti, a development Toussaint encouraged. "The merchants at Le Cap are all agents of American firms and the Americans are more Jewish than the Jews," Leclerc later wrote to Napoleon. There occasionally appeared at the table d'hôte a small, unassuming Negro in general's uniform, who readily engaged such of the visitors as spoke French in conversation and astonished them by his intelligence and courtesy. When later they would inquire of the hotelkeeper who the general was they learned with surprise that they had been conversing with Toussaint Louverture.

## 2

When Toussaint wished to relax he went to Ennery. He had four plantations at Ennery – Descahaux, Sancey, Beaumont and Rouffelier. His wife and other members of his household usually stayed at the Descahaux plantation, so it was there he stopped most often. His son Isaac and his stepson Placide were still in France, and his youngest son, Saint-Jean, lived with his white tutor, Monsieur Granville, at Gonaïves. The household consisted of Toussaint's wife, Suzanne, his father – now one hundred and four years old and blind – his foster mother Pélagie, and his two nieces, Eleonore and Louise Chancy.

Whatever philandering Toussaint might have indulged in, his heart remained true to Suzanne. Enormous of girth, good-natured, unaffected and wholly devoted to her family, she was like a restful haven to which he returned after stress and storm. Toussaint, dressed in white and wearing a big straw hat, would ride about the plantation, watch the cultivators at their work or discuss improvements with his manager. It was his ambition that his plantations should be models for others to follow. He was a kind but strict employer. His relations with his workmen and their families were patriarchal. He interested himself in everything that went on in the laborers' quarter, and woe to the Negro who ill-treated his family or showed an inclination towards voodooism! When he was on the plantation he often attended the devotions of his workmen and he frequently asked questions to ascertain their understanding of the Christian religion. He liked to watch them dance the *chica* and sometimes he and Suzanne would join in the dancing. He often entertained white men on his plantation and they pronounced him an incomparable host.

He had three hobbies – horses, precious and semiprecious stones and weapons of all kinds. His stable was the largest and finest in the colony and he had a positive affection for his stallion Bel-Argent. A Jewish merchant at Gonaïves, a certain Nathan, the only man of his faith in the colony, had a standing order to acquire new specimens for his collections, which Toussaint delighted in showing to his guests.

# CHAPTER IV

## The Constitution

ONE day Toussaint said to the white general, Vincent: "It is impossible for me to stop in my gigantic undertaking. I feel as if some occult power were urging me on. I am unable to resist it." At another time he mused: "I have taken my flight in the domain of the eagles. I must be careful where and how I alight. My footing must be upon a rock, which can only be constitutional government that will guarantee me authority for the remainder of my life."

He was the *de facto* ruler of Haiti; *de jure* he was Commander in Chief of the army, nothing more. Bonaparte had announced that the laws of France no longer applied to Haiti, which was to be ruled by special decree. We have seen what was one of the decrees he contemplated. Toussaint decided to forestall him by giving the country self-government.

He called an election. Ten men, two from each of the five departments (the Spanish colony had been divided into the Departments of Engana and Samana), were to be chosen to a Central Assembly whose business it was to frame a Constitution and a code of laws. One of the ten died before the first meeting. Of the remaining nine six were white and three mulatto. They had little to do with the framing of the Constitution, which appears to have been the work of Toussaint, Bernard Borgella and Father Molière. Considering time, place and circumstances the document did not lack merit. Slavery was abolished for all time. All citizens, irrespective of color, were eligible to public office. The Catholic religion was to be the State religion. Toussaint was to be Governor for life, was to receive a salary of 300,000 francs and was to have the right to appoint his successor. After that Governors were to be elected for five years. The Governor was to propose laws to the Assembly and was to be responsible for their execution. Immigration from Africa was to be encouraged.

Notwithstanding some provisions which appeared to limit Toussaint's power, that power remained absolute. Democracy would have been impossible in St. Domingo at that time. It was insecure even in the United States, where a proposal "that a dictator be established in the commonwealth who should have the power of disposing of the lives and fortunes of the citizens thereof without being subject to account" had found numerous supporters.

The fact that the Constitution did not provide for the appointment of a single functionary by the French Government, and that France was not granted any privilege not enjoyed by all other countries, made the Constitution a veritable Declaration of Independence. That Toussaint had been planning such a move for some time we know from a report of Edward Stevens, who, on February 3, 1800, wrote to Timothy Pickering: –

> Everything announces a speedy dissolution of those ties which once connected this important colony with the Mother Country. While I was uncertain of the real intentions of Toussaint, I was loth to say anything about them. Now that I think I know them, it is my duty to announce them to you. *He is taking his measures slowly, but securely. All connection with France will soon be broken off. If he is not disturbed he will preserve appearances a little longer. But as soon as France interferes with this colony he will throw off the mask and declare it independent.**

Anticipating Toussaint's intention to make St. Domingo an independent State, a distinguished American who had contributed much towards framing the American Constitution penned a Constitution for St. Domingo. It was none other than Alexander Hamilton. He sent the document to Pickering with the recommendation that it be pressed on Toussaint. "This," he writes, "cannot be done *officially*, but he [Edward Stevens] will know how to use it." At the same time he recommends: "The United States must not be committed on the independence of St. Domingo. No guaranty – no formal treaty – nothing that can rise up in judgment."

We do not know if Stevens ever presented Hamilton's draft to Toussaint.

## 2

The Constitution was solemnly proclaimed at the Place d'Armes at Le Cap, on July 7, 1801. To escape the heat of the day the ceremony was scheduled to take place immediately after sunrise. The tolling of bells and the roll of drums awakened the citizens at three o'clock in the morning. An hour later the garrison stood massed on the square, surrounded by a great con-

* Italics are those of Stevens.

course of people. Every house displayed a flag. Balconies and windows were crowded. The Altar of the Fatherland – a wooden structure commemorative of the emancipation proclamation of Sonthonax and Polverel – from which the speakers were to address the crowd, was decorated with bunting and fronds of palms.

At five in the morning the civil, military and ecclesiastical authorities arrived in solemn procession. Toussaint wore the dress uniform of a general. He looked grave rather than triumphant. To proclaim the Constitution without submitting it to the approval of the French Government meant to drop all pretense – to forgo even the appearance of loyalty.

The venerable Negro mayor of Le Cap, Télémaque, spoke first. He was followed by the President of the Central Assembly, Bernard Borgella, who read the proclamation and made a speech in which he alluded to Toussaint as "a phœnix risen from the ashes." Then Toussaint arose and was greeted with deafening cheers. His speech was that of a benevolent autocrat. He reminded the civil and military authorities of their duty and told each class of citizens what was expected of them. When he finished bells tolled, cannon boomed, cheer after cheer rang out. The slave of the Bréda plantation had reached the zenith of his career.

The ceremony at the Place d'Armes was followed by a *Te Deum* at the principal church. That night there was a banquet at the Palace attended by six hundred people. The city was illuminated and the merrymaking lasted all night. Heralds were dispatched to proclaim the Constitution in every parish. General amnesty was proclaimed for all prisoners except those guilty of the most serious common law offenses. A new commonwealth had been born.

## 3

The zenith had been reached, and now, almost immediately, began the descent – slow at first, with only a few haunting shadows reaching up from the abyss that eventually was to engulf the Negro leader. Disturbing rumors reached Toussaint's ears. He learned that his generals were terrified at his boldness. Their thoughts did not, like his, soar into the future. They had no dreams of the greatness of a people. They possessed power, wealth, social position, and were afraid to risk them. Christophe said to General Vincent: "The Constitution is a crime. It is foolish to imagine that we can govern ourselves. We should be grateful if they allow us to occupy a few offices. I will revolt against Toussaint rather than support his pretensions." And Moyse: "What does the old fool want? He thinks he is King of St. Domingo. Against whom is he arming? Where will he get his soldiers? For it won't be we, General, who will lead our men [against the French]. We shall see what we shall see."

Besides hesitation and disloyalty in his own camp, Toussaint noticed an increasing coolness on the part of the planters. The threat of higher taxes was partly responsible for this, but even more the rumor that Napoleon might soon be in a position to intervene and that he favored the restoration of slavery. The planters did not doubt for a moment that in a conflict with Napoleon's soldiers Toussaint would be crushed like an eggshell. They added their machinations to those of the absentee planters, who left no stone unturned to bring about the consummation of their ambitions. Toussaint had never really trusted the planters. In 1797, when they were engaged in a similar campaign, he had written concerning them to the Directory: "Blind men that they are! Do they not realize that far from recovering what they pretend to have lost, they are risking total ruin for themselves and the colony? Do they really believe that men who have tasted liberty will calmly submit to have it taken from them? The Negroes submitted to slavery because they knew no happier lot, but having thrown off the yoke, if they had a thousand lives they would sacrifice them all rather than to take it up again."

But Napoleon was a terrible adversary. Toussaint began to wonder if perhaps he had been overbold.

## 4

He sent for General Vincent.

Among the venal, rapacious, timeserving crew France sent to St. Domingo, General Vincent, Commander of Fortifications, stands out like a beacon of light – a man of character and principle, remarkably free from race prejudice. He respected Toussaint and never ceased to defend him, but did not hesitate to take issue with him, any more than with Napoleon. He was convinced that in proclaiming the Constitution without the consent of the French Government, Toussaint had made a fatal mistake. He was wrong. An expeditionary force would have been sent had Toussaint never thought of the Constitution. What in fact proved fatal to Toussaint was that he tried to retrace his steps and did not boldly proclaim his independence. Says de Lacroix: "The veil of dissimulation behind which he had hidden while climbing to supreme power became an impediment when he was attacked. It interfered with his military measures and was thus responsible for his defeat."

Vincent had been Toussaint's envoy at the time of the war with Rigaud. The Negro leader now proposed that he should take a copy of the Constitution to France and get it approved by the First Consul. The French general was skeptical about the success of the mission. He replied that the document should have been presented for approval before it had been proclaimed. He found fault with the Constitution, saying that it did not provide for the appointment of a single functionary by the French Government.

"They can appoint a Commissioner," Toussaint replied.

"Say rather an Ambassador. The United States, England and Holland can do the same, and undoubtedly will."

When Toussaint told him that it was a printed copy he meant him to present to Bonaparte, Vincent lost patience. A printed copy was a *fait accompli.* A manuscript copy should have been sent long ago.

"I see you don't want to go."

Vincent reproached him with ingratitude towards France – the only nation that had freed the slaves. Then Toussaint had one of his rare outbursts of temper. He shouted that there were men who were anxious to destroy him, but that he was far from being at their mercy. He flung out of the room, called for his horse, vaulted into the saddle and rode into the open country, to be alone with his thoughts.

General Vincent finally consented to undertake the mission and departed for France by way of the United States. From Alexandria, Virginia, he wrote reproachfully to Toussaint: "Nothing is talked about here except your Declaration of Independence. They refer to you as the King of St. Domingo."

# CHAPTER V

## Moyse

TOUSSAINT's nephew, Moyse, was a score of years younger than his uncle.* We know little about him except that he was a full-blooded Negro, a capable military commander, had lost an eye in battle and was courageous and ambitious. He owed a great deal to Toussaint, which, however, did not deter him from thinking that the old leader had been in the saddle long enough and that it was time for a younger man to assume supreme command. The younger man he had in mind was of course himself. Even

* It has been claimed that while Moyse referred to Toussaint as his uncle, no family relationship existed between them. This can be neither proved nor disproved.

before the conquest of the Spanish colony, General Chanlatte had found occasion to report to Bonaparte: "Moyse shows a desire to supplant his uncle."

Moyse was opposed to the Constitution, which he considered a needless provocation to the French. He could hardly have hoped, however, to build up a personal following on this issue. He found two other issues far more popular: the maintenance of the large plantation system and forced labor.

Most of the Negroes failed to realize how long and arduous the battle for freedom really is. They considered that battle already won and failed to understand why they should not benefit to a far greater extent from their victory over the planters. They believed the land still in the hands of the planters and that sequestered by the State should be divided among the cultivators. Already at the time when Toussaint's agents had roused the populace against Roume, there had been cries of "Land! Land! We want land!" But Toussaint knew that the battle was yet far from won, that the mightiest blow was still impending, and was feverishly preparing to parry it. He knew that to abolish the large plantation system and divide the land among the cultivators would deprive him of the means with which to parry the blow. He also knew that liberty in Haiti could only be saved by forced labor, as liberty in France had been saved by forced military service – conscription.

One can hardly blame a primitive, childlike people, accustomed to living for the moment, for failing to comprehend this. But although few of the Negroes understood Toussaint's policies, most of them trusted him. Under his leadership they had gained much. If Papa Toussaint did not give them more (even though it seemed he could) he must have good reasons. But there were others who were dissatisfied and grumbled. Moyse encouraged their grumbling. He made it known that once things were in his hands short work would be made of the remaining planters. The big plantation system would cease to exist. Every Negro would have his own farm and could work as he pleased. When production lagged in the Department of the North, of which Moyse was Military Commander, and Toussaint reproached him for it, the General said to his friends: "No matter what my old uncle does, I'm not going to become the executioner of my color. He upbraids me in the name of France. That, to me, means the interest of the whites, and I'll never love the whites until they have given me back the eye I lost while fighting them."

It has been claimed that Moyse was sincere in his opposition to Toussaint's policies. If we grant his sincerity the fact nevertheless remains that he was working in the interest of the enemy by stirring up discontent during a most critical period. Leclerc, whose mission it was to restore slavery, made use of propaganda remarkably like that of Moyse. Referring to Leclerc's propaganda Toussaint writes in his memorandum: "Did he not try to instigate the laborers to rise by attempting to persuade them that I treated them like slaves and that he had come to break their chains?" But there are circumstances that throw serious doubt on Moyse's sincerity. He owned a plantation in the Department of the North, and he who objected so vehemently against land being left in the hands of the whites could think of nothing better than to lease his plantation for 20,000 francs a month to a white syndicate! When Toussaint learned of the transaction he ordered Moyse to cancel the lease.

## 2

Toussaint was on his way to the Spanish part of the island in the company of Dessalines when a courier overtook him with dispatches from the Department of the North. The news he read was serious. Hundreds of soldiers belonging to Moyse's command were making common cause with cultivators who were massacring the whites, looting plantations, occupying towns. Moyse, the dispatches stated, was making no attempt to suppress the rebellion; worse than that – his name was the rallying cry of the rebels and he had even been seen among them acknowledging their cheers.

Toussaint was now fifty-seven, but had lost none of his resolution. He read the dispatches to Dessalines and ordered him to hurry back, collect his troops and march north. Dessalines had nothing to gain and much to lose by the success of Moyse's rebellion. Thirty plantations in the Departments of the West and the South were under his direct supervision. A division of the land would have deprived him of enormous revenues, most of which were illegitimate, but which Toussaint thought it better not to question. He departed immediately, while Toussaint set out for the disaffected territory.

He arrived in record time, collected garrisons that had remained loyal and fell upon the rebels like a thunderbolt. The mob of marauding soldiers and cultivators fled before the attack. In the meantime Christophe, Commander of Le Cap, scattered the rebels in the environs of that city. Dessalines, marching up from the south, completed the rout. Order was restored, but three hundred whites and more than three times that many Negroes had perished. Much property was destroyed.

Hundreds of prisoners had been taken, whom Toussaint now ordered lined up. A firing squad stood ready. Grim as he had seldom been, Toussaint appeared on horseback before the line of prisoners. He addressed them, telling them they had shamed him and the Negro race and had endangered the liberty of the blacks. Then, with outstretched arm, he counted and ordered the tenth man to present himself before the firing squad. The man looked up at him, saluted and went. When the muskets had spoken Toussaint counted again. This went on until the end of the long line had been reached. Not one begged for mercy, not one had to be forced to obey.

Then Toussaint sent for Moyse. Madiou claims that after the interview Toussaint sent his nephew away unguarded, ordering him to hold himself at his disposition, but hoping that he would flee. Moyse made no attempt to escape and was arrested a little while later. He was court-martialed – *in absentia*. Why *in absentia?* He was in prison and could have been produced. We do not know why he was not given an opportunity to defend himself. The first verdict of the court-martial was favorable to him. Toussaint practically ordered that the death penalty be imposed. Of Moyse's guilt there can be no doubt.

Moyse, his eyes unbandaged, himself gave the order to fire.

# *PART FOUR*

# *Toussaint's Fall and Death*

## CHAPTER I

## Napoleon Hesitates

On March 4, 1801, the young, energetic First Consul, in his palace of the Tuileries, dictated a letter to his secretary. It was addressed to Toussaint Louverture, with whom in the past he had always communicated through the agency of the Minister of Marine. The letter read: –

I am instructing the Minister of Marine to forward to you your commission as Captain General of the French part of St. Domingo. The Government could hardly offer you greater proof of its confidence in you. Use your influence to the utmost for the maintenance of peace and the encouragement of agriculture. Train and organize the National Guard and the troops of the line. I hope the time is not far distant when an army from St. Domingo will be able to contribute to the extension of French possessions and glory in your part of the world.

I salute you affectionately,

Bonaparte

Then he wrote to the Colonial Prefect: "The policy adopted by the Government makes Toussaint the Republic's foremost functionary in St. Domingo. Rally all the inhabitants around him."

Neither letter was sent. Both remained in Napoleon's personal file.

There would come a time when he would regret not having

sent them. On St. Helena, dictating his memoirs to Las Cases, he was to say: "I have to reproach myself the attack upon this colony. I should have contented myself with ruling the island through the intermediary of Toussaint."

The invasions of St. Domingo, Spain and Russia were Napoleon's three capital blunders. From the historical perspective the invasion of St. Domingo surpasses the two others in importance. The setback to the Grand Army in Spain, its virtual destruction on the steppes of Russia, had important repercussions on the history of that time and hastened Napoleon's downfall. But had Spain and Russia not been invaded, Europe would still have emerged from the Napoleonic adventure the Europe of the Congress of Vienna. The invasion of St. Domingo, however, was responsible for the loss by France of its richest colony, and, as a result of that loss, for the sale of the Louisiana Territory to the United States. The sale of the Territory affected the future of the American Continent and of the world to an extent that cannot be overestimated.

The Grand Army's losses in St. Domingo were almost as serious as those it suffered in Spain – 70,000 were lost in Spain, 63,000 in St. Domingo.

## 2

What did Napoleon mean when he wrote to Toussaint: "I hope the time is not far distant when an army from St. Domingo will be able to contribute to the extension of French possessions and glory in your part of the world"?

He had already sent Berthier to Spain to negotiate with Charles IV the retrocession of the Louisiana Territory. In the Foreword I have quoted Henry Adams as saying that Bonaparte, wishing to restore the French colonial empire, with Haiti for keystone, needed the Louisiana Territory to render the island independent of the United States for its food supply. But there exists another possibility. Napoleon was planning world domination, a "global" war. He had his eye on the Occident as well as on the Orient. He might have wanted the Louisiana Territory as a base for military operations against the United States. Stevens' letter to Maitland (quoted in the Foreword) indicates that an attack on the United States had already been planned by the Directory, whose ambitions did not soar nearly as high as Bonaparte's. The unsent letter to Toussaint and the order to the Colonial Prefect, together with the demand for the retrocession of the Louisiana Territory, tend to indicate that Napoleon at one time meant to use Toussaint and his Negro army to attack the United States. Leclerc underestimated Toussaint and the Negroes, Napoleon did not. The size of the expedition he sent against them proves this. But after writing the letter Napoleon must have reconsidered. Why did he reconsider? Did he think Toussaint would steadfastly refuse to become involved in an overseas expedition, or did he fear the power the Negro might wield if he were victorious on the American continent? The latter seems more probable, since Napoleon later expressed the conviction that unless Toussaint was overthrown, "the scepter of the New World would sooner or later pass into the hands of the blacks."

## 3

Before the French Revolution two thirds of the French import and export trade had been with St. Domingo. Toussaint was practising a free trade policy. His overthrow could not help being popular with the commercial classes of France. Thiers claims that Napoleon likewise wished to reconcile the nobles of the Vendée, who had been large property owners in St. Domingo. It was impossible to restore to them the property they had lost in France. A restoration of their lands and slaves in St. Domingo was bound to mollify them. Bonaparte's wily Minister of Police, Fouché, gives in his memoirs still another reason for Napoleon's decision: –

The real reason for this disastrous expedition must be sought in the recesses of the First Consul's mind. He seized with avidity the opportunity to send to a remote part of the world a great number of regiments and general officers fashioned in the school of Moreau. He wished to include all such general officers as he judged insufficiently devoted to him and to his interests, or whom he believed to be still attached to republican institutions.

In other words, planning to make himself Emperor, he wished to get rid of the men of the heroic phase of the Revolution, who were confirmed republicans.

It became common talk in Paris that this was one of Napoleon's reasons. The rumor reached the First Consul, who remarked to Fouché: "I hear your Jacobins claim that it is the soldiers and the friends of Moreau whom I want to send to St. Domingo to perish. They are a parcel of fools. Let them chatter. If one allowed oneself to be deflected from one's purpose by defamation and calumny it would be impossible to govern."

Yet the Minister of Marine, Forfait, has claimed that the man who later was to say to Metternich: "What are the lives of a million soldiers to a man like me?" said to him: "There are sixty thousand men whom I want to send as far away as possible."

## 4

One of the reasons usually given for Napoleon's decision is the influence of his wife, Josephine, who was a Creole from Martinique. Her first husband, the Marquis de Beauharnais, had owned a plantation in St. Domingo, near Léogane, to which she had fallen heir. In her memoirs Josephine disclaims responsibility: —

He [Napoleon] condescended to consult me regarding the form of government he should grant to St. Domingo. He had, however, already decided to place General Leclerc at the head of the administration. I made no secret of my opinion that such a move would be fatal and might result in a permanent loss of this beautiful colony to France. Keep Toussaint Louverture at the head, I told him. He is the man you need to govern the blacks. Now that the Negroes have established their supremacy over the colony they will be dissatisfied when they see the reins of power torn from the hand of their foremost general. They will constantly fear a renewal of slavery. I was never able to convince him. He assured me that he would have no difficulty in trapping Toussaint Louverture and that he expected to have him deported to France, where imprisonment in a fortress would be the best guarantee of his loyalty.

There is no reason to disbelieve her. Excellent politician that he was, Toussaint had the Beauharnais plantation cultivated at government expense and sent the revenue to her. She was so pleased that when she heard Toussaint's son Isaac was at the Colonial Institute in Paris, she had him visit her at Malmaison. Isaac Louverture was then only fourteen, but looked three years older. An official memorandum says of him: "He is an excellent pupil, very apt to learn, but lacks courage and is reserved and solitary." He must have pleased Josephine, for the visit was renewed several times. He, on his part, was so impressed that he wrote poems to her, some of which have been preserved. *Honi soit qui mal y pense.*

# CHAPTER II

## Toussaint Prepares

TOUSSAINT had not yet abandoned hope that Napoleon would relent, and anxiously awaited a letter from the First Consul that would dissipate his fears.* He would pounce upon the mail

* It has been claimed that Toussaint once wrote a letter to Napoleon with the superscription: "From the First of the Blacks to the First of the Whites." No such letter was ever sent.

arriving from France and tear open the envelopes eagerly, but there would only be the usual official communications from the Minister of Marine. He would toss them contemptuously to his secretaries with the words: "Worthless trash! You fellows can attend to that," or "It isn't worth bothering with. Cabinet Minister – lackey!"

Once he said to a white acquaintance: "Bonaparte is wrong in not writing to me. He must have listened to my enemies. If he had not would he deny me the satisfaction of a personal letter – me, who has rendered greater services to France than any other general? The British and the Spanish Governments show more consideration than that for generals who have rendered valuable services."

He was at this time in a chastened mood and to prove his good intentions restored the republican calendar he had abolished. He would have been willing to make important concessions to France, but no compromise offer was made and he prepared for the worst. He strengthened the coast defenses and issued an order that warships were not to enter the ports of the island without his special permission. He had quantities of war material moved from the coast cities into the interior and stored in secret hiding places. He called a meeting of prominent mulattoes at Port-au-Prince and appealed to them to let bygones be bygones and to rally to his support.

He was worried about the fate of his two sons, who were still in France, and had written a number of times asking that at least one be restored to him, but the request had been ignored. Shortly before the proclamation of the Constitution he had sent his secret agents Huin and d'Hébecourt to Paris with instructions to abduct the boys. General Maitland and several *émigrés* were persuaded to give their assistance. The boys were to be taken to Dover, where a Negro named Kina was waiting to take them to Jamaica. But the French Government got wind of the affair and the boys were so closely guarded that nothing came of the scheme.

## 2

No measure Toussaint took proved of greater importance than the organization of practically the entire Negro and mulatto population into a militia. When Leclerc later undertook to disarm the cultivators he reported to his government that he had confiscated 30,000 muskets, but that at least as many more remained in the hands of the Negroes. De Lacroix says, however, that all Leclerc succeeded in doing was to disarm the Negroes of the principal cities and towns. If the yield from this was as stated by his chief, then Toussaint must have distributed upward of 100,000 muskets among the cultivators. He did more. He trained the men in guerrilla warfare.

One day, while reviewing a militia contingent he took a musket from the hand of a cultivator, held it aloft and cried: "This is your liberty!" He was right. It was this citizen army that eventually drove out Napoleon's soldiers and saved the Negro population from slavery.

When news reached the island that peace was about to be concluded between France and England the toadying of the white colonists changed to arrogance. They taunted Negroes by saying that the day of reckoning was coming. Toussaint, who had been so free from race prejudice, felt a wave of bitterness surge over him. There was to come a time when he would write to one of his generals: "Don't trust the whites. They will betray you if they can."

One day he appeared at a review holding a glass jar filled with black maize, over which a thin layer of white maize had been spread. "This represents St. Domingo," he said. "The whites are on top, but look . . ." He shook the jar vigorously and the white maize disappeared. "That is what will happen to the whites if the Negroes rise in their might," he said.

He issued a proclamation of warning to the whites. Those who conducted themselves properly could count on his protection.

Those who did not would be deported. At the same time he addressed a stirring appeal to the army. "I am a soldier," he wrote. "I fear God, but I fear no man. If I must die I will die like a soldier, with honor unsullied and without self-reproach . . . You must conquer or die at your posts."

Unfortunately the diplomat as well as the warrior took a hand in drafting the proclamation, which contains these lines: "A child who understands the right that nature has given his parents over him, is obedient and submissive. If in spite of this his parents are so unnatural as to wish to destroy him, he must leave their punishment to God. . . . The orders and emissaries of France should be received with filial piety and respect."

Thus in one paragraph he bids the soldiers to die at their posts, in another he preaches submission. He had worn a mask so long that he found it difficult to discard it when it became a danger to him. Instead of giving his generals to choose between loyalty and disloyalty, the choice he put before them was between two loyalties.

## 3

A white colonist who had been on particularly friendly terms with Toussaint came to him and asked for a passport. The conversation between the two men has been recorded by de Lacroix. The Negro leader looked at the white man, aggrieved, and said: "Why do you wish to leave? You whom I love and esteem?"

"Because I am white and because in spite of your kind feelings towards me you are about to become the wrathful leader of the blacks. For the last few days you are no longer the protector of the whites. You have ordered a number of them deported because they showed satisfaction about the imminent arrival of Europeans."

"Yes," said Toussaint, "they have had the impudence and the stupidity to rejoice at the news of the early arrival of a European army. As if the expedition did not spell the doom of the colony and their ruin as well as mine. But since you wish to go, I'll not detain you, only let your voyage be of some benefit to St. Domingo. I'll give you a letter to the First Consul. I'll beg him to listen to you. Paint to him Toussaint as he really is. Tell him about the prosperity of agriculture and commerce under my rule. Tell him about my work. It is by that I want to be and should be judged. I have taken up arms for the liberty of the people of my color, which France alone has proclaimed, but which she no longer possesses the right to revoke. Our liberty is no longer hers to do with as she pleases. It belongs to us. We shall know how to defend it or perish."

In his anxiety to save his people from slavery Toussaint became involved in a questionable transaction. He contracted with British slave traders to bring 20,000 able-bodied blacks from Africa, whom he wished to turn into soldiers. Let our judgment not be too harsh. Kidnaping freemen to serve in the armed forces was a common practice at that time and was later to involve England in war with the United States. Toussaint probably reasoned that the slave traders were transporting Negroes from Africa anyway and that having them brought to St. Domingo, far from adding to their misery, saved them from bondage. But, on the other hand, the contract served to stimulate the slave traffic. The peace of Amiens intervened and the Africans were never delivered.

# CHAPTER III

## The Expeditionary Force

TOUSSAINT's envoy, General Vincent, arrived in Paris on October 1, 1801, a few days after the order for the expeditionary force had gone forth. He threw himself with ardor into the hopeless task of getting it revoked. During his interview with the First Consul he argued that England might object to the expedition, to which Napoleon replied: "The Cabinet of St. James has no desire to oppose my plans to send a fleet to St. Domingo. I merely notified them that if they did not consent, I would give Toussaint unlimited power and recognize the colony's independence. They withdrew their objections." He showed his animosity towards the Negro race by exclaiming: "I will not leave an epaulette upon the shoulders of a single black!"

Vincent was not dismayed. He wrote a memorandum, which he submitted to the Minister of Marine, Decrès, with the request that it be shown to the First Consul. Concerning Toussaint he writes: –

In command of these vast resources is a man of indefatigable energy. It may be said without exaggeration that he is ubiquitous and can be found especially where danger is greatest and where his cool reasoned judgment is most needed. He is frugal in his habits and has the unique faculty of being able to do without rest. After the most fatiguing journey he throws himself into administrative work, answers a hundred letters a day, exhausts his secretaries. More than that, he has the ability of cajoling and beguiling everybody, which he sometimes carries to the point of deceit. In short, a man so much superior to all those surrounding him that respect for his person and submission to his orders reach the point of fanaticism with many of his followers. His power over them is unbounded. He is absolute master of the island. His will is law. A few of the blacks realize the danger of this, but are powerless to change it.

Then follows this eloquent plea: –

Sire, leave it alone! It is the happiest spot in your dominions. God meant this man to govern. Races melt beneath his hand. He has saved you this island, for I know of my own knowledge that when the Republic could not have lifted a finger to prevent it, George III offered him any title and any revenue if he would hold the island under the British Crown. He refused and saved it for France.

Bonaparte rewarded the disinterested counselor with banishment to Elba, where Vincent still occupied a government post when Napoleon himself was banished to the island.

Advice more in keeping with the First Consul's own views was offered him by General Kerverseau, who outlined a plan of campaign against Toussaint and wrote: —

> Let there be no mistake. As long as he [Toussaint] remains in the colony he will be the sovereign. He may rule in the name of France, but only so long as France is willing to bow to his will. There will be order, but it will be the kind he wants. Laws will be enforced, but they will be of his making. There will be authority, but it will be his. If he deigns to receive the representatives of France, they will be like the pachas of the Porte in Egypt – honored captives without a vestige of authority. The moment they incur the displeasure of this easily-offended and distrustful personage they will be ignominiously driven out. It is for the Republic to decide whether after having laid down the law to all the monarchs of Europe, her dignity will permit her to have a rebellious Negro tell her what she can or cannot do in her own colony.

Napoleon adopted Kerverseau's plan of campaign and incorporated it in his "Secret and Confidential Instructions" to General Leclerc.

## 2

Never in the history of France or of any other nation had so large an overseas expedition been fitted out. "All the preparations," wrote the First Consul, "are to be made secretly, as in time of war." The first contingent was to consist of 20,000 men, to be immediately followed by a second contingent of equal strength. After that reinforcements were to be sent monthly. Spain and Holland agreed to co-operate in transporting the army. England promised to send supplies from Jamaica and Spain was to do the same from Cuba. A fleet of eighty-six war vessels and transports was assembled in the harbors of Brest, Orient,

Rochefort, Toulon, Havre, Cádiz and Flushing. The sexagenarian Admiral Villaret-Joyeuse was to be in command of the fleet, assisted by seven vice-admirals – five French, one Spanish and one Dutch.

In command of the army Napoleon placed his brother-in-law, General Leclerc. He appears to have hesitated between Leclerc and Bernadotte, about whom Leclerc says in a letter to Bonaparte: "I have especial reason to be pleased with the considerate conduct of General Bernadotte towards me. I have been the more sensible of it because he expected to have command of the expedition."

Leclerc died of yellow fever in St. Domingo, Bernadotte lived to found a dynasty.

Charles Victor Emmanuel Leclerc had married Napoleon's favorite sister Pauline. He was twenty-nine and had distinguished himself in Italy, on the Rhine and in Portugal. His cast of countenance resembled Napoleon's, but had an effeminate touch, notwithstanding the lush sideburns with which he adorned it. Thirteen generals of division and twenty-seven brigadier generals were to be under his command. There were men among them whose names were known throughout Europe – Rochambeau, who had seen service in Martinique and in the Tyrol; Dugua, the hero of the battle of the Pyramids; Humbert, who under the Directory had made a landing in Ireland; Boudet, whose name is inscribed on the *Arc de Triomphe* in Paris and who made the victory of Marengo possible by leading the French artillery over the St. Bernard; the capable de Lacroix, Hardy, Debelle, Claparède, etc. There was besides a staff of administrators and technicians headed by Bénézech, former Minister of the Interior. The commissary left much to be desired. Leclerc wrote to Napoleon: "Never have suppliers cheated more shamelessly." Shirts and trousers, he wrote, were beyond description; headgear became like a sponge when it had been out in the rain; shoes did not last two days; medical supplies were spoilt.

The suppliers were not alone in their greed for profit. If

Leclerc is to be believed practically all the generals and administrators were principally concerned about filling their pockets, and stole and looted shamelessly. General Mayart, who had left France penniless and was killed a few weeks after his arrival, managed in that short space of time to accumulate $30,000 and a quantity of silver plate.

Napoleon's young brother Jérôme, the founder of the American branch of the Bonaparte family, and Leclerc's wife and three-year-old son were to accompany the expedition. Miss Hassall, in a letter to Aaron Burr, says of Napoleon's favorite sister: "She is small, fair, with blue eyes and flaxen hair. Her face is expressive of sweetness, but without spirit. She has a voluptuous mouth, and is rendered interesting by an air of languor which spreads itself over her whole form."

Pauline intended to live sumptuously in St. Domingo and took with her a magnificent wardrobe, a quantity of elegant furniture and a staff of decorators, musicians, actors, dancers, etc. At the last moment she seems to have changed her mind about going. There was a rumor that she had to be taken aboard forcibly.

## 3

Among those who were to accompany the expedition were the mulatto leaders who had fled the colony or had been deported – Rigaud, Villate, Pétion, Boyer and several others. They, too, were slated for betrayal. Napoleon's secret instructions were that if Leclerc found it unnecessary to avail himself of their services they were to be deported to Madagascar.

A special role was assigned to Toussaint's son and stepson – Isaac and Placide.

They had been placed at the Colonial Institute, in Paris, a government school for the sons of distinguished mulattoes and Negroes, under the management of the Abbé Coisnon. The Abbé was informed that he and the two boys were to accompany General Leclerc and were to be presented to the First Consul.

Isaac was then sixteen and Placide twenty-one. Of Placide Séraphin Clère a government report says: "He possesses little schooling and is without marked ability, but appears to have a penchant for a military career. His complexion is darker than a mulatto's, he being what is known in the colony as a 'griffe.'" He had been sent to Toulon, where he served as aide-de-camp to General Sahuguet, but was now ordered to return to the Institute.

On the appointed day the Abbé presented himself with his two charges at the office of the Minister of Marine. The ministerial carriage was waiting and together with Decrès the visitors mounted into the vehicle, which sped towards the Tuileries. Isaac has given an account of what took place at the Palace.

An aide-de-camp received them and conducted them to Bonaparte's work cabinet, where the great man was conferring with General Leclerc. Decrès made the introductions.

"Which one is Toussaint's son?" asked the First Consul.

When he had been told, Napoleon turned to Isaac and said: "Your father is a great man. He has rendered important services to France. You will tell him that I, the First Magistrate of France, promise him protection, honor and glory. Do not be deceived into thinking that it is the intention of France to wage war upon St. Domingo. The army that is being sent there is not intended to combat the forces of your country, but to strengthen them. This is my brother-in-law, General Leclerc, whom I have named Captain General and who will be in command of the army. Orders have been given to take you to St. Domingo fifteen days in advance of the expedition, so you may acquaint your father with its arrival."

No such orders had been given. The boys departed with the expedition, not in advance of it.

The First Consul put some questions to them concerning their studies and professed to be satisfied with their answers.

Decrès then conducted them to the carriage and invited them and the Abbé to a dinner he was giving the following day in their honor at the Ministry of Marine.

Important men were present at the dinner – Generals Leclerc and Vincent, Vice-Admiral Bourgainville and high colonial functionaries. Vincent must have thought about Napoleon's exclamation: "I will not leave an epaulette upon the shoulders of a single black!" and have wondered about the fate in store for the two guests of honor and their father.

Before Isaac and Placide departed for Brest each was presented, in the name of the First Consul, with a gorgeous uniform and a set of sidearms of Versailles manufacture. They went aboard the frigate *La Sirène* in high spirits, prepared to sing the praises of their generous benefactor.

## 4

While Leclerc was given extensive civil and military powers, his course was carefully mapped out for him. The First Consul had dictated a set of instructions which prescribed the mode of attack in case resistance was encountered and the course to follow after the landing. A proclamation signed by Bonaparte was to assure the blacks that slavery would not be restored. Toussaint and his generals were to be assured that they would remain undisturbed in the enjoyment of their posts and prerogatives. This was called the First Phase and was not to last over a fortnight. During the Second Phase, of about equal length, the iron fist was to emerge from the velvet glove. Power was to be withdrawn from the Negro leaders and the black troops were to be disbanded. Then would come the Third Phase, during which Toussaint, his generals and appointees, of whatever color, were to be deported to France and the population was to be disarmed. The Fourth Phase (not mentioned in the instructions, but definitely decided upon) was the restoration of slavery.

Leclerc was further instructed to deport to France "all white women who have prostituted themselves with Negroes." The disaster which this threatened to genteel colonial society was averted by the gallantry of General Boudet, who burned the letters he found in Toussaint's palace at Port-au-Prince.

Napoleon's notion of promoting education among the Negroes is contained in this paragraph: –

> No public instruction of any kind shall exist in St. Domingo. All the [white] Creoles shall be required to send their children to France to be educated.

Discussion of the rights of the Negro was not to be tolerated: –

> Anybody, irrespective of rank or services rendered, who discusses the rights of the Negroes, should, on one pretext or another, be sent back to France.

## 5

Napoleon's "Secret and Confidential Instructions" contain an interesting reference to the United States. He writes: –

> Jefferson has promised that the moment the French army sets foot in the colony all necessary measures will be taken to starve out Toussaint and to aid the army.

If Jefferson made such a promise he must have received assurances that the interests of the large number of Americans in the colony and of the still larger number who traded with St. Domingo would be protected. It was evidently meant that these assurances should be broken, for the Instructions read: –

> During the First, Second and Third Phases, Americans are to be allowed to trade with the colony, after that the French trade monopoly existing before the Revolution is to be restored.

As the combined length of the three Phases was not to exceed a few weeks, this could hardly have been the agreement the American Government had entered into. Thus the Negroes, the mulattoes and the Americans were, each in turn, to be duped.

The French Government evidently expected some difficulty as a result of its disregard of American interests, for on June 16, 1802, Decrès wrote to Leclerc: –

The only nation towards whom you may be obliged to assume a hostile attitude is the United States, which may be seized with a fit of madness [*un accès de délire*]. Two warships and a few frigates will suffice to keep them in check.

The "fit of madness" was not long in coming. Decrès's letter crossed one of Leclerc, in which the Captain General wrote: "They breathe fire and flame against us in the United States. They accuse us of being brigands."

Such were the "Secret and Confidential Instructions" of the man who was to say of himself: "Having been called by the orders of Him from whom all things emanate to bring back to earth justice, order and equality, I shall be unperturbed when my last hour strikes."

# CHAPTER IV

## Burning of Le Cap

"History has no record of a military enterprise employing a larger maritime force or one more wretchedly handled," wrote Leclerc's Chief of Staff, Pamphile de Lacroix.

The flotillas, setting out from ports in France, Holland and Spain, lost several weeks in vain attempts to make a junction. They finally proceeded separately, in the hope of meeting in the Bay of Samana, on the east coast of Haiti. On January 29, 1802, only two of the squadrons had arrived, that of Admiral

Villaret-Joyeuse and of Vice-Admiral Latouche-Tréville. Yet it was a formidable fleet that Toussaint, on horseback, watched from a height overlooking the bay – so formidable that he turned in consternation to his officers and said: "We are doomed. All France is about to invade us. France has been deceived and has come to avenge herself by reducing the blacks to bondage."

Then he gave his horse the spurs and rode off in the direction of the French part of the island, where he expected the attack to take place.

Leclerc held a council of war on board the flagship *L'Océan*. The two squadrons carried a force of only 12,000 men, but the Captain General decided to attack. Kerverseau, with two frigates and 1400 men, was to sail to Santo Domingo City. Rochambeau, with 2000, was to occupy Fort-Dauphin. Boudet and de Lacroix, with 3500, were to sail to Port-au-Prince. Leclerc himself, with the remaining 5000, was to land at Le Cap. There was a sharp disagreement between him and Villaret-Joyeuse. The General wished to modify the First Consul's plan to fit existing circumstances, the Admiral insisted on strict observance of Napoleon's orders. Leclerc threatened to arrest the Admiral, but thought better of it and agreed to abide by the instructions. De Lacroix is of the opinion that in doing so he committed a fatal blunder. There were to be many disagreements among those in charge of the expedition. In his letters to Napoleon, Leclerc complains about practically everybody in his entourage, about the French Ambassador to the United States and about the Minister of Marine, Decrès, who, in his opinion, had "bats in his belfry." The only one of whom he expresses a favorable opinion is his enemy, Toussaint Louverture, about whom he writes: "He is not an ordinary man. He has brains and strength of character."

## 2

If there was disagreement concerning tactics in the camp of the French, there was no greater unanimity in the camp of the

Negroes. Toussaint had 20,000 troops of the line. To defend the coast meant to scatter his army over a vast territory. Even then landings could not be prevented, since the French would have numerical superiority at the points of attack. Defending a coast city against a powerful fleet was moreover a far more difficult task then than now. In our own day naval guns are seldom a match for coast defenses, but we have the assurance of a naval expert, Admiral Latouche-Tréville, that this was not the case in Toussaint's time. Coastal batteries were then so little maneuverable that they could easily be silenced by the guns of war vessels. Toussaint wished, therefore, to leave only a small garrison in each of the principal coast cities and to retire with his army into the interior. When a town was attacked it was to be the duty of the garrison to set fire to it and to fall back instantly, burning everything on its way and arousing the cultivators. Toussaint then meant to attack the landing parties one by one with a vastly superior force and annihilate them.

That this tactic would have brought him victory is attested by de Lacroix, who writes: –

> If Toussaint had kept his army united and had had it fight under his personal command, none of the chiefs would have deserted. With the superiority in numbers this mode of defense would have given him there can be no doubt that he would have been victorious.

Indeed, knowing Toussaint's military genius, it was a grave error on the part of Kerverseau to recommend to Napoleon that landings be made at widely scattered points. If Kerverseau's mode of attack did not result in immediate disaster it was due to an unforeseen circumstance – the opposition of Toussaint's generals to the strategy he proposed.

Toussaint appears to have had the same difficulty with his subordinates that Washington had with Gates and Putnam. The generals had their private ambitions. They wished to keep important forces under their personal command and to oppose landings in their territory. Christophe was to say later to de Lacroix: "If instead of joining battle our system of defense had consisted of retreating and arousing the cultivators, you would never have got the best of us. Old Toussaint kept dinning it into our ears, but we would not listen to him. We had arms. It hurt our pride not to make use of them. This was our undoing."

Thus Toussaint, against his better judgment, was forced to scatter his army. What he feared happened. Wherever the French landed they found an inferior force confronting them and Toussaint was deprived of the personal supervision over his generals which would have prevented defection.

## 3

The first to reach his objective was General Rochambeau, who captured Fort-Dauphin with the loss of only fourteen men. Prisoners taken by the French were massacred. Rochambeau thus began the series of atrocities which finally received its answer in Dessalines's "War for war, crime for crime, atrocity for atrocity." Toussaint himself, whose rule had always been "no retaliation," was to become affected.

The main body of the fleet had sailed to Le Cap, where Henri Christophe was in command. The future King of Haiti was a native of the British Antilles and spoke English as well as French and Creole. He was a full-blooded Negro freed before the Revolution for faithful service, had been a waiter at a hotel at Le Cap and had acquired some outward polish. He was at Fort Picolet when the squadron was sighted and immediately sent word to Toussaint of the arrival of the fleet. At the same time he ordered the Negro harbormaster Sangos to go aboard the flagship and inform the Admiral that the Governor General was in the Spanish part of the island and that without his permission warships could not enter the harbor. Admiral Villaret-Joyeuse did not wish to risk entering without a pilot and asked

Sangos to serve in that capacity. The Negro refused and was placed under arrest.

A boat was now lowered and the Admiral's aide-de-camp, Lebrun, was rowed to Fort Picolet, where Christophe received him and asked if he was the bearer of a written communication from the Commander of the expedition. Lebrun replied that he was, but that he could deliver it only to Toussaint Louverture. Christophe suggested that they go to the city for a parley. The aide-de-camp consenting, a horse was furnished him, and escorted by several officers they rode into the city. In his report Lebrun comments on the sullen looks of the mulatto and Negro officers and the ill-disguised satisfaction of their white colleagues.

The appearance of the city surprised Lebrun. Not a trace remained of the conflagration of 1793. The houses of hewn stone had an air of solidity and prosperity. Streets were crowded. Fountains played in the squares. There were many handsome public edifices. The Frenchman was, however, not so dazzled as to neglect the purpose of his mission. When opportunity offered, he dropped a bundle of printed proclamations. They were later returned to him, but not before the municipal officers and numerous citizens had read these words addressed to the population by Bonaparte: –

No matter what your origin, you are Frenchmen, equal before God and the Republic.

France, like St. Domingo, has been a prey to factional strife, and has been torn by civil and foreign wars. But this is now over. All nations have now become reconciled with France and have vowed to maintain peace and friendly relations with her. Frenchmen, too, have settled their differences and have sworn to be friends and brothers.

It is now your turn to welcome the French and to rejoice at the arrival of your brothers from Europe.

The Government sends you Captain General Leclerc.

He commands a powerful army, intended for your protection against your and the Republic's enemies. If anybody tells you that these forces are meant to deprive you of your liberty, give him this answer: The Republic has given us liberty; the Republic will not tolerate that it be taken from us.

Rally around the Captain General. He brings you peace and plenty.

Whoever dares to separate himself from the Captain General is a traitor to his country, and the anger of the Republic will devour him as fire devours dry sugar cane.

## 4

On his arrival at the Government Palace Lebrun found more to wonder about. The imposing proportions of the edifice, the well-kept gardens and tasteful furnishings, the smartly dressed officers and soldiers of Toussaint's bodyguard, the liveried servants – it was not thus he had imagined a country ruled by *nègres dorés*. He was ushered into a room hung with gold brocade. Here Christophe informed him that he was empowered to receive any communication intended for Toussaint. Lebrun conceived the notion that Toussaint was hiding in the Palace, and thinking Christophe meant to take the message to him, surrendered the envelope. It contained a copy of Napoleon's proclamation and a demand that suitable quarters be provided for the army which was about to land.

Christophe left the room, returning an hour later. Leaving the door open, so officers in the adjoining room might hear, he made this formal declaration: "Without an order from Governor General Toussaint Louverture, who is at present in the Spanish part, I cannot receive the squadron and the army it has on board."

Lebrun approached him and said in an undertone: "If you will receive the army before Toussaint's return, the Captain General will shower you with honors and favors."

Christophe drew back and roared: "No, sir! I can't listen to any proposal without an order from the Governor General.

The proclamations you have brought are the fruit of tyranny and despotism. I will have my soldiers swear to maintain liberty at any cost."

The windows of the room gave out upon the sea and Christophe noticed that the fleet had departed. He added in a milder tone: "The squadron has left. It is no longer visible. You will rejoin it tomorrow. In the meantime you are to remain here."

Having said this he left the room.

Again Lebrun found himself alone. When darkness fell four liveried servants entered, drew the curtains, lit the candles in the candelabra and laid a table with snow-white damask and heavy silver plate. Lebrun was asked to seat himself and a dinner was served to him such as he had seldom tasted. Any attempt to question the servants proved, however, fruitless. They served him with courtesy and efficiency, but never opened their lips.

In this weird atmosphere, among the evidences of Toussaint's wealth and power, Lebrun must have been reminded of a sinister tale current in France. It was claimed that Toussaint had had a great vault constructed in the Cahos Mountains to which he had transferred a treasure variously estimated at from 40,000,000 to 250,000,000 francs. When the treasure had been safely stored the four hundred Negroes engaged in the work were said to have been executed. The story was a fable, but found credence with Bonaparte and his advisers.

## 5

In the meantime Christophe sat in Toussaint's work cabinet dictating to his mulatto secretary. At midnight a delegation from the Municipality was announced. It was headed by Mayor Télémaque, a venerable old Negro who had been a freedman before the Revolution. He pleaded with Christophe to welcome the French and save the city from bombardment by the fleet. Had not Toussaint himself said: "The orders and emissaries of France should be received with filial piety and respect"?

Christophe replied that he was a soldier and recognized no other chief than Toussaint Louverture. What proof was there that the fleet had been sent by the French Republic? He had seen foreign ensigns floating from the mastheads of some of the vessels. If France had any orders to give she would not entrust them to foreign squadrons, but would send a dispatch vessel. If this so-called Captain General insisted on forcing his way into the roadstead, the city would burst into flames before he had time to drop anchor.

Aghast at this threat Télémaque begged permission to call with a delegation on the commander of the expedition. He would try to obtain a forty-eight-hour delay, by which time Toussaint would have returned. Christophe consented.

In the early morning, the fleet having reappeared, Télémaque and four white men accompanied Lebrun to the flagship. Two were leading citizens, one was the parish priest, the fourth was Tobias Lear, Consul General of the United States, successor to Edward Stevens. The delegation was courteously received. Leclerc expressed his admiration for Toussaint and Christophe, but refused to grant the delay, fearing no doubt that it would be used to strengthen the city's defenses. If within half an hour after the delegation had set foot on shore he did not receive assurances that he would be welcomed, he would resort to force. He penned a letter to Christophe and sent his aide-de-camp with the disconsolate delegates to deliver it and bring him the answer. The letter read: –

I learn with indignation, Citizen General, that you refuse to receive the French squadron and the army I have the honor to command. You give as a pretext that you have received no order to that effect from the Governor General.

France is now at peace with England and her Government is sending an army to St. Domingo fully capable of imposing its will upon rebels, if there are such in the colony. I should be chagrined, General, to be forced to the conclusion that you are a rebel.

I warn you that if you fail to turn over to me today the forts of

Picolet, Belair and all the coastal batteries, fifteen thousand men will be landed. Four thousand are landing this very moment at Fort-Liberté and eight thousand at Port-Républicain.

I enclose a proclamation. It states clearly the Government's intentions. I value very highly the services you have rendered, but will hold you responsible for the course of events.

The delegates, who had accompanied the aide-de-camp to the Palace, noticed with dismay that the ultimatum, far from intimidating Christophe, seemed to incense him. One of the leading citizens, a certain La Garde, tried to allay the threatening storm by reasoning with Christophe. The black general turned on him savagely. "You talk like a planter!" he shouted. "Like a property owner! I have no confidence in you!"

Tobias Lear asked permission for the white inhabitants to embark. Christophe replied that Americans could do so; all others must remain. He then dictated his reply to Leclerc, of which this is the most significant paragraph: –

I am awaiting the Governor's orders. Until I hear from him I cannot permit you to land. If you use force, I will resist, and if you succeed in making a landing, you will enter a city reduced to ashes. Even on those ashes I will continue to combat you. As for the troops that you say have already landed, you are building a house of cards that will be scattered by the wind.

The aide-de-camp departed with the letter and immediately reinforcements were rushed to the forts. But the wind having turned Leclerc was unable to make good his threat and the fleet withdrew a second time.

## 6

In the morning a crowd of women, children and old men, of all colors and representing every social class, marched slowly through the streets towards the Government Palace. Arrived before the building they knelt and stretched forth their arms in supplication. This impressive demonstration, organized by the Municipality, proved unavailing. Ignoring the petitioners, Christophe rode off to the Place d'Armes, where he reviewed the garrison, addressed the soldiers and had them swear to resist invasion unto death.

In the meantime Télémaque had Bonaparte's proclamation, in French and Creole, posted throughout the city.

When darkness fell the squadron had not yet reappeared, but Christophe had no illusions. At midnight he went to the municipal building, where the Council was in permanent session, and informed the councilors that when Fort Picolet found it necessary to fire the first shot, the torch would be applied. He suggested that they take immediate steps to evacuate the population.

Télémaque replied heatedly that by virtue of his authority as first magistrate of the city, he forbade him to carry out his threat. He turned to the commander of the Municipal Guard and ordered him to suppress disorder of any kind. Christophe took up the challenge and said that the Guard would be confined to their barracks.

On the morning of the fourth of February the fleet reappeared. That day soldiers went from door to door warning the people to leave. Uneasiness spread and grew into panic. Towards evening there was a veritable exodus. In carriages, in sedan chairs, on foot, on horseback, the people fled. Rich, poor, white, mulatto and black intermingled. Creole ladies sat in their carriages amidst an avalanche of boxes. Negro women balanced towering loads upon their heads. Naked children clutching bundles perched upon handcars laden with household goods. Horsemen struggled with their mounts. Like a viscous lava stream the mass of humanity pushed upward along the winding road to Haut-du-Cap. At the foot of the mountain that broods over the city they halted and made camp.

The sun dropped below the horizon and the sudden darkness characteristic of that latitude enveloped the country. Except for the military, a few shopkeepers who sat behind closed shutters and some human hyenas intent on looting, Le Cap was deserted. Lights blazed in the Government Palace, where Christophe issued orders and officers came and went.

## 7

The commander of Fort Picolet watched the lights of the fleet in the offing. He saw a dark shape detach itself from the main body of the fleet and draw nearer. Slowly, cautiously a frigate glided towards the fort. The officer knew that if he fired a warning shot the city would burst into flames. But he dared not risk a broadside. He shouted a command and the cannon boomed.

No sooner had the sound of the explosion, cast back by the mountain, reverberated through the city, than soldiers carrying lighted torches swarmed into the streets. Le Cap boasted eighty-three public buildings. During the conflagration of 1793 nearly all had been spared. Now they were the first to be sacrificed. Squads of soldiers under the command of officers entered the buildings, methodically set fire to them. Soon flames poured from the windows of the customhouse, the bureau of marine control, the government warehouses, the barracks, the municipal building, the theater, the great church, the Government Palace. Then doors were broken open, shops and private dwellings entered and fired. The straight narrow streets became pathways of flame. Here and there a desperate shopkeeper tried to defend his property. He was stabbed or beaten to death, his body flung into the street or cast into the flames.

Christophe, on horseback, galloped about directing his men. In his gold-braided uniform, his black face and dark eyes shining in the weird illumination, he was a terrifying figure. He had acquired one of the city's most imposing mansions and had furnished it with regal splendor. He now galloped towards the mansion, from which his family had fled, dismounted, snatched a torch from the hand of a soldier and went inside. Holding up the torch he looked about at the treasures he had accumulated, then mounted the stairway and going from room to room set fire to curtains, bedding, the contents of clothes closets.

### 8

The refugees at the foot of the mountain had heard the shot that doomed their city. They had seen fires spring up, intermingle in a vast holocaust. Some wept, some prayed, some cursed, others gazed in mute fascination. Suddenly there was a fearful explosion. Flames leaped high into the air. The arsenal had blown up. The earth shook. Boulders detached themselves from the side of the mountain and crashed into the midst of the shrieking multitude.

# CHAPTER V

## Capture of Port-au-Prince

On February 3, 1802, the squadron of Vice-Admiral Latouche-Tréville appeared before Port-au-Prince. The colonial capital was no longer the small city of 8000 inhabitants which a decade earlier had reminded de Wimpffen of a Tartar camp. It was now a flourishing city of 30,000, but the houses were still of wood and the broad, unpaved streets still turned into a quagmire after a rain. The city was under the jurisdiction of Dessalines, who was with Toussaint in the Spanish part of the island. The garrison was commanded by the white general Agé.

When Brigadier General Sabès and Naval Ensign Gémont stepped from a dinghy and in the name of General Boudet asked that the French army be allowed to land, Agé would have given his consent, but his second in command, the mulatto colonel Lamartinière, demanded that the request be denied and the two French officers be kept as hostages. Agé found himself obliged to inform Boudet that the officers were being detained pending the arrival of Dessalines, but the messenger was instructed to inform Boudet privately that General Agé was not a free agent.

Boudet addressed an appeal to the Negro and mulatto chiefs in the city, assuring them that his intentions were peaceful, that he had come to reinforce the garrison and that they need not have the slightest fear of losing their freedom or their military rank. Lamartinière replied that at the first sign of a landing the city would be fired and the whites throughout the Department massacred. He inspected the forts, and noticing that they lacked ammunition, demanded the key of the arsenal from Lacombe, the white Commander of Fortifications. Lacombe refused. Lamartinière drew his pistol and shot him.

## 2

Notwithstanding Lamartinière's threat a landing was made, but at some distance from the city, at a point named Lamentin. The landing party, consisting of 1200 grenadiers in tall bearskins and a battery of field pieces, was commanded by Boudet and de Lacroix. They marched swiftly towards the city and at noon arrived before Fort Bizoton. Boudet ordered a halt and himself advanced towards the fort. The Negro captain Séraphin came to meet him and informed him that if the French advanced another step the fort would fire. The French general turned towards his men and shouted: "Comrades, you are on French soil, where you should find only friends. Keep your muskets on your shoulders. Let them kill you if they wish, so those who come after us may have reason to avenge our death and the dignity of France." Then turning to Séraphin he added: "Go and tell your battalion what you have just heard. Fire on us if you dare. But if you do, defend yourselves well, sell your lives dearly, for you're lost." Then again to his soldiers: "Long live the Republic! Long live liberty! Forward, march!"

The flag carried at the head of the French column was the same that floated over the fort. The garrison of the fort was composed mainly of mulattoes who had served under Rigaud. When some of them cried: "Long live France! Long live our brothers!" others took up the cry. The gates were opened and Boudet marched into the fort. Séraphin placed himself under his orders.

The French continued their advance until they reached the breastworks protecting the city. Here again they halted and Boudet demanded the right to pass. From behind the breastworks men motioned to him to advance. There were cries of "We have orders to receive you!" The grenadiers advanced, only to be met by a deadly salvo that stretched a hundred dead upon the ground. There were two hundred wounded, including de Lacroix. The enraged grenadiers re-formed and took the breastworks at the point of the bayonet.

The coast defenses had opened fire on the squadron, but Latouche-Tréville made good his boast that land batteries were no match for a fleet able to maneuver while it fired. He silenced the batteries and a fresh landing was made.

Lamartinière tried to set fire to the city, but the French advance was so swift that he did not succeed. A sum of 2,500,000 francs in the treasury fell into the hands of the invaders. Lamartinière withdrew in good order, taking with him most of the whites as hostages.

Agé, who had managed to elude his terrible subordinate, went to meet the conquerors at the head of a delegation of white and mulatto citizens, among whom was the Apostolic Vicar Lacune. It was the same Lacune who had once eulogized Toussaint in such glowing terms. He now thanked the Almighty and his instrument Boudet "for having delivered the colony from the reign of a monster."

# CHAPTER VI

## Toussaint Writes to His Generals

CHRISTOPHE's messenger reached Toussaint and his escort at a considerable distance from Le Cap. Soon afterwards, a second messenger arrived and Toussaint speeded up his horse so that his companions had difficulty keeping up with him. Between San Raphael and San Michel he met Dessalines. They were to have gone together on a tour of inspection, but Toussaint now ordered him to hasten back to Port-au-Prince, while he pushed on to Le Cap. The falling of darkness did not interrupt his journey. While rounding the brow of a mountain he saw a reddish glow on the horizon. The meaning of this did not escape him. Thus Toussaint and Leclerc learned practically at the same time that the city had been given over to the flames.

He reached the environs of Le Cap in the early morning. The roads were crowded with refugees. When he arrived at Haut-du-Cap, where he had been a slave, the panorama of the city and the surrounding country lay before him. The city was still burning and the valley was veiled in smoke, but he could see the French squadron in the harbor and soldiers debarking on the quay. There was the intermittent crash of artillery, for the warships were shelling the road over which the garrison was retreating. On the Plaine-du-Nord plantations were burning.

Christophe came trotting up and saluted. The two men reviewed the situation. In his memorandum to Bonaparte, Toussaint writes: "I asked him who had ordered the city fired. He replied that it was he. I reprimanded him severely for having employed such rigorous measures. 'Why,' said I to him, 'did you not rather make some military arrangements to defend the city until my arrival?' "

That Toussaint ordered every city or town where a landing was made fired is proved by documentary evidence. He apparently considered the firing of Le Cap premature in view of the strength of the force under Christophe's command. He quotes Christophe as replying: "What do you wish, General? My duty, necessity, the circumstances, the repeated threats of the general commanding the squadron forced me to do it."

He now ordered Christophe to withdraw to Grande-Rivière. He himself departed for the Héricourt plantation, intending to reach Gonaïves, where he wished to set up temporary headquarters. The road over which he had to pass was under fire and his horse was wounded before he reached the plantation.

At Héricourt, Toussaint received a letter from General Rochambeau, who informed him that he had occupied Fort-Dauphin and expressed indignation at having met with resistance. Rochambeau did not deny having put to death prisoners he had taken, whom he had chosen to regard as traitors to the Republic. Toussaint replied that they were soldiers, acting under orders, and that Rochambeau had committed an outrage. "I will fight," he wrote, "to the last to avenge the death of these brave men, to preserve my liberty and to restore tranquillity and order in the colony."

## 2

After his arrival at Gonaïves Toussaint wrote to his principal generals. To Maurepas, stationed at Port-de-Paix, he wrote that if the town was attacked, he was to resist, but if a landing was made he should set fire to the town and retreat into the interior.

To Dessalines he wrote: –

> There is no reason to despair, Citizen General, if you can succeed in depriving the troops that have landed of the resources of Port-Républicain. Endeavor by force or cunning to set fire to the city. It is entirely built of wood, so a few faithful emissaries should be

able to do the work. Are there not men under your command sufficiently devoted for this service? Ah, my dear General, what a misfortune that there was a traitor in that city and that your orders and mine were not carried out.

Watch for the moment when the garrison will have been weakened by expeditions into the plains, and then try to take the city by surprise.

Do not forget that while we await the rainy season, which will deliver us of our enemies, fire and destruction remain our only resource. Bear in mind that soil bathed with our sweat must not be allowed to furnish the enemy with any means of subsistence. Render the roads impassable. Throw corpses of men and horses into all the wells. Order everything burned and destroyed, so that those who have come to enslave us may have constantly before their eyes an image of that hell they so richly deserve.

The messenger was intercepted and the letter fell into the hands of General Boudet.

To Colonel Dommage, in command at Jérémie, in the Department of the South, Toussaint sent his nephew Bernard Chancy with a letter in which he says: –

I have given orders to Brigadier General Laplume to set fire to Les Cayes, to all other towns and to plantations in the plains, when he is no longer in a position to defend them. The garrisons of these towns and the cultivators will come to swell your forces at Jérémie. You and General Laplume should come to an understanding regarding the best way to carry out these measures.

There is a paragraph in his letter to Dommage which biographers who prefer their Toussaint faultless have suppressed, even when ostensibly they give the letter in full. After telling of Agé's treason, Toussaint writes: –

The whites of France have united with those of the colony to deprive us of our liberty . . . Don't trust the whites. They will betray you if they can. Consequently I give you *carte blanche*. Whatever you do will be well done.

This can have only one meaning: if Dommage thinks it best to put the whites to death without further ado, Toussaint will not object. In fairness to him it should be said that the letter was written under the stress of emotion caused by the burning of Le Cap, the treason of Agé, whom he had showered with favors, and the massacre of Negro prisoners by Rochambeau and Hardy. The latter, who had landed at Acul, had butchered six hundred Negro prisoners he had taken. During the succeeding campaign Toussaint did not follow the policy implied in his letter to Dommage. On the contrary, he did what he could to protect white prisoners and hostages. Shortly after Hardy's butchery some two hundred white soldiers were brought to his camp by the guerrilla chieftain Sylla. They had lost their way in the labyrinth of mountains, had been wandering about for days and were famished and footsore. Toussaint had an ox killed and roasted for their benefit and gave each a pair of shoes before sending them to the prison camp at Marmelade. On many occasions he appointed trusted men to protect white prisoners against the fury of the Negroes.

Toussaint's letter to Dommage had the same fate as his letter to Dessalines. Bernard Chancy was stopped and Boudet got the dispatch.

## 3

Toussaint's letters to Dessalines and Dommage had merely served to acquaint the French with his plans. A letter he sent to the mulatto general Clerveaux, ordering him to fall back on San Raphael, was likewise intercepted, and soon after the mulatto was induced by Bishop Mainvielle to place himself under Leclerc's orders. But the worst mischance was reserved for a dispatch the Negro leader sent to his brother Paul, at Santo Domingo City.

As soon as the warships with Kerverseau's battalion on board appeared before the capital of the former Spanish colony, Paul sent a messenger to Toussaint to ask for orders. The population of the Spanish part of the island was friendly to the French, so Toussaint, fearing his messenger might be stopped, resorted to a ruse. He gave the messenger two letters. In the first, which was to be carefully hidden, he told his brother to resist a landing, but to burn the city and retreat to San Raphael if his position became perilous. The second letter, which was to be destroyed when the messenger arrived at his destination, was to be carried so it could easily be detected. It instructed Paul to welcome the French. It was reasonable to suppose that in the event the courier was stopped, the contents of the second letter would assure him safe passage.

But fate intervened. The messenger was killed and both letters were found in his clothing. They were delivered to Kerverseau, who had made a landing a short distance from the city. He immediately sent an officer to Paul with the second letter and the explanation that it had been found on a messenger who had been killed. Paul, acquainted with Toussaint's policy, pronounced the letter a forgery, but his officers were unanimous in their opinion that the signature was genuine. He remained obdurate until Bishop Mainvielle intervened. The ecclesiastic, back from his successful mission to Clerveaux, reminded Paul of Moyse's fate when he had disobeyed Toussaint's orders. The bewildered Paul gave up the struggle, surrendered the city undamaged and placed himself under the command of Kerverseau.

Mainvielle, who owed his office to Toussaint, later offered to raise a force of 7000 men in the Spanish part of the island to combat his benefactor. Napoleon rewarded him by confirming him in his episcopate.

# CHAPTER VII
## Toussaint and His Sons

On his return to the flagship Lebrun had given an enthusiastic description of Le Cap and the splendor of the Government Palace. Leclerc and his young wife had been interested listeners. Pauline saw herself reigning in an exotic Versailles. But, alas! Two days later she stood on the deck of the flagship and watched flames consume the city around which her dreams had hovered. When finally she went ashore an appalling scene met her eyes. Out of over 2000 houses 59 remained habitable. The government buildings were smoking ruins. The streets were filled with debris, among which lay half-burned corpses of men and animals. The property damage was estimated at over 100,000,000 francs.

Miss Hassall, who landed in the city on June 10, more than four months after the conflagration, wrote to Aaron Burr: –

On landing we found the town a heap of ruins. A more terrible picture of desolation cannot be imagined. Passing through the streets choked with rubbish, we reached with difficulty a house which had escaped the general fate. The people live in tents, or make a kind of shelter, by laying a few boards across half-consumed beams; for the buildings being here of hewn stone, with walls three feet thick, only the roofs and the floors have been destroyed.

Concerning Leclerc and Pauline she writes: –

General Leclerc is small, his face is interesting, but he has an appearance of ill health. His wife, the sister of Buonaparte, lives in a house on the mountain till there can be one in town prepared for her reception. She is offended, and I think justly, with the ladies of the Cape, who, from a mistaken pride, did not wait on her when she arrived because having lost their clothes they could not dazzle her with their finery.

The American girl went to pay her respects to Pauline: –

She was in a room darkened by Venetian blinds, lying on her sofa, from which she half rose to receive me. When I was seated she reclined again on the sofa and amused General Boyer, who sat at her feet, by letting her slipper fall continually, which he respectfully put on as often as it fell. She was dressed in a muslin morning gown. I gave her one of the beautiful silver medals of Washington, engraved by Reich, with which she seemed much pleased. The conversation languished and I soon withdrew.

In a later letter she complains: –

We have neither public nor private balls, nor any amusement except now and then a little scandal. The most current at this moment is, that Madame Leclerc is very kind to General Boyer, and that her husband is not content, which in a French husband is a little extraordinary.

She was, however, charmed with the flaxen-haired, blue-eyed Pauline, with her voluptuous mouth and her air of languor, and remarks: –

. . . Those most disposed to condemn would exclaim on beholding her –

*If to her share some female errors fall,*
*Look in her face and you'll forget them all.*

## 2

Leclerc was dismayed by the destruction Christophe had wrought. If Toussaint meant to lay the whole country waste, it was a serious business. Such evidently was his intention: in the wake of Christophe's retreating army plantations were burning. Leclerc decided to keep force in abeyance for a while and to see what results could be achieved by more subtle means.

He sent for Toussaint's confessor and offered to confer the title of bishop upon him if he managed to get the Negro leader to relent. Father Lantheaume declined to make the attempt and other priests were equally unwilling. Then Leclerc summoned the Abbé Coisnon and Toussaint's two sons.

Placide and Isaac were far from happy. What they had witnessed did not rhyme in the least with Bonaparte's assurances. A letter of protest they had sent to Leclerc had remained unanswered. When they now appeared before the Captain General their faces showed their distrust. Leclerc did his best to reassure them. Isaac quotes him as saying: –

"I have the greatest hope of coming to an understanding with your father. He was away and unable to make proper arrangements. You will bring him this letter from the First Consul, so he may learn my intentions and the high regard I have for him."

He handed the Abbé a gold-enameled box tied with a ribbon from which two seals depended. Leclerc's friendliness, coupled with the attitude of Coisnon – who believed, or professed to believe, that there had been merely an unfortunate misunderstanding – served to give the two boys a more hopeful view of the situation. They felt flattered by the mission entrusted to them and declared themselves willing to use their influence with their father.

Together with the Abbé they departed on horseback at eleven o'clock that same evening. Rain fell in torrents. The light of torches carried by their attendants and bivouac fires struggling against the rain alone relieved the darkness. When they reached the furthest French outpost they dismounted, were entertained for supper by the company commander and went to sleep in a tent.

When, in the morning, they resumed their journey, the sky had cleared. Isaac and Placide, who had been abroad six years, were enchanted with the familiar scenes of their childhood. News of their arrival traveled before them and at settlements through which they passed they received an ovation. They had sent a courier to notify their family, and when on the second day, at nine o'clock in the evening, they arrived at Ennery, a crowd awaited them at the plantation gate. Their mother and cousins received them with rejoicing. A messenger had been sent to Toussaint, who was on a tour of inspection, and he was expected at any moment. After supper the old Abbé retired, while Isaac and Placide regaled the family with an account of their adventures.

Towards midnight there was the sound of trumpets. Toussaint's carriage came rolling up the avenue of palms. The Negro leader leaped from the carriage and embraced his sons. The Abbé was called, and as Toussaint met him with outstretched hand, the old priest said: "Is this Toussaint, the friend and servitor of France who is offering me his hand?"

"Can you doubt it?" asked Toussaint.

He thanked the Abbé for the care he had given his children and said he regretted having to welcome him in the midst of a war, for which there was no excuse. The priest then handed him the gold-enameled box containing the First Consul's letter. Toussaint broke the seals, opened the box and read the first and only communication Bonaparte ever deigned to address to him.

## 3

When one compares Bonaparte's letter to Toussaint Louverture with his "Secret and Confidential Instructions" to General Leclerc, and with letters exchanged by Bonaparte, Leclerc and Decrès concerning St. Domingo, one is amazed at the cold-blooded perfidy of the Napoleonic policy. The first note he strikes in his letter to the Negro leader is one of fulsome praise: –

We have conceived a high regard for you, and it pleases us to recognize the great services you have rendered to the people of France. If the French flag still floats over St. Domingo, it is to you and to your valiant blacks that the credit belongs. You have put an end to civil war, stopped persecution, placed religion and the worship of the Almighty – the source of all blessings – in the place rightfully due them.

He next refers to the Constitution, which, he says, contains many excellent provisions, but also some incompatible with the dignity of the French nation. This, he grants, is not Toussaint's fault, since, owing to the blockade, he was frequently unable to communicate with the French Government and had to rule the colony as if it were a sovereign state. That necessity no longer existed. Bonaparte trusts that Toussaint, "whom France counts among her most illustrious citizens," will recognize this. If he fails to do so, he will forfeit the right to the gratitude of the French nation. An abyss will open beneath his feet and will swallow him. What is more, such a course "will bring misery to the valiant blacks, whose courage we admire and whom we should be loath to have to punish as rebels."

Having first caressed and then tried to intimidate his victim, the First Consul now proceeds to reason with him: –

What is it you want? The liberty of the blacks? You know quite well that wherever we have gone we have brought liberty to people who had none. Do you desire personal consideration, honors, fortune? After the services you have rendered and can still render, and considering the high regard we have for you, can you doubt that you will receive them in full measure?

Bonaparte demands that Toussaint recognize the authority of the Captain General and get his people to recognize it. Nobody need have the least fear of being punished for what happened during the civil war. The past would only be considered when the question arose of rewarding those who had distinguished themselves in the war against France's former enemies, Great Britain and Spain. The First Consul closes with the admonition: "Count on our esteem and conduct yourself as becomes a leading citizen of the greatest nation on earth."

## 4

Toussaint glanced over the letter and laid it aside, saying that he would read it carefully later. He writes in his memorandum: "I then asked the Citizen Coisnon if General Leclerc had not given him a communication for me or charged him with something to tell me. He replied in the negative, advising me, however, to go to Le Cap and confer with the General. My children added their solicitations to persuade me to do so."

Having listened to their arguments, Toussaint replied: "You, Monsieur Coisnon, are my children's tutor and an envoy of France. Are you not forced to admit that the First Consul's words in the letter he has sent me are in direct contradiction with General Leclerc's conduct? One talks to me of peace, the other wages war upon me. If General Leclerc really wants peace, let him cease his aggressions. I will write him a letter, which you, Monsieur Granville – the tutor of my youngest son – and my children will take to him. It depends entirely on him whether France will lose or preserve the colony. I am ready to enter into any reasonable arrangement with him, and am willing to submit to the orders of the French Government, but General Leclerc must show me the orders of which he is the bearer and above all must cease every species of hostility."

Coisnon again urged him to regard Leclerc and his army as friends.

Toussaint shook his head. "That is no longer possible," he said. "The war has begun. The rage of battle is in everybody's blood. My military chiefs are on the point of burning and destroying everything. If, however, General Leclerc will suspend hostilities, I will do the same."

All now retired for the night, but Toussaint was up long before dawn and had another interview with his sons. Then he departed for Gonaïves.

## 5

That same day, Granville arrived with Toussaint's letter to Leclerc.

The Negro leader reproached the Captain General for the method he had adopted in taking over the command, for violating the rights of the Negroes and for delivering the First Consul's letter to him three months after it had been written. He proposed an armistice during which he promised to reach a decision concerning his future course and carried his punctiliousness so far as to write that he was sending back his sons so the French might have no claim upon his gratitude.

Leclerc's reply was brought him at Gonaïves by his two sons, unaccompanied by their tutor. The Captain General threw the blame for what had occurred at Le Cap upon Christophe, and begged Toussaint to help him save the colony. "No matter what forces you may have at your disposal, the final result cannot be doubted. But what should influence a man of your generous spirit even more is the thought of the misery which is bound to result from war. The solemn declaration the First Consul made in his proclamation and in his letter to you, should set your mind at rest concerning the liberty of your people. Their right to enjoy that liberty has been too dearly bought to be taken from them. The First Consul has no intention of doing so. I am waiting for you. Come and talk things over with a comrade in arms." He would order the army based upon Le Cap to refrain from hostilities for four days, which would give Toussaint sufficient time to let him know if he was coming. Placide and Isaac were moreover instructed to tell their father that the office of Lieutenant Governor was being reserved for him.

The sincerity of Leclerc's letter may be judged by comparing it with this passage in the "Secret and Confidential Instructions":

> During the First Phase you will not be exacting. You will negotiate with Toussaint. You will promise him anything he might ask, so as to enable you to occupy the cities and gain a foothold in the country. When this first goal has been attained, you will become more exacting. You will demand that he reply categorically to my proclamation and to my letter. You will get him to come to Le Cap. His submission will not be complete until he has done so, and in the midst of the French army has sworn fealty to the Republic. That day, without scandal, without insult, but with consideration and show of honor, you will have him put aboard a ship and send him to France.

The Instructions were not quite so secret and confidential as Bonaparte supposed. Decrès, Boudet and de Lacroix knew their contents. Others, too, must have known. It appears probable that Toussaint's secret agents, Huin and d'Hébecourt, had acquainted him with their general purport. When Toussaint said to Coisnon "Leclerc must show me the orders of which he is the bearer," he may have alluded to the Instructions. But whether Toussaint knew, or merely suspected, the conciliatory tone of Leclerc's letter failed to pacify him. In fact, immediately after the receipt of the letter he ordered his guard to assemble, addressed the soldiers and told them that he considered it his duty to resist invasion unto death. The men cried in unison: "We will all die with you!"

Toussaint then turned towards his sons and said that he did not blame them for being attached to the country that had given them their education. But between him and France was the cause of the blacks. He could not compromise the future of his people by leaving them to the mercy of the French. If now, when the Negroes still possessed means of defense, they received such treatment, what would be their lot when they were powerless? "You must choose, but remember, no matter which way you choose, you will remain dear to me."

Then Isaac cried peevishly, "I won't bear arms against France!" turned on his heel and walked away. But Toussaint's stepson said in a firm voice: "Father, I will remain with you. I fear the future. I fear slavery. I am ready to fight so it may never be restored. I renounce France!"

Toussaint opened his arms and embraced Placide. That day he appointed him his aide-de-camp.

Isaac went to Ennery, where his mother prevailed upon him to remain, but he wrote to Leclerc that he would never bear arms against France.

Concerning the reply he sent to Leclerc, Toussaint writes in his memorandum: –

> I replied plainly to the General that I would not report to him at Le Cap, that his conduct did not inspire me with sufficient confidence, that I was ready to transfer the command to him in conformity with the orders of the First Consul, but that I would not be his Lieutenant Governor. I added in conclusion that if he persisted in his invasion, he would force me to defend myself. I sent the letter with the utmost dispatch by an orderly, who brought me back word that "he had no reply to make and had taken the field."

Leclerc had, in fact, recovered from the shock the burning of Le Cap had given him. Good news had arrived from Port-au-Prince and from the Spanish part of the island. The belated squadrons of Gentheaume and Linois were due to arrive at any moment with heavy reinforcements. When a delegation of citizens from Gonaïves came to call on him and begged him not to resume hostilities, he curtly replied that he had sworn not to remove his boots until he had arrested Toussaint Louverture.

On February 17 the two squadrons dropped anchor at Le Cap. Soldiers and cannon poured ashore. Leclerc issued a proclamation placing Toussaint, Dessalines and Christophe outside the pale of the law. Five French armies began their march into the interior.

# CHAPTER VIII

## At Grips with Napoleon's Armies

LECLERC was now master of the principal coast cities, of the former Spanish colony, of a large part of the Department of the North and of the Department of the South. In Rigaud's former capital, Les Cayes, General Laplume had gone over to the enemy. At Jérémie, Colonel Dommage had been arrested by his subordinates, who had turned the town over to Boudet. The commander of Jacmel allowed himself to be bought. In buying him, the French made an excellent bargain: warehouses containing 12,000,000 francs of commodities fell into their hands.

Toussaint and the generals remaining loyal to him were hemmed in by armies totaling 25,000 men. Desfourneaux, Hardy and Rochambeau were converging upon Gonaïves, where Toussaint had his temporary headquarters. Debelle's division was being rushed by sea to Port-de-Paix, where the Negro general, Maurepas, was proving more than a match for the French general, Humbert. Boudet was marching upon St. Marc, which Dessalines abandoned and fired.

Gonaïves not being fortified, Toussaint decided not to defend the town. He ordered the mulatto general, Vernet, to fight a delaying action with Hardy, whom Christophe had been unable to keep in check, and with 5500 men rushed to the Ravin-à-Couleuvre, a mountain pass through which Rochambeau was advancing. The force under Toussaint's personal command consisted of 1500 grenadiers of the guard, 400 dragoons, 1200 infantrymen and 2400 armed cultivators. Rochambeau commanded 5000 of Napoleon's veterans. Nevertheless the French general was soundly trounced and thrown across the Lacroix River, leaving many prisoners in Toussaint's hands. It was a bitter pill to swallow for a general who had said in his order of the day: "It is only slaves you have to fight today – men who dare not look you in the face and who will flee in every direction. You have not come eighteen hundred miles to allow yourselves to be beaten by a rebellious slave."

Rochambeau, however, had something to console him. He intercepted Toussaint's treasury, which was being transported from Gonaïves. In the meantime Hardy had made a valuable prisoner – Toussaint's youngest son, Saint-Jean, who had become separated from his mother when Suzanne fled before the advancing enemy.

## 2

Maurepas was giving an excellent account of himself. He had evacuated Port-de-Paix, made untenable by the guns of the fleet, and had set fire to the town. General Humbert had occupied the ruins, but when he tried to go further afield was thrown back with heavy losses. When Debelle arrived with reinforcements he tried again, with no better result. Leclerc wrote to Napoleon: "General Humbert has dishonored himself at Port-de-Paix by his cowardly conduct."

Leclerc now ordered Desfourneaux and Hardy to march north and attack Maurepas in the rear. Lubin Golard, Rigaud's fanatical adherent in the Department of the North, who after his defeat by Toussaint had taken refuge in the mountains, came to the assistance of the French with his Maroon Negroes. Hemmed in on all sides, Maurepas asked Humbert for an interview, the upshot of which was that he dismissed the armed cultivators who had flocked to his banner and with the 9th demi-brigade went over to the enemy.

## 3

Toussaint had evolved a plan to keep the French occupied until August, when rains and yellow fever would cripple the invaders and enable him to take the offensive. In the mountains east of St. Marc was the fortress Crête-à-Pierrot, built by the French engineer Brothier at the time of the British invasion. Together with Fort Verrette and Fort Laveaux, it had barred the way into the interior. A strong garrison stationed at Crête-à-Pierrot would be a constant menace to Leclerc's communications and make penetration into the interior impossible. Leclerc would be obliged to reduce the fort at any cost, which would require so large a part of his effectives that many strategic points would be poorly guarded. This would enable Toussaint and his generals to operate behind the enemy lines, cut communications, capture supplies and threaten the coast cities.

He stationed 1200 men at the fort under the command of Magny, the black commander of his bodyguard. The mulatto Lamartinière was second in command. They were to take their orders from Dessalines, who was to operate in the immediate vicinity, while Toussaint and Christophe harassed the enemy further north.

Leclerc realized the danger of the maneuver and ordered Debelle to take the fort by assault. The French general engaged a small Negro force outside the fortifications. The Negroes quickly retreated with the French in hot pursuit. When Debelle's men were within easy range of the guns of the fort, the Negroes suddenly disappeared, as if by magic. They had jumped into a deep trench especially dug for that purpose. The fort now opened up with all its effectives. Four hundred Frenchmen fell dead or wounded. Debelle was seriously injured. The French beat a hasty retreat.

Dessalines now took command at the fort, while the enraged Leclerc ordered Dugua and Boudet to renew the assault.

Dessalines, standing near an open powder barrel, a lighted torch in his hand, addressed the garrison. "I want only brave men here," he said. "Those who are content to be the slaves of the French have my permission to leave. We are going to be attacked. If the enemy manages to set foot in the fort, I'll blow it up. We will all die for liberty." Then he ordered a sortie.

Unbelievable as it may seem, the hero of the battle of the Pyramids and the hero of the St. Bernard fell into the same trap that had proved so disastrous to their predecessor. They drove back the blacks who sallied forth from the fort, and pressed on swiftly, intending no doubt to gain admittance together with the fugitives. But again the Negroes suddenly vanished and again a murderous fire belched forth from the fortifications. Boudet lost 500 men, Dugua 300. Both generals were wounded.

## 4

It was evident that only a prolonged siege could force the fort to surrender. As Toussaint had expected, Leclerc was forced to employ the greater part of his effectives. The divisions of Rochambeau and Hardy were sent down from the north. De Lacroix took command of Boudet's and Dugua's shattered forces. Bourke arrived with a fresh division. More than 12,000 of Napoleon's best soldiers, commanded by some of his ablest generals, laid siege to a fort held by 1200 Negroes.

Dessalines had left Crête-à-Pierrot, expecting to harass the enemy in the rear. Before leaving he showed Magny a ring and told him that if a messenger arrived with that token, he was to cut his way through the enemy lines. Day and night the French artillery now pounded the fort. The besieged ran short of provisions. There were 500 dead and wounded. The water supply was giving out. But from the four corners of the fort defiantly floated a red flag, signifying *No Quarter*.

Often the besieged intoned the Marseillaise and their voices could be heard clearly by the French. De Lacroix tells of the effect this produced on the French soldiers. These men, for whom the word "Liberty" had once been a sacred shibboleth, were beginning to wonder what it all meant. Was it true that Bonaparte meant to restore slavery? Were they, the soldiers of the Republic, to be used for that? There would come a time when a French captain, Gabriel Véret, would leave the ranks of his countrymen, hold out his hand to the mulatto general Pétion, who finally ranged himself on the side of the Negroes, and say: "Your cause is that of human freedom. It is the cause I have always fought for. I am a soldier of liberty. I renounce France as you have renounced her." There would come a time when Leclerc, dying of yellow fever, would say to the physician attending him that men who loved liberty as did the Negroes of St. Domingo and men as valiant as the French soldiers deserved a better fate than that to which the First Consul had doomed them.

De Lacroix makes no secret of the fact that he himself felt a sense of shame. He was staying at the house of an old Negro warrior, a certain Paul Lafrance, who, believing in Napoleon's assurances, had joined the French. The rumor that slavery was to be restored had grown more persistent and Lafrance said to him: "General, you look like an honest man. Tell me truthfully: did you come here to restore slavery?" The chief of staff of Leclerc's army betrayed his embarrassment and did not reply. The Negro covered his face with his hands and moaned: "My daughters! My poor daughters! Oh, I cannot bear it!" But holding hospitality sacred, he added: "Fear not, General. Old Paul Lafrance will not harm you."

## 5

One day a decrepit old couple approached from the direction of the fort. The man, apparently blind, was led by the woman, who supported herself with a stick. The French attempted to question them, but found they were dealing with deaf-mutes. An officer, who believed they were shamming, ordered them beaten until they decided to talk. The stick was vigorously applied, but without effect. De Lacroix intervened and ordered them released.

The aged couple continued their hesitant way along the bank

of the Artibonite. Suddenly both dived into the stream and swam across with vigorous strokes. Having reached the opposite bank they executed a fantastic dance and showed by various indelicate gestures their contempt for the French, whose amusement at these antics affected their aim. Finally, agile as goats, the fugitives scampered off to safety. Later the French were to learn that the two impostors were messengers from Dessalines, returning from a mission to the fort, which they had managed to reach unobserved.

That same night Magny and Lamartinière led a desperate sortie. So unexpected was the attack that Rochambeau's men were thrown into confusion and he had to flee in his nightclothes. When the French re-formed the enemy had vanished. "The retreat which the commander of Crête-à-Pierrot conceived and executed," writes de Lacroix, "was a remarkable feat of arms. More than 12,000 of us surrounded the fort, yet he got away, leaving us only his dead and wounded."

Leclerc forbade his officers to mention in their private correspondence the losses he had suffered before Crête-à-Pierrot. He reported that he had lost 500 men. In reality his loss was four times that number. The truth, however, must have leaked out, for Decrès wrote to him: "The affair of Crête-à-Pierrot, during which through an unfortunate fatality Generals Debelle, Deveaux, Dugua and Boudet were wounded, and the loss of so many brave men, has affected the First Consul painfully."

## 6

All this time Toussaint had not been idle either with sword or pen. In reply to Leclerc's decree outlawing him, Dessalines and Christophe, he issued an edict placing Leclerc, Rochambeau and Desfourneaux outside the pale of the law. He sent forth this proclamation to the army and the armed cultivators: –

You are combating enemies devoid of faith, law or religion. They promise you liberty, but aim to enslave you. The mother country, seduced by the First Consul, has become a cruel stepmother to you. Have you forgotten the abject servitude, the tortures, the cruelties inflicted upon you in the course of three centuries? Bare your breasts and you will see upon them the mark of the branding iron.

It is not for liberty or for their fatherland that the French make war upon us, but to satisfy the spite and ambition of the First Consul. Their bodies are not mutilated by the branding iron. Their wives and children do not share their hardships. The tombs of their fathers are beyond the ocean.

Those whom our sword fails to strike down will be slain by our avenging climate. Their bones will lie scattered among these rocks and these mountains or will be bleached by the waves of our sea. Never will they see their fatherland again or receive the tender embraces of their wives, sisters and mothers. Liberty will flourish upon their graves.

He recaptured in quick succession San Michel, Marmelade, San Raphael and Dondon and set up permanent headquarters at Marmelade. Colonel René occupied Limbé. The guerrilla leader Sylla captured strategic Plaisance. Christophe threatened Le Cap, where Admiral Villaret-Joyeuse hastily debarked sailors, lest the garrison prove insufficient to defend the city.

One day, observing the enemy through his telescope, Toussaint recognized the uniform of the 9th demi-brigade of Maurepas. It was his first intimation that the general had changed sides. Without a moment's hesitation he galloped towards the regiment and cried: "Soldiers of the 9th! Will you fire upon your General and upon your brothers?" Thirteen years later, Napoleon, on his return from Elba, finding his way barred by his former soldiers, made almost exactly the same gesture. It does not appear impossible that consciously or unconsciously he imitated Toussaint, with whose history he was well acquainted. But Napoleon's gesture succeeded; Toussaint's failed, owing to the presence of a white regiment that opened fire. A company of dragoons hurled itself between the enemy and their leader and at the cost of several casualties saved him from death or injury.

## 7

Leclerc's situation was becoming alarming. In two months he had lost 5000 men in battle; 8000 ill or injured were hospitalized. Toussaint's position, on the other hand, was improving steadily. Thousands of cultivators had joined his ranks. He and his four principal generals – Dessalines, Christophe, Belair and Vernet – occupied strong positions in the mountains, from which Leclerc did not even attempt to dislodge them. Sylla, Sans-Souci, Macaya, Petit-Noël, Prieur and a score of other guerrilla chieftains were waging a war of extermination upon the French. They made roads impassable by felling trees, burned bridges, devastated plantations. Huge boulders detached themselves from mountain slopes and crashed into marching columns. Men, horses and cannon were trapped in cunningly disguised pits. Sentries died at their posts. Regiments marching through the mountains sometimes lost half their complement of men without even catching sight of the enemy. "It is like warring against Arabs," Leclerc wrote to Napoleon. "No sooner have we passed than the blacks occupy the woods on both sides of the road and cut our communications." De Lacroix exclaims with a note of admiration: "Like a hundred-headed hydra they were reborn after every blow. At an order of Toussaint Louverture they sprang out of the ground. The earth was covered with them. His name was on everybody's lips. They talked only of him."

With his fortunes steadily rising and those of the enemy falling, Toussaint suddenly reached the seemingly inexplicable decision to come to terms with Leclerc.

# CHAPTER IX

## Toussaint Decides to Submit

General Hugo, member of the French General Staff, discussing the situation existing in St. Domingo at that time, avows himself puzzled at Toussaint's peace move. He writes: —

His [Leclerc's] progressive losses enabled him to foresee the time when his army would have ceased to exist. It is more difficult to comprehend why the Negro chieftains decided to make peace at a time when such a move was of greater advantage to the enemy than to them.

General de Lacroix, however, appears to have resolved the question quite satisfactorily in his own mind when he wrote: —

When the Captain General decided to accept the *apparent* submission of Toussaint Louverture, the army had already lost more than 5000 men in battle. An equal number of sick and wounded were hospitalized. Out of 23,000 men who had arrived up to that time, hardly 12,000 remained.

The word *apparent* tells the whole story. Toussaint's submission was feigned.

### 2

It will be remembered that in his "Secret and Confidential Instructions" Napoleon had ordered Leclerc to receive the Negro generals who wished to submit with open arms. During the First Phase, which was to last only fifteen days ("If it lasts longer than that we shall be dupes"), the generals who had submitted were to be left in command of their troops. During the Second Phase they were to be relieved of their commands and the

Negro troops were to be disarmed and disbanded. During the Third Phase the generals were to be arrested and sent to France. Leclerc, however, had found himself unable either to deprive the generals of their commands or to disarm and disband their troops. His white army was melting too fast to enable him to run the risk of such a move. Hence, on April 27, he reported to Decrès that his army was composed of 11,000 white and 9000 Negro soldiers, and made it plain that the Negro soldiers could not be relied upon.

Now Toussaint knew as well as, if not better than, Leclerc what went on in the French camp. He knew that Leclerc's wastage of white soldiers was considerably greater than the reinforcements he was receiving. The yellow fever had made its appearance earlier than usual that year. On May 7, Leclerc wrote to Napoleon that from 30 to 50 white soldiers were dying daily from that cause alone – a death toll that was to mount to 120 in September. Since Leclerc was not in a position either to deprive the black generals who submitted of their commands or to disband their troops, why not have all the Negro soldiers join Leclerc's army, wait a few months until the yellow fever had still further decimated the ranks of the French, then calmly step in, arrest the Captain General and his staff and send them back to France? That this plan would have succeeded, had Dessalines and Christophe remained loyal to him, may be judged from the fact that on September 26 Leclerc reported to Decrès: "The last month we have lost 3000 men from sickness alone. My entire army is destroyed, even the reinforcements you have sent." To Napoleon he wrote: "I do not have 200 men fit for service."

Toussaint, as well able as Leclerc to calculate when the French army would cease to exist, considered it a useless waste of life and property to go on with the war when the same result could be achieved by "apparent submission."

## 3

A too sudden reversal of policy might awaken Leclerc's suspicion, so Toussaint proceeded cautiously. He had never replied to Bonaparte's letter. A reply could be sent only through the medium of the Captain General, hence furnished an excuse for getting into communication with him. So Toussaint wrote a letter to Bonaparte. He maintained the fiction of loyalty to France, but said that if the First Consul wished hostilities to cease he must recall Leclerc. He chose a somewhat roundabout way of placing the letter in Leclerc's hands.

It will be remembered that before attacking Port-au-Prince, General Boudet had sent two emissaries to General Agé, and that the two officers, Sabès and Gémont, had been retained as hostages, on the demand of Lamartinière. When forced to abandon Port-au-Prince the mulatto general had taken the officers with him, and they were now in the prison camp at Marmelade. Toussaint sent for them, gave them a safe-conduct and a letter to General Boudet, in which he enclosed his letter to Napoleon. He asked Boudet to forward the letter to Leclerc, expressed his regret for the arrest of the two officers and said he hoped Boudet would release his nephew Bernard Chancy.

In the course of time Bernard Chancy arrived with a letter from Boudet, in which the French general assured the Negro leader that his dispatch to Napoleon would be forwarded. Soon Bernard Chancy departed with a second letter to Boudet, about which Toussaint says in his memorandum: –

From my nephew's report and after reading the letter of General Boudet, I thought I recognized in him a frank and honest nature, worthy of a French officer qualified to command. I therefore addressed myself confidently to him, begging him to persuade General Leclerc to enter into negotiations with me that might lead to conciliation. I assured him that ambition had never been my guide, but only honor; that I was ready to give up the command in obedience to the orders of the First Consul, and to make all necessary sacrifices to arrest the spread of the evil.

## 4

If Toussaint was anxious to enter into negotiations, Leclerc's reasons for wishing to do so were far more pressing. He had, however, given up hope of coming to an understanding with Toussaint and hence tried to seduce as many of his generals as possible. He undoubtedly realized that once they joined his forces they would be so many Trojan horses, but their adherence, however temporary, would give him a breathing spell. It would enable him to conserve more of his rapidly dwindling white army while awaiting reinforcements. So he had Rochambeau write a letter to the Negro general Belair, who was Toussaint's nephew and favorite, assuring him that if he would abandon his chief he would be richly rewarded. Belair turned the letter over to Toussaint.

Christophe received a letter from a mulatto named Vilton, with whom he had been on intimate terms. Vilton suggested that he and Christophe meet and talk things over. General Hardy had assured him that if Christophe changed sides he would be showered with favors. Shortly after Hardy himself wrote and suggested a meeting. Christophe sent copies of both letters to Toussaint, who notes in his memorandum: "General Christophe communicated to me a letter he had received from a citizen named Vilton and another from General Hardy, both asking for an interview. I gave permission to General Christophe to hold those interviews, recommending to him to be very circumspect."

## 5

Leclerc was worried about Christophe's delay in replying to Vilton and furthermore thought that the black general should have been given a hint of what was expected of him. Before Christophe had had time to arrange the interviews authorized by Toussaint, he received this letter from the Captain General: –

You can put entire trust, Citizen General, in everything Citizen Vilton has written you in the name of General Hardy. I will keep the promises that have been made you. But if it is your intention to offer your submission to the Republic, think of the great service you can render by enabling us to secure the person of Toussaint Louverture.

Christophe's reply does him honor: –

You propose to me, Citizen General, that I furnish you the opportunity to secure the person of General Toussaint Louverture. That would be a perfidious and treacherous act. I see in this degrading proposal a demonstration of your inability to attribute to me any susceptibility to the demands of honor and fair play. He is my chief and my friend. Is it your opinion that friendship is compatible with such monstrous and cowardly conduct?

Leclerc hastened to reply that Christophe's refusal to set a trap for Toussaint only strengthened the high opinion he already had of his character. He proposed that Christophe meet him at Haut-du-Cap, and gave him his word of honor that if they failed to reach an understanding he would be allowed to depart unhindered. Christophe sent copies of the correspondence to Toussaint, who says in his memorandum: "He sent me a copy of his [Leclerc's] letter and of his reply and asked my permission to go to the appointed place. I gave him permission and he went."

Christophe went therefore to meet Leclerc as Toussaint's envoy. Leclerc knew this, for at the conclusion of the interview he gave Christophe a letter for Toussaint.

## 6

It was obviously to Leclerc's interest to get Christophe to come to an immediate private arrangement with him regarding the army he personally commanded. This would make it difficult for Toussaint to break off negotiations. For Christophe to enter into such a private agreement was of course equivalent to treason. How the man who only a few days before had indignantly repudiated the suggestion that he betray his chief was persuaded to follow such a course, we do not know. The only excuse he ever offered is that "he was tired of living like a savage" and that "circumstances got the better of him." It is possible that he feared Toussaint might change his mind and wished to force his hand. Anyway, he and Leclerc reached this understanding: –

Christophe was to turn over certain strategic points to the French and was to release 2000 white hostages he was holding. He was to dismiss the armed cultivators with his army and with his 1500 regulars was to join Leclerc's forces. He was to retain his rank and his command and most of his other prerogatives.

Leclerc then gave him a letter for Toussaint in which he expressed the hope that they might soon come to an understanding, but said not a word concerning the private agreement he had made with his envoy. Christophe evidently was conscious of guilt, for when he called on his chief to deliver the letter and to report, he, too, said nothing concerning the agreement he had concluded.

Toussaint, however, was not to remain long in the dark. When Christophe returned to his headquarters and began taking measures to carry out his pact with Leclerc, he found a near-mutiny confronting him. Colonel Barade sent a messenger to Toussaint and the commander of Dondon refused to turn the town over to the French. Christophe arrested Barade and several others, but numerous officers and soldiers deserted and went to join Toussaint's forces.

Toussaint found it difficult to believe that having treason upon his conscience Christophe would have come to report to him. He thought there must be a misunderstanding and sent an aide-de-camp to Christophe to ask him to come and explain matters. The general replied that he would come "if circumstances did not get the better of him." He never came and Toussaint was forced to accept the fact that he had been deserted by still another general. Isaac Louverture writes: "The affair of Christophe having become known among the people and the soldiers, the air was filled with reproaches against him and a crowd gathered before the house of Toussaint Louverture to assure him of their devotion, resolution and loyalty."

## 7

Toussaint wrote an angry letter to Leclerc, accusing him of bad faith and reminding him that he would "always be strong enough to lay the country waste and to sell his life dearly." That his position remained strong is confirmed by de Lacroix, who writes: "Entrenched in the heart of the colony, in the midst of inaccessible mountains, whence he could sally forth and spread destruction and revolt, he would have never ceased being formidable. The evil he had already done was proof of what he was still capable of doing."

So Leclerc thought it best to reply in a conciliatory fashion and to invite further negotiations. Toussaint proposed that they meet at Héricourt. Leclerc made the counterproposal that Toussaint send emissaries. Toussaint appointed the Jewish merchant Nathan, who had become his secretary, and his aide-de-camp Couppé. They traveled to Le Cap, and this agreement was drawn up between them and Leclerc, subject to Toussaint's approval: –

Toussaint was to retire from active service, but could retain his staff and reside where he wished.

The liberty of the Negroes and mulattoes of St. Domingo

was not to be infringed upon, and their rights as citizens were to be respected.

All Negro and mulatto officers were to preserve their rank and were to remain in active service.

In a letter to Napoleon, Leclerc claims that Toussaint had demanded the office of Lieutenant Governor for himself, and for his generals continued jurisdiction over the territory they had supervised before the invasion. The fact, however, is that the terms were unimportant. Neither side meant to abide by them. The French had no more intention of respecting the liberty of the blacks than Toussaint had of remaining in retirement. Convinced as he was that the French meant to enslave his people, how could he have done so? As for the Negro officers remaining in active service, they would do so only as long as Leclerc felt too weak to run the risk of dismissing them.

A number of matters had been left at loose ends by the emissaries. The principal one concerned Dessalines. The French had such a horror of a man who massacred whites with no more compunction than they themselves showed in massacring Negroes that they refused to have any dealings with him. Toussaint, however, felt that he could not dispense with Dessalines and insisted that he must retain his command. It was therefore decided that he and Leclerc should meet at Mornets, eight miles from Le Cap, to settle this and other matters.

# CHAPTER X

## Toussaint and Leclerc

It was generally believed that Toussaint would reconsider and the meeting at Mornets would not take place, but before the advent of the day appointed for the interview, Toussaint suddenly announced that he meant to beard the lion in his den –

call on Leclerc at Le Cap. He departed in the early morning of May 6, taking with him Isaac, his staff and an escort of four hundred dragoons of his bodyguard, under the command of Colonel Morisset.

At an advance post he met the French general Fressinet, whom he had known in the days of Laveaux. Fressinet greeted him cordially and joined his party. Rumor of the Negro leader's coming had reached the city, and as Toussaint, side by side with Fressinet, rode through the ruined streets, crowds assembled to see him pass. Negroes and mulattoes cheered, but a group of white men booed him and made insulting remarks. Toussaint turned to Fressinet and said: "That is how men are. I have seen them crawl at my feet – these men who now insult me. They may yet live to regret me."

*They did live to regret him.* Miss Hassall writes to Aaron Burr: "Many of the Creoles who had remained on the island during the reign of Toussaint, regret the change and say that they were less vexed by the Negroes than by those who have come to protect them." Toussaint had taxed them 25 per cent of their revenue, Leclerc and his successor Rochambeau demanded 50 per cent and extorted large subsidies besides. Toussaint had done away with vagabondage, but under Leclerc's rule the French soldiers became mendicants. Miss Hassall writes: "The poor soldiers, badly clothed and still more badly fed, are asking alms in the streets and are absolutely dying of want." It may not have been true, as she charges, that Leclerc, at the instigation of Pauline, had "a superb service of plate made with the money intended to pay the army," but vast sums were squandered on lavish entertainment while the soldiers received no pay and short rations.

## 2

As Toussaint and his escort rode towards the Government House an incident occurred that may well have had a decisive effect on the future course of events. A Negro officer, Colonel

Robillard, who served under Christophe, came riding up, saluted, and pressing close to his former chief, so that the flanks of their horses almost touched, said in an undertone: –

"I have been sent by General Christophe, who is awaiting your orders."

Either Toussaint's resentment at Christophe's breach of faith was too great to allow him to put further trust in the Negro general, or he suspected a trap; anyway he said coldly: "I am pleased to see you, Colonel, but as far as your mission is concerned, I have no reply to make."

A moment later his eyes blazed with anger, for he had sighted a Negro officer, one of the first who had deserted to the enemy, astride his favorite charger Bel-Argent. Hardy had got possession of the horse when he raided Toussaint's plantations at Ennery, and had presented the animal to the Negro.

## 3

Leclerc was lunching with Vice-Admiral Magon on board the flagship when news reached him of Toussaint's unexpected arrival. He ordered that the forts and the warships fire a salute and sent word to Generals Hardy and Debelle to receive Toussaint with full military honors. A fashionable convent school near the seashore – the only large building in the city that had escaped the flames – had been transformed into a Government House, and as Toussaint and his escort rode up, commands rang out and white soldiers presented arms. Morisset's dragoons ranged themselves opposite the building and throughout Toussaint's long visit remained in the saddle, swords drawn, faces grim, ready to intervene at a moment's notice.

As Toussaint and his staff were ushered into the reception hall, they found Hardy and Debelle, surrounded by high-ranking officers, standing under a full-length portrait of the Captain General. There were military salutes and courtesies. A collation was served. Soon after, Leclerc himself, slight and vivacious, came bustling into the room. He wore a general's undress uniform and had a handkerchief knotted about his head. He rushed up to Toussaint, seized his hand with a show of cordiality, then linked his arm through his and led him into the adjoining work cabinet. Here he bade him seat himself upon a sofa and sat down beside him.

"Your presence," he said, "is proof of your magnanimity and good faith. Our reconciliation will make this island, of which you have been the restorer, blossom anew."

Toussaint remained cold and distant and switched the conversation to their disagreement concerning Dessalines. Isaac Louverture writes: "He [Leclerc] promised to employ Generals Belair and Vernet, but not General Dessalines, about whom a difficulty arose, which, however, was soon smoothed out when Toussaint pointed out that to make such an exception would be an infraction of the treaty they had made." Toussaint writes in his memorandum: "General Leclerc said to me, 'But tell me if General Dessalines will obey my orders and if I can rely on him.' I replied that he could; and that General Dessalines might have his faults, like any man, but that he understood military discipline."

It is one of the ironies of fate that Toussaint was insisting on the retention in active service of a man who was to be principally responsible for his arrest, and who, until he became convinced that the French cause was hopeless, proved the most solid prop of the invaders.

But the concession concerning Dessalines did not put Toussaint in a better humor. He reproached Leclerc with the manner in which he had assumed command and with the misfortunes he had brought upon a country that had been peaceful and prosperous before his arrival. The Captain General, anxious to gain his confidence, so as to avoid fresh difficulties he was ill prepared to meet, humbled himself to the extent of saying: "It is true, I was lacking in self-control. But let us forget the past. Everything will be made right. Let us rejoice at our conciliation,

General. Your son, the officers that are with you, my own generals and officers must witness our accord."

He got up, threw open the door and bade all those assembled in the reception room to enter.

Among those who entered was Toussaint's brother Paul. Toussaint had been deeply grieved by his defection, not suspecting that the ruse he had employed in communicating with him was responsible. As his brother approached him with outstretched hand, he frowned, took a step backward and said: "Stop! I should have heard of your submission only after I myself had decided to lay down the sword. You should have regulated your conduct by mine, as time is regulated by the sun."

Then he turned his back upon Paul, who withdrew, hurt and puzzled.

The Negro leader's face relaxed, however, when the eleven-year-old Saint-Jean, whom Hardy had captured during his attack on Gonaïves, came running into the room and threw himself into his father's arms. Leclerc, who was responsible for the reunion, was pleased with the effect it had produced and now asked Toussaint and his officers to remain for dinner.

During the dinner Toussaint sat in the place of honor on Leclerc's right, but remained moody and noncommittal. Although tempting viands and choice wines were offered him, he partook of nothing except a piece of cheese and a glass of water. When Leclerc asked him, "Tell me, General, if the war had continued, where would you have obtained arms and supplies?" he replied gruffly: "I would have taken them from you."

At eleven o'clock that same evening Toussaint and his escort departed for Marmelade.

## 4

It had been agreed that Toussaint's bodyguard was to enter the service of the French. The grenadiers, under Magny, were to depart for Plaisance; the dragoons, under Monpoint and

Morisset, were to be stationed at Le Cap. On his return to Marmelade Toussaint reviewed the guard and addressed the men, lauding their valor and their loyalty and bidding them farewell. He shook hands with each officer and then, motionless in the saddle, watched the guard depart.

He had announced that he meant to retire to the Desfourneaux plantation, and immediately after the review left for Ennery, accompanied by his sons and his staff. At Ennery a great crowd had assembled. Negroes and mulattoes had come from as far as L'Arcahaye. But there was no acclaim. Faces were mournful. In the eyes lifted up to his Toussaint read silent reproach. Then a voice cried: "Papa Toussaint, have you forsaken us?"

He drew himself up and according to the testimony of Isaac gave this significant answer: "No, my children. Your brothers are under arms; the officers of all ranks are at their posts."

# CHAPTER XI

## Toussaint's Arrest

Napoleon's orders were to arrest Toussaint as soon as opportunity offered, but that order could not have been carried out had not several of the most powerful Negro generals insisted on the arrest and deportation of their former chief.

De Lacroix and Leclerc have testified that Toussaint's former generals demanded that he be deported. "All the generals, even Dessalines, came to me with charges against Toussaint Louverture," writes Leclerc. That all the generals did so is untrue. Toussaint's nephew, Charles Belair, remained loyal to him, as did Toussaint's brother-in-law, the mulatto General Vernet.

Paul Louverture, who had found an opportunity to explain to his brother the circumstances leading to his submission and had become reconciled with him, also was of his party. But that Maurepas, Clerveaux and Christophe should have feared Toussaint's return to power need not surprise us. They had betrayed him and feared the fate in store for them if Toussaint carried out his plan to overthrow Leclerc when the yellow fever had still further decimated the French army – an intention they either knew or suspected. Christophe, who evidently regretted his breach of faith and had wished to make amends, had met with a rebuff when he had sent Robillard to his former chief. His instinct of self-preservation told him that his only safety now lay in making Toussaint's return to power impossible.

But why Dessalines? He had not submitted until Toussaint had told him to do so. "I urged him to submit, as I myself had done," Toussaint writes in his memorandum. Yet de Lacroix informs us that Dessalines came to Le Cap with the express purpose of urging Toussaint's arrest. The explanation must be sought in Dessalines's mentality and character.

There can be no question of Dessalines's military ability, but he was unprincipled and had no more sentiment for the people of his race than the African chieftains who sold their subjects into slavery. He had remained loyal to Toussaint because he felt he had nothing to hope for from the whites, having massacred prisoners and hostages. Now, however, that Leclerc had agreed to keep him in active service, he decided to make himself indispensable to him. This involved massacring the guerrillas, who had not laid down their arms – a course of procedure Toussaint was sure to resent. In addition to this he had a grudge against Toussaint, who, convinced that Dessalines was unfit to be a ruler, had made no secret of the fact that when the time came for him to retire permanently, he meant to appoint Charles Belair as his successor. It became Dessalines's policy not only to get Toussaint out of the way, but also to undermine his colleagues, so he would have no rival for Leclerc's favor. "Dessalines has begun bearing tales against Christophe and Morpas [Maurepas]," Leclerc wrote to Napoleon.

Toussaint evidently had not counted on the defection of Dessalines. With Dessalines, Belair and Vernet to support him there can be no doubt that September of that same year would have witnessed the arrest and deportation of Leclerc and his staff and the return to power of Toussaint Louverture.

## 2

Leclerc was anxious to carry out Napoleon's order to arrest Toussaint if this could be accomplished without great hazard. The stand taken by Dessalines made this appear possible. He decided, however, to proceed with caution and began by greatly increasing the French garrison at Ennery. Hitherto only fifty white soldiers had been stationed there, now five hundred were sent under the command of Colonel Pesquidon. This was not to Toussaint's liking and there followed an acrimonious correspondence between him and the Captain General. Toussaint complained that the soldiers were terrorizing the Negro inhabitants and were committing depredations upon his plantations. Leclerc countered by accusing Toussaint of encouraging Sylla and other guerrilla leaders and of maintaining a private military force.

Assuming that Toussaint meant to regain power, maintenance of relations with the guerrillas appears logical. As for the second accusation, Toussaint's bodyguard had proved so insubordinate that it had to be dismissed. Officers and men had found their way to Ennery and had been taken back into service by Toussaint under the guise of overseers and laborers. There is reason to believe that they acted in accordance with a preconceived plan.

Toussaint wrote a reply and dispatched his son Isaac to deliver it. The reply – a general denial of the charges – contained a covert threat. He said that unless the annoyances ceased, he would leave Ennery and take up his residence on a property he owned in the Spanish part of the island. This may well have meant that he would go into the mountains and resume hostilities. Leclerc decided there was no time to lose. To place Toussaint under arrest at Ennery, where he was in position to offer armed resistance, was out of the question, so he gave Isaac this letter to Toussaint: –

Since you persist, Citizen General, in thinking that the number of troops [stationed at Ennery] frightens the laborers, I have instructed General Brunet to confer with you regarding the transfer of a part of these troops to Gonaïves and Plaisance.

At the same time he sent his aide-de-camp Ferrari with instructions to Brunet to invite Toussaint to his headquarters and place him under arrest.

Soon after Isaac's return Toussaint received a letter from General Brunet, of which this is the most significant portion: –

We have, my dear General, to reach an understanding concerning measures which it is impossible to take up by correspondence, but which an hour's conference will settle. If I were not worn out by work and petty cares I would have come today instead of writing to you; but since I am unable to leave, will you not come to me?

If you have recovered from your indisposition, let it be tomorrow. When good is to be done, there should be no delay. You will not find in my house all the comforts I should like to put at your disposal, but you will find a frank and honest man, whose only ambition is to promote the welfare of the colony and your happiness. If Madame Toussaint, whose acquaintance I am very anxious to make, wishes to accompany you, it will give me pleasure. If she needs horses I will send her mine.

I repeat, General, you will never find a sincerer friend than you have in me.

## 3

Warnings had reached Toussaint from numerous sources that Leclerc meant to have him arrested. Paul Louverture had sent him a warning. General Vernet had done the same. Ferrari, passing through Ennery on his way to Brunet with the order of arrest, had boasted about his mission and the boast had been reported to Toussaint. When the Negro leader went to Ennery he noticed that French officers and soldiers no longer saluted him. From Gonaïves came word that two boatloads of soldiers had arrived and that Toussaint's arrest was imminent. It remains a mystery why in the face of all this Toussaint, one of whose favorite proverbs was "Distrust is the mother of security," went to call on Brunet. He knew that he could no longer rely on Dessalines, for Leclerc had shown a letter to Isaac in which the black general accused his former chief of complicity with the guerrilla leader Sylla. What seems most probable is that Toussaint was deceived by the tone of Brunet's letter.

It has been said of Benjamin Franklin that he was exceedingly cunning, but was the soul of candor when dealing with a candid man. This was also true of Toussaint. He believed he saw candor in Brunet's letter and banished all suspicion. On the morning of June 7 – almost exactly a month after his visit to Leclerc – he departed for Brunet's headquarters on the Georges plantation accompanied only by Placide and his aide-de-camp César.

## 4

Toussaint arrived on the Georges plantation at eight o'clock that same evening. He writes in his memorandum: "When he [General Brunet] met me, I told him that I had received his letter and a letter from the Commander in Chief requesting me to act in concert with him, and that I had come for that purpose. I said that I had not brought my wife, as he requested, because she never left home, being very occupied with domestic duties, but that if sometime, when he was traveling, he would do her the honor of visiting her, she would be pleased to receive him."

He then handed Brunet Leclerc's letter. The General glanced at it and said that he had not yet heard from the Captain General concerning the matter. He asked Toussaint to be seated, begged to be excused for a moment and left the room. Toussaint was not to see him again. "He had probably hid himself to escape my merited reproaches," he later wrote to Napoleon.

It was still light, but the sun was nearing the horizon. The Negro leader sat and waited. He did not know that immediately after he had entered the house soldiers with fixed bayonets had surrounded the building. Suddenly the door opened and Ferrari entered, a pistol in one hand, a sword in the other. Behind him was a company of soldiers. Toussaint sprang to his feet and drew his sword. Ferrari advanced, sword lowered, and said: "General, the Captain General has ordered your arrest. Your officers are already in custody. Our men are everywhere. If you resist you are a dead man. Your power in St. Domingo is at an end. Hand over your sword."

Toussaint sheathed his sword and said: "I rely on the protection of General Brunet. He has given me his word of honor."

Ferrari gave a signal. The soldiers threw themselves upon the Negro leader, took away his sword and tied his hands behind his back. He protested vainly against the indignity.

A carriage and an escort of dragoons were waiting. Toussaint was hustled into the carriage, Ferrari seated himself opposite him, and the vehicle drove off towards Gonaïves. Detachments of soldiers were stationed at short intervals along the road to the town.

It was midnight when the carriage reached Gonaïves and drove through the deserted streets towards the harbor. Toussaint was rowed to the warship *Créole*, which immediately lifted anchor and sailed for Le Cap. The captain of the ship treated Toussaint with great courtesy and offered him money and a change of linen. He was not the only man in the French army who sympathized with him and disapproved of the manner of his arrest. The French soldiers henceforth referred to General Brunet contemptuously as "the Gendarme."

Four miles from Le Cap, Toussaint was transferred to the frigate *Héros* and confined to a cabin, with a sentry guarding the door. The ship remained in the offing for several days until another ship arrived with Toussaint's family. They, too, were transferred to the *Héros*, which set sail for Brest.

General Severin, in charge of the prisoners, has testified that when Toussaint boarded the frigate he uttered these prophetic words: "In overthrowing me they have only felled the tree of Negro liberty in St. Domingo. It will shoot up again, for it is deeply rooted and its roots are many."

## 5

Leclerc issued a proclamation in which he said: "He [Toussaint] had sent his accomplices to General Dessalines to explain to him that his surrender was not to be in good faith. General Dessalines told me so himself." He likewise published two letters allegedly written by Toussaint to his aide-de-camp Fontaine, at Le Cap. The letters, if genuine, would furnish conclusive proof of Toussaint's intention to overthrow Leclerc as soon as the yellow fever had sufficiently weakened the French army. Toussaint has claimed that the letters were forged and the charge appears well founded. The forgery must have been a clumsy one, for when Decrès, wishing to bring Toussaint to trial, wrote for proof of the Negro leader's guilt, the Captain General replied: "I have plenty of evidence to convict him, if it is desired to use documents relating to his conduct before the amnesty I accorded him. I have none dating later than that."

This can only be interpreted as an admission of the apocryphal character of the Fontaine letters; nevertheless Fontaine was executed for having been the recipient.

But apocryphal or no, the letters accurately reflect the Negro leader's intentions. Knowing – as he unquestionably did – what Napoleon's plans were concerning the restoration of slavery, Toussaint's surrender *could* not have been final. Had it been final then he would have been guilty of treason towards his own people.

# CHAPTER XII

## Toussaint's Imprisonment and Death

THE *Héros* with the Louvertures and Chancys on board set sail for Brest on the fifteenth of June. During the journey Toussaint was kept a prisoner in his cabin and was not permitted to see his family. He wrote to Bonaparte: "I endured every species of hardship, while my wife and children received treatment from which her sex and their rank should have preserved them." He would have frequent occasion to complain about the treatment meted out to him in captivity. "Doubtless," he writes in his memorandum, "I owe this treatment to my color. But my color – my color – has it prevented me from serving my country with zeal and loyalty? Does the color of my skin affect my honor or my valor?"

When on the ninth of July the ship dropped anchor at quarantine, Placide was given permission to serve his stepfather as secretary. Toussaint dictated letters to the First Consul and to the Minister of Marine. He protested against his arrest and especially against that of his family. "My wife has no accounting whatever to give," he wrote to Napoleon. "I alone am responsible to the Government." He tried to intercede for the members of his staff and his secretaries, all of whom had been taken into custody. "Whatever they have done, they did by my orders. Their arrest is not justified," he wrote to Decrès.

Soon word came that the family was to be dispersed. Suzanne, Isaac, Saint-Jean and Louise Chancy were to live at Bayonne. Placide was banished to Belle Ile. Bernard Chancy was ordered to Toulon. Toussaint was to be kept in the citadel of Brest, until the authorities had decided on a permanent place of confinement. His servant, Mars Plaisir, was to remain with him. The Negro leader was permitted to bid farewell to his family and was then led away.

## 2

Toussaint felt confident that Bonaparte would find it difficult to make out a legal case against him and repeatedly demanded a trial: "I demanded that General Leclerc and I be judged before a tribunal; that Government order my correspondence to be brought. By this means my innocence and all I have done for the Republic will be established." But just as he had allowed Moyse to be condemned without giving him an opportunity to be heard, so a hearing was now denied him by Napoleon. And the Corsican's turn, too, would come – he complained on St. Helena: "I was condemned without having received a hearing and without a trial."

Leclerc was opposed to trying Toussaint. "Under present circumstances," he wrote, "his trial and execution would still further inflame the Negroes." He advised: "He should be put in a fortress in the center of France, so he will never have the opportunity to escape and return to St. Domingo, where his influence is that of a religious chief. If this man were to return after three years, he could still undo all that has been accomplished." In another letter he writes: "You can't keep Toussaint far enough from the sea or in too secure a prison. This man has so fanaticized this country that his presence would suffice to set it on fire again."

In keeping with this advice, the Fort de Joux, in the Jura, near the Swiss frontier, was chosen to serve as the place of confinement. The Fort crowns the summit of a mountain of solid rock the sheer sides of which soar to a height of five hundred feet above the valley of the Doubs. The surrounding mountains are covered with snow eight months of the year. Since its erection in the ninth century the Fort has been altered and enlarged. It commands roads leading to the four points of the compass and in the Middle Ages was considered impregnable.

The history of the Fort contains pages that should satisfy the most exquisite taste for the gruesome. In the court the visitor is shown a well cut in the solid rock to a rivulet five hundred feet below. If a stone is dropped no sound ascends to announce its arrival at the bottom. The work was done by serfs, who, when depth was gained, were not permitted to ascend, but lived in recesses in the walls, where most of them died. The well, intended to serve when rain water gave out during a siege, has never been used.

The gray stone walls of the castle are twelve feet thick. In an outside wall the visitor is shown a recess, four feet long, three high, three deep, and provided with a heavy door in which there is a small barred window. Here a feudal lord of the castle, a certain Amoury, kept his seventeen-year-old wife, Berthe de Joux, imprisoned until her death ten years later. She had been unfaithful to him while he was on one of the Crusades. Through the barred window she could see, on the mountain opposite, the vultures wheel around the body of her lover, kept hanging from a gibbet throughout her imprisonment.

A more cheerful page has been furnished by the irrepressible Mirabeau, who beguiled a short imprisonment with a piquant love affair.

This grim stronghold, situated in a region where, in winter, the thermometer drops far below zero, and where even at the height of summer there is frequently a chill in the air, was chosen to house a man accustomed to a tropical climate. Toussaint might well have made the plaint Napoleon later uttered on

St. Helena: "Here they will sooner reach the goal they have in view."

## 3

The Ministers of War and of Marine shared responsibility for the prisoner, but he was considered of sufficient consequence likewise to engage the attention of the civil authorities – the Ministers of General Police and of Justice, prefects, sub-prefects, etc. The precautions taken in transferring him from the citadel of Brest to the Fort de Joux were so extensive as to suggest that Toussaint's sympathizers in France must have been fairly numerous and it was feared they might attempt a delivery. A coach and a chaise were purchased by the government to transport the prisoner and his servant. The coach was to be drawn by four horses, guided by two postilions. A carefully selected guard of twelve artillerymen, two gendarmes and an officer, all mounted, were to be the escort. The route the vehicle was to travel was kept secret and gave a wide berth to all important centers of population. The military commanders and prefects of all the departments through which the prisoner was to pass received orders to have the roads guarded and to exercise particular vigilance. When at d'Arcenis a small group of horsemen was sighted, the military commander of the district was immediately notified. He sent a message to the Minister of War, who communicated with the Minister of Marine, who wrote to the Minister of General Police, who notified the Minister of Justice, who ordered the prefects of two departments to investigate and send a detailed report.

There was one incident during the journey. The coach was to pass through a town where a regiment was stationed that in happier days had served in St. Domingo. When the officers learned the identity of the prisoner they decided to welcome him. Throughout the journey the curtains of the coach were carefully drawn, so it must have been with a feeling of alarm that Toussaint suddenly saw the doors fly open and a mob of officers take the vehicle by storm. But they merely wanted to shake his hand. Some even embraced him. It was the last pleasant experience fate had in store for him.

## 4

The Commandant of the Fort, Baille, an old curmudgeon, was not particularly happy about having Toussaint as a boarder. Two rebel officers from the Vendée, entrusted to his care, had recently given him the slip by filing the bars of their window and bribing a guard. Another such occurrence might compromise him gravely. The escape of the officers may have been responsible for the particularly severe instructions given regarding the watch to be kept over Toussaint. The Prefect of the Department wrote to the Subprefect: "The orders of the Minister are precise. Toussaint must not see anyone, nor may he be permitted to leave the room in which he is confined under any pretext whatever. The guard of the Fort should be set with the greatest exactness, and without relaxation of vigilance. Only the General of Division can modify the rigor of the orders, and I know that he will not do so without being authorized by the Minister. The Commandant must sleep at the Fort, unless especially authorized to the contrary by his superiors. The supplies of the prisoner have been prescribed. They must not be exceeded under any pretext. Every excess will be stricken off from the account."

Toussaint arrived at the Fort on the twenty-fourth of August. He was dressed in the uniform of a French general, the same he had worn the day of his arrest. Baille and an officer conducted him to the room he was to occupy. They crossed the court and went up a stoop to the guardhouse, where two heavy doors were unbolted and unlocked. They then entered a series of three gloomy corridors separated from each other by heavy iron-studded doors. Water dripped from the ceiling and in the third corridor had accumulated to a depth of six inches. The officer opened still another door and Toussaint beheld the place in which he was to be entombed for the remaining seven months of his life.

With its low, concave ceiling, the room resembled a burial vault or a section of a tunnel. It was twenty feet long by twelve wide. The deeply-embrasured window had been bricked up to two thirds of its height and light seeped in through a horizontal row of three small glass panes. Even these were obscured by a fine-meshed screen, to prevent the passing of notes. A narrow ribbon of sky and the roof of a barracks were dimly visible. The furniture consisted of a curtainless bedstead, a chest of drawers, a table and two chairs. The walls were clammy, but a small fireplace on the right gave promise of warmth and a little cheer.

Instructions were that the prisoner was to retain nothing reminiscent of his former rank and was to be known only as Toussaint. So, to his indignation, the Negro leader was now told to remove his uniform and to put on the clothes Baille handed him. "I have received," he wrote to Napoleon, "the old half-worn clothes of a soldier and shoes in the same condition. Was it necessary to add this humiliation to my misfortunes?" The Empress Josephine, who in her memoirs shows such sympathy with Toussaint, wonders if retributive justice was responsible for the treatment Bonaparte later received on St. Helena. When Napoleon complains: "Each day he [the Governor] invents new ways of tormenting and insulting me and makes me suffer fresh privations," it indeed sounds like an echo of the plaint Toussaint uttered at the Fort de Joux.

The prisoner was not searched, but was told to surrender weapons, money, jewelry or papers he carried upon his person. He kept back several gold pieces and two letters and was allowed to keep his watch.

Mars Plaisir was housed in the adjoining room, but after two weeks the authorities decided that the prisoner could do without a servant and the faithful Negro was sent to Nantes, whence, eventually, he returned to St. Domingo.

## 5

Toussaint was accustomed to an outdoor existence and to ceaseless activity. The climate of St. Domingo might be deadly to Europeans; with him it had agreed. Notwithstanding his fifty-eight years he had been able to endure fatigues and privations without ever incurring a serious illness. But now, in this alien climate, confined in a cellar-like room, where only the ghost of sunlight penetrated, condemned to inaction, brooding about the past, his decline was rapid. Almost from the beginning he needed the services of a physician. He suffered from headaches, a stomach disorder and rheumatism. His lungs became affected. His teeth troubled him and an army surgeon came and pulled five. The prisoner was given wood for his fireplace and continually kept a fire going, yet shivered with the cold. Three weeks after his imprisonment, Napoleon's aide-de-camp, Caffarelli, who came to interview him, wrote: "I found him trembling with cold and ill. He suffered a great deal and was barely able to speak."

He became querulous. The man who even at the height of his career had led a Spartan existence overwhelmed Baille with complaints about food and clothing. He must have more sugar. He must have coffee. He must have collars of a certain kind. He must have handkerchiefs to tie around his head. He must have a hat. When four handkerchiefs were brought him instead of the six he had asked for, he grumbled, and he complained about their quality. The Prefect writes: "I notice, Citizen, that the prisoner Toussaint makes every day new demands, either for objects that are out of place in a prison or for articles of food the abuse of which might injure his health rather than improve it. It is the intention of the Government to furnish him what he really requires, but not to be prodigal."

Prodigality in the maintenance of its political prisoners was not one of the Government's weaknesses, but the charge that Toussaint was systematically starved is unfounded. Four francs a day (about eighty cents), which the Government paid to a tavernkeeper in the town below for Toussaint's food, washing and mending, did not condemn a man to starvation. Many a student in the Latin Quarter of Paris lived on less than half that amount. The food was served cold to Toussaint, but he had facilities for heating it. At nine o'clock in the morning a daily supply was brought to his cell. Salt meat, cheese, bread and wine are mentioned in the reports, and Baille wrote that the prisoner put sugar into everything he drank.

The Commandant tried to humor him. When Toussaint complained about the scanty sugar ration he gave him sugar from his own pantry, but wrote to the Prefect that he would be unable to continue doing so. He was the only person with whom the prisoner was allowed to converse. "I see Toussaint every day," he wrote to the Minister of Marine. "He talks to me about his situation, which seems to affect him greatly, and about his political affairs, concerning which, I find, he often varies. I have noticed that when he tells something that is manifestly untrue and imagines I believe him, he can't resist smiling a little. To hide his smile he covers his mouth with his hand."

Toussaint had asked for writing material and the privilege had been granted. When he told Baille that he wished to write a report and a letter to the First Consul, but was used to dictating, the Commandant sent him his secretary Jeannin. He dictated to Jeannin his famous memorandum, which is partly a recital of his campaigns, partly a statement of his grievances. He writes in the first paragraph: "I will relate the facts with all the simplicity and frankness of an old soldier, adding to them the reflections that naturally suggest themselves. In short, I will tell the truth, though it be against myself."

But he no more told the truth than Napoleon has done in his Memorial of St. Helena. Both men wrote for purposes of self-justification. Toussaint wished to justify himself before Bonaparte; Bonaparte wished to justify himself before posterity. Napoleon was too shrewd a man to be deceived by Toussaint, and the legend Napoleon's memoirs created with the help of Béranger, Hugo and other romantics has not lasted. Nobody today believes that he was "a crowned Washington," "the martyr of an immortal cause." He fascinates precisely because he was completely amoral, because at the sacrifice of every moral principle known to man he dared "to live his dreams while others dream their lives." Conscience was to him what it was to Richard III in Shakespeare's play of that name: –

> . . . but a word the cowards use,
> Devised at first to keep the strong in awe.

## 6

Toussaint wrote to the First Consul that he had important revelations to make. Now, there were a number of things on which Bonaparte desired enlightenment. He wished to know the principal clauses of the secret treaty Toussaint had made with Maitland, and where Toussaint had hidden his treasure – for that a treasure existed he did not doubt for a moment. Most of all he wished Toussaint to confess that independence had been his goal. Things were going from bad to worse with the Leclerc expedition and murmurs were heard against Bonaparte's colonial policy. Even Josephine, who regretted the loss of the revenue from the Beauharnais plantation, had joined the critics. The *émigré* planters had lost all their enthusiasm for the expedition, and those who had remained in the colony sighed for the order and security they had enjoyed under Toussaint. All this was very annoying to the man who wished to make himself Emperor. Nothing would have justified him more before public opinion than an admission on the part of Toussaint that he had striven for complete independence. No sooner therefore had Bonaparte received the Negro leader's letter than he dispatched his aide-de-camp, Caffarelli, to interview him. The choice of Caffarelli proves the importance he attached to the matter, for the General was one of his ablest negotiators. Two years later he sent him to Rome on a particularly delicate mission – to persuade the Pope to come to France and crown him Emperor.

It was on the fifteenth of September that the dapper young general (he was then in his thirty-sixth year) waded through the flooded corridor to Toussaint's room. What he saw must have shocked him. He had come to interview a man with whose name two continents had buzzed, who had provoked the sending of the largest fleet and the most powerful expeditionary force that had ever crossed the Atlantic, whose growing power France, England and Spain had regarded as a menace to their possessions in the New World, whom the Directory and Napoleon had considered sufficiently strong to wage war upon Great Britain and the United States – and he saw a little, shrunken old Negro, dressed in a worn, ill-fitting soldier's uniform, with a handkerchief tied about his gray hair – a man shivering with ague, whose features were twisted with pain. But Caffarelli was a man of the world and gave no inkling of his surprise. "I told him," he writes, "that it was a great satisfaction for me to meet a man whose name had gained such renown, who had done or had attempted to do such extraordinary things, and that, if he was willing to tell me about them I should be pleased to listen."

He then intimated that if the interview turned out to be satisfactory Toussaint's lot would undergo a favorable change.

Toussaint's trembling made it difficult for him to speak, but with an effort of the will he mastered it and launched into a spirited account of all that had taken place in St. Domingo. Caffarelli listened attentively and promised to return on the morrow.

During his second visit Toussaint gave him the memorandum he had dictated, which, however, contained nothing that could be of value to Napoleon. Caffarelli made seven visits to the prisoner, the last on September 27, but gained no useful information. In his report he writes: "This man, willfully deceitful and secretive, self-possessed, adroit and subtle, speaking with a great show of sincerity, had his thesis all prepared and said nothing except what he wanted to say."

The negotiator put a number of questions to Toussaint. What were the principal clauses of the secret treaty he had made with Great Britain? Since they were less damaging than Napoleon undoubtedly imagined, Toussaint told him. Where had he hidden his treasure? He replied that he had none; he was "rich in land and cattle, but not in money." Was it not a fact that he had six of his guards bury his treasure and then had them executed? "He made a spirited denial and said that it was an atrocious calumny invented by his enemies." Did he not possess bank deposits in England, Jamaica or the United States? Toussaint untruthfully replied that he did not. "I've lost other things far more precious than money," he added.

All this, however, was of secondary importance. The really important thing was to get him to confess that it was Washington's example he had sought to imitate. But Toussaint would admit nothing. He kept repeating stubbornly that he had been faithful to the Republic, loyal to the First Consul. He conceded that it had been a mistake to proclaim the Constitution before submitting it for approval, nothing more. Then Caffarelli tried another tack. "I said to him," he writes, "that what he had told me thus far was unworthy of a man like him; that he was the foremost man of his race; that he had won military glory; that now he was broken, without hope of ever regaining his former state, but that there was another kind of glory, unknown to him, to which he might aspire. He could gain it by having the courage to step from behind the rampart of negation he had built around himself and boldly declare that he had driven out the Agents of the Republic because they had interfered with his plans, had organized the army and civil administration, had negotiated treaties, created a treasury, stocked the arsenals and powder magazines – all with the single purpose of achieving independence. By taking such a stand he would gain a glory such as could only be attained by genuine courage, and many things would be forgiven him."

One has the feeling that Caffarelli's purpose in making this appeal was not merely to be useful to his master, but that he wanted this captive and mortally wounded eagle to die as an eagle should – screaming defiance at his enemies. For a moment it seemed as if he might succeed. Toussaint remained silent and seemed to be meditating. But the habits of a lifetime are not cast off in a moment. All his life, in his intercourse with white men, he had had to gain his ends by devious means – to dissimulate, to pretend, to humble himself. He was, like Napoleon, a consummate actor, but heroic posturing was not in his line. His model was Ulysses. He again replied that he had been a faithful servant of the Republic and was attached to the First Consul.

Caffarelli notes with evident satisfaction that on two occasions he showed "elevation of spirit." The soldier's uniform that had been given him was a temporary expedient. "A warm coat and trousers, gray or brown in color, amply cut and comfortable, a round hat – such must be his clothing," the Minister of Marine had prescribed. The new clothes were brought to the prisoner during one of Caffarelli's visits. Toussaint had objected to exchanging his general's uniform for the worn clothes of a private; still, a soldier's uniform was a recognition of his military status. But this miserable outfit, such as a galley slave might wear – no, it was too much! He burst into vigorous invective, which did not displease the French general.

The second time was when Baille asked him to give up his razor. "He said," writes Caffarelli, "that those who required him to do so must be small-minded persons, since they imagined that he lacked the fortitude to bear his lot. Besides, he had a family and his religion forbade suicide."

Caffarelli assured Toussaint that he need feel no uneasiness concerning his family and undertook to forward a letter to his wife. He promised to intercede for him with Napoleon and to place the memorandum and a letter Toussaint had written in the First Consul's hands. Before turning the memorandum over to Caffarelli, Toussaint picked up a pen and in his queer phonetic spelling added this pathetic plea: –

"First Consul, Father of all soldiers, defender of the innocent, a man more unfortunate than guilty awaits your verdict. Cure my wounds, which are profound. You alone can apply to them the healing potion that will keep them from festering. You are the physician. My position, my services merit your attention. I count entirely on your sense of fairness and justice and send you my respectful salute."

Caffarelli's report contains this covert plea on behalf of Toussaint: "The prisoner is patient and resigned and expects from the First Consul the justice which he feels is due him."

For a short time after the visit Toussaint lived in hope. When it began to fade, he tried to revive it by writing to Caffarelli, whom he reminded of his promise, and to Bonaparte. The letters remained unanswered. The First Consul, displeased with the result of the interview, was not inclined to show mercy.

Then an incident occurred that greatly aggravated the lot of the prisoner.

## 7

In early October there came to the Fort a man named Dormoy, who represented himself as a doctor and asked for the privilege of examining Toussaint. Considering the strict orders issued from Paris against the admission of visitors, and the fact that an army surgeon could be obtained at Pontarlier, it is difficult to understand how he succeeded in gaining admittance. He was not a doctor, but an ex-priest and seminary teacher, who had been mayor of Dijon. What his purpose was in visiting Toussaint we do not know. It appears unlikely that he came with the intention of helping him to escape. He may have been driven by curiosity, or may have been a sympathizer who merely wished to shake his hand and say a few encouraging words. His identity was discovered shortly after the visit and he was arrested.

Whatever Dormoy's intention, his visit had serious consequences for Toussaint. Bonaparte himself took notice and Baille received a letter from the Minister of Marine in which that official says: "I am instructed by the First Consul to inform you that you are answerable with your life for the safekeeping of the prisoner."

A threat like that from Bonaparte meant exactly what it said. Baille was thrown into a panic. He had hitherto been amazingly lenient. Toussaint, in the letter to his wife he entrusted to Caffarelli, speaks of him as "humane." His failure to search the prisoner on his arrival, the gifts of sugar from his pantry, the loan of his secretary, the admission of Dormoy – all prove that he was inclined to indulge the prisoner. As so many white men before him he was impressed by some quality in Toussaint that had not deserted the Negro leader in his misfortune. In a letter to the Prefect he relates that a captain who had served in St. Domingo had told him Toussaint was often referred to in the colony as "His Majesty."

But now, with Bonaparte's threat hanging over him, Baille dared take no further chances. Accompanied by two subordinates he entered Toussaint's cell and ordered him to surrender every article of whatever kind he had brought with him to prison. When Toussaint demurred he threatened to have him searched and said that if anything was found he would put him in irons. Toussaint surrendered several gold pieces and two letters. His watch, too, was taken from him. The castle clock, which struck every quarter-hour, could be heard in the room and Baille said that this must suffice.

Henceforth nobody was permitted to see the prisoner. The Commandant himself brought him his food and even did such menial tasks as carrying out the slop pail. "I assure you," he wrote contritely to the Prefect, "that the Government can feel entirely safe concerning the prisoner, who is not seen by anybody except myself. I am the sole guardian of the keys and padlocks that keep him in confinement." He informed the Minister of Marine that unless he received orders to the contrary, no doctor (not even the army surgeon) would be allowed to visit Toussaint. He considered a doctor superfluous anyway, for – "the constitution of Negroes being entirely dissimilar from that of Europeans, the services of a doctor or surgeon could be of no possible use to him."

The Minister did not contradict this piece of anthropological wisdom, and although Baille reported Toussaint's condition as becoming steadily worse, no order was issued to admit a physician.

Baille's sudden severity convinced Toussaint that Bonaparte meant to have him executed and that these were the preliminaries. He wrote a letter to the First Consul and to the Minister of War and handed Baille a written protest, in which he says: "Nothing can compare with the humiliation to which you subjected me today. You have taken away my watch and the money I had in my pocket. I hereby serve notice on you that these objects are my personal property and that I will call you to account for them on the day I am executed, when I shall expect you to remit them to my wife and children."

This protest, dated November 1, 1802, was the last piece of writing he did in prison. Shortly after, an order came from Paris that writing material was to be taken from him, so he could no longer annoy officials with his epistolary complaints.

He now lived in expectation of the firing squad. This and the progress of the disease that was undermining him affected his disposition. When Baille came to see him he would talk sharply, stamp his feet and sometimes, in impotent rage, beat his head with his fists. He dropped all pretense of respect for the French and told the Commandant that they were a nation of "character assassins, wicked and unjust." He believed Leclerc's machinations to be mainly responsible for the harsh treatment he was receiving and when he spoke about the Captain General there was no end to his invective. To Napoleon he had written concerning Leclerc: "I can but compare him with the Roman Senate, pursuing Hannibal to the depths of his retreat." Curiously, Napoleon was to say on St. Helena about the British: "They are like the Romans who pursued Hannibal into the very depths of Bithynia."

## 8

Responsibility for the prisoner was beginning to weigh heavily upon the shoulders of the aged Commandant. He had begged the Prefect to allow him to buy a few planks, so he would not have to wade daily through the flooded corridor. He now wrote to the Minister of Marine that he must have a trusted assistant to share responsibility with him. "My duties at the Fort de Joux are so numerous that I have hardly a moment to myself. I am forced to fulfill the functions of commandant, janitor and hotel-keeper."

The result was what might have been expected. The Minister of War, Berthier, notified the Minister of Justice that he was relieving Baille from his command and had appointed Battalion Chief Amiot to take his place. He describes the new Commandant as "a young officer covered with wounds, whose morals are irreproachable and whose devotion to duty is unbounded." The change had the same consequences for Toussaint that the appointment of Hudson Lowe in the place of Admiral Cockburn had for the prisoner of St. Helena.

Amiot's devotion to duty was such that, not satisfied with frequent searches by day, he made repeated nocturnal visits to Toussaint's room. In the dead of night, in the midst of winter, the door would open, Amiot would enter followed by a subordinate carrying a lantern, order Toussaint out of bed and into the room formerly occupied by Mars Plaisir. Here the mortally ill man would sit shivering with the cold while his bed and room were searched. "He wants to shorten my life by constantly irritating me," Napoleon was to say of Hudson Lowe. Perhaps Amiot had a similar intention.

The result of this treatment was soon apparent. Amiot's successive reports reveal the increasing gravity of Toussaint's condition: –

Toussaint complains of pains in different parts of the body. I have also noticed that he has a dry cough.

He complains a great deal about stomach pains and does not eat as usual.

He has vomited a number of times. For several days I have noticed that his face is swollen.

His face is swollen. He complains continually about pains in the stomach. He has a very bad cough.

He coughs incessantly. He wears his arm in a sling because it hurts him. Since three days I have noticed that his voice has changed. He has never asked for a doctor.

Often the prisoner remained in bed all day and left his food untouched. One moment he burned with fever, the next he shivered with ague. The cough racked him. He breathed with difficulty. The pain in his stomach was a constant torture. When able to get up he would make a fire, and in a little earthen pot brew some herbs he had asked Amiot to procure for him. He would sit and sip the brew, watching the flames, or the snowflakes as they settled on the window panes – a novel sight to him. The wind would howl in the chimney and bluster about the eaves. Every quarter-hour the castle clock would strike. Had it known time's secrets it could have told Toussaint: "It is only twelve years until Waterloo."

With thoughts for his only companions the past must have often risen up before him. For himself he had given up all hope, but the future of his country must have often occupied him. He had prophesied that the tree of Negro liberty would shoot up again. It would have cheered him had he known that it was already doing so. Leclerc and several of his generals had followed thousands of officers and soldiers to the grave. There had been a mass uprising of the cultivators. Rochambeau was fighting a losing battle. But though he did not know, his faith in the ultimate victory of his people remained unshaken throughout his imprisonment. There is significance in the fact that in his conversations with Baille, with Caffarelli, with Amiot, and in his memorandum, so full of invective against Leclerc and his entourage, he does not make a single accusation against the Negro and mulatto generals who had abandoned and betrayed him. When Caffarelli tried to draw him out concerning Dessalines and Christophe, he curtly replied: "I do not wish to compromise anybody." It is as if he foresaw that sooner or later, for one reason or another, they, too, would join the battle for freedom. He, Toussaint Louverture, might be dying in prison in a hostile land, but the gate that he had opened could never be closed.

## 9

On April 3, 1803, Amiot found himself obliged to journey to Neufchâtel. He expected to be gone three or four days, but did not dare take the risk of turning over the keys of the prison to a subordinate. He told his second in command, Captain Colomier, that Toussaint would not need anything and departed.

Toussaint's biographers have charged that the journey was arranged for the express purpose of having the Negro leader die of starvation. If such had been the intention either of Amiot or of the Paris authorities the Commandant would have remained away longer. People do not usually die as a result of a four days' fast. Nor is there any certainty that he did not leave the prisoner a supply of food sufficient to last during his absence. Since the food was served cold he might easily have done so.

Sometime between April 3 and the forenoon of April 7,

when Amiot returned, Toussaint felt well enough to get up from bed and make a fire. He took a chair, placed it close to the wall, by the side of the fireplace, and sat down. Sitting there watching the flames he heard the castle clock strike for the last time. His heartbeats stopped; the light faded in his eyes; his body slumped against the wall; his head drooped; his right arm fell limp. The fire burned low and finally expired. Half an hour before sunset a soldier closed the shutter from the outside.

In the forenoon of the seventh of April Amiot returned from Neufchâtel. He took a tray of food and went to the dungeon. He entered Toussaint's room, placed the tray on the table and spoke to him. The prisoner did not reply. Amiot drew nearer, touched the motionless figure and saw that Toussaint was dead.

The autopsy throws no light on the probable time of his death, possibly to save embarrassment to Amiot. The cause is given as apoplexy and pneumonia. An examination of the stomach failed to disclose the reason for the frequent stomach pains.

Toussaint was buried in the basement of the chapel, in the presence of a priest. The grave was not marked.

Between 1876 and 1880, when Joffre, future Marshal of France, was Commandant of the Fort de Joux, alterations were ordered. The chapel was demolished. The skeletons found under the basement floor were thrown in pell-mell with the rubble later used in the construction of the new buildings. Embedded in the wall of one of these are the remains of the Greatest of the Blacks, the man who, Napoleon feared, might wrest the scepter of the New World from the hands of the white race.*

* A skull, supposedly Toussaint's, was for a long time exhibited in the room the Negro leader had occupied at the Fort de Joux. An official examination has established that it was the skull of a white man.

# EPILOGUE

The arrest of Toussaint Louverture had had immediate repercussions in St. Domingo. "After the deportation of Toussaint," Leclerc wrote to Decrès on June 11, "a few men attempted to start trouble. I have had them deported. Since then some of the colonial troops have shown a disposition to revolt. I have ordered the ringleaders shot and at present these troops hide their discontent." On the same day he wrote to Napoleon: "I have issued a proclamation concerning his conduct, but there have been tumultuous gatherings. I am sending the black generals to suppress them. Today one of Toussaint's mistresses has been arrested, who came here for the purpose of assassinating me."

Charles Belair, Toussaint's nephew, raised the standard of revolt. He was inveigled into a conference by Dessalines and arrested in the same treacherous manner as Toussaint had been. He and his heroic wife, who encouraged her husband to die in a manner worthy of him, faced the firing squad.

Daily the situation became more ominous. Leclerc reported nightly gatherings in the Plain and in Le Cap and avowed himself unable to discover the leaders. He decided that he must risk an attempt to disarm the cultivators, with the result that on August 6 he was forced to report: "When I wished to disarm the North a general insurrection broke out."

The situation became acute when news reached the colony that slavery had been restored at Guadeloupe. When Toussaint had warned the Negroes that nothing short of the restoration of slavery was Napoleon's intention, many, beguiled by the First Consul's and Leclerc's assurances, had not believed him. Now there could be no further doubt. Leclerc reported: "Immediately after the arrival of the news that slavery had been restored at Guadeloupe, the insurrection, which until then had been partial, spread to the entire colony." *

It was as spontaneous an uprising as history makes record of. Henry Adams has remarked: "The idea that leaders were everything, and masses without leaders nothing, was a military view of society which led Napoleon into all his worse speculations." Bonaparte had imagined that by arresting a handful of *nègres d'orés* he would render the Negroes of St. Domingo impotent. Now Toussaint was in prison and his generals in the camp of the enemy, but new chiefs were found under whose leadership the former slaves fought with frenzied courage. "The men die with a fanaticism that is unbelievable. They laugh at death. It is the same with the women," wrote Leclerc. And again: "There is veritable fanaticism in this insurrection. These men allow themselves to be killed to the last man, but will not surrender."

Who was it that now attempted to have the Negroes bow their necks under the yoke of slavery? Leclerc no longer possessed a white army. He had written to Napoleon that he did not have more than two hundred white soldiers fit for service. The men who had taken over the task of restoring slavery in St. Domingo were Dessalines and Christophe. "Dessalines and Christophe are doing well. I am under veritable obligation to them," Leclerc wrote to Decrès. To Napoleon he wrote: "Dessalines is at present the butcher of the blacks. I make use of him to carry out the most odious measures. He has already begged me not to leave him behind if I feel it necessary to depart." Of Christophe he writes: "To make up for his mistake of having espoused the cause of the blacks he has since maltreated them

* In his "Secret and Confidential Instructions" the cynical First Consul had told Leclerc to give the St. Domingo Negroes this assurance: "Never will the French nation put the chains of slavery on the wrists of men whom she has declared free. The Blacks will therefore live as free in St. Domingo as they live today at Guadeloupe."

in such a manner that they loathe him. I could have him deported without the slightest fear of an insurrection."

To restore slavery Leclerc thought it necessary to carry out this ambitious program he proposed to Napoleon: "All the Negroes of the mountains, women as well as men, must be put to the sword. Only children of less than twelve should be spared. As for those of the plains, about half should be killed. Not a Negro who has ever worn epaulettes should be left in the colony."

But it soon became obvious that Dessalines and Christophe would be unable to keep their men in line. On September 17 Leclerc writes: "The greater part of my colonial troops have deserted to the enemy." On September 25: "Every day the forces of the rebels grow stronger, mine weaker." On September 27: "The blacks are leaving me every day." Dessalines and Christophe realized that they would soon be generals without an army. They began throwing out anchors to windward. Leclerc writes of Dessalines: "A month ago when I would send him on an expedition, he would destroy arms. Now he no longer does so and he no longer maltreats the blacks as he did then."

It became evident that the generals were only waiting for a favorable opportunity to change sides once more. Maurepas, who had never wholeheartedly supported the French, seemed especially untrustworthy and Leclerc had him arrested in the hope that this would deter the others. The exact opposite happened. All the Negro and mulatto generals mutinied. Indeed, they had no other choice. Had they waited longer they would have been either arrested by Leclerc or killed by their own men.

The guerrillas were not at all enthusiastic about receiving the traitorous generals who had attempted to exterminate them. Sylla swore that he would split Christophe's head the first time he saw him. Eventually, however, the cultivators realized that the military talents of the generals could be of incalculable value to them and accepted their leadership. It is needless to say, however, that neither Dessalines nor Christophe should be credited with Haitian independence. But for their treason Toussaint would have maintained independence without sacrificing nearly a third of the black and almost the entire white populations.

## 2

The black plague that swept Europe in the Middle Ages could hardly have been more devastating than the yellow fever epidemic in St. Domingo proved to Europeans in the summer and autumn of 1802. Every evening after sunset carts preceded by drummers with crape-hung drums moved through the straight narrow streets of Le Cap, picking up the corpses laid out on the pavement. The bodies were buried in trenches dug on the outskirts of the city. Sometimes "a corpse" protested feebly that it was not yet ready for burial. A few shovelfuls of quicklime silenced the protest.

Under the leadership of Pauline the white inhabitants tried to forget the yawning grave in a continual whirl of amusement. "Nothing is heard of but balls and concerts," Miss Hassall writes. Love had many devotees, but there was no time for preliminaries: "In three days a love affair is begun and finished and forgotten; the first is for the declaration, the second is the day of triumph, if it is deferred so long, and the third is for the adieu."

The adieu was usually for eternity. Soldiers numbering 20,000 died; 9000 sailors, 3000 hangers-on of the army, 1500 officers, 700 doctors. Generals Debelle, Hardy, Dugua, Pambour, Perrin died. The Colonial Prefect Bénézech died. On November 1, 1802, Leclerc himself lay on his deathbed, cursing the ill-fated expedition.

Leclerc was thirty years old when he died. The repentant Pauline cut off her beautiful blond tresses and laid them in the coffin, which she accompanied to Marseilles. The man who came to St. Domingo to restore slavery lies buried in the Panthéon in

Paris, where is the sepulcher of Rousseau, who dreamt of liberty for the whole human race.

## 3

His uniform was *à la hussar*, and very brilliant; he wore red boots: – but his person is bad; he is too stout; a Bacchus-like figure.

This is the description Miss Hassall gives of Leclerc's successor, Rochambeau. The son of the Marshal of France, under whose orders he had fought to restore "the liberties of America," wrote to the Minister of Marine: "Slavery should be proclaimed in these regions and the Black Code should be made much more severe. I believe even that for a time the masters should have the right of life and death over their slaves."

To bring about this desirable state of affairs Rochambeau demanded 35,000 men. He received 20,000 and inaugurated a Reign of Terror that makes the notorious Carrier appear like an angel of mercy. His favorite method of disposing of his victims was the same as Carrier's: he drowned them by the shipload. He drowned so many that the Negroes refused to eat fish, "for fear they eat their own relatives." The salubrity of the coast cities was not enhanced by the corpses the sea washed ashore, which remained unburied on the beaches until birds picked the bones clean.

He did not confine himself to drowning. He fusilladed, made use of the hangman, buried alive, asphyxiated with sulphur fumes, indulged in such sadistic experiments as having sixteen Negro officers chained by the neck on a small uninhabited island, without either food or drink, and receiving daily reports concerning their condition. The last one died after seventeen days.

He tried his hand at the slave trade. For a while ships of the Republic that had *Liberté*, *Égalité*, *Fraternité* for its device hawked about slaves at bargain prices in the Caribbean. They found no takers. Nobody wanted Negroes from St. Domingo. When the ships returned, the unsalable human cargo was thrown overboard.

He had a taste for the gruesomely fantastic. Once, at Port-au-Prince, he invited the leading Negroes and mulattoes to a ball at the Palace. At midnight the music stopped. A double-winged door swung open, revealing a black curtain. It was drawn aside and the guests were invited to enter the adjoining room. It was hung and carpeted in black, with a frieze of skulls and crossbones. Bronze lamps suspended from the ceiling threw a sepulchral light upon coffins placed in the corners. An invisible orchestra struck up a mournful dirge and the amiable host said: "You are invited to dance your funeral dance."

Having learned that the Spaniards made use in Cuba of especially trained dogs to hunt slaves, he imported four hundred of the brutes, at a cost of 660 francs each. The boatload of man-eating canines arrived at Le Cap on March 1, 1803. Rochambeau decided to celebrate the occasion by having a Negro devoured for the entertainment of his friends. The spectacle took place in the court of the former Jesuit monastery. Officers dressed *à la Mameluc*, courtesans in gay attire, planters and their wives, wealthy merchants – the elite of the colony – occupied mounting tiers of seats in the cloister. A young Negro was brought in and chained to a post in the center of the court. The military band struck up a lively tune and several large, vicious-looking dogs bounded in. They had been starved in preparation for the event and it was expected that their slavering jaws would immediately fasten upon the black flesh. But nothing happened. The creatures ran about, barked, sniffed the helpless man, but did not harm him.

Rochambeau was furious. He felt cheated – shamed before his friends. General Boyer came to the rescue. It was the same Boyer who had spent a delightful afternoon restoring Pauline's slipper to her shapely foot – the same of whom Miss Hassall writes: "His form and face are models of masculine perfection; his eyes sparkle with enthusiasm; and his voice is modulated by a sweetness which cannot be heard without emotion." He sprang into the arena, drew his big cavalry sword from its shining scabbard and with one well-aimed blow laid open the Negro's belly. He was rewarded with applause. At the sight of the blood gushing forth from the gaping wound the dogs became interested and before the young hero had regained his seat they were tearing out the entrails of the shrieking black man.

Lest it be thought that Rochambeau has been slandered, here is a letter, dated May 6, 1803, which he sent to General Ramel, Commander of Tortuga: —

> I am sending you, my dear Commandant, a detachment of fifty men of the National Guard of Le Cap, commanded by Monsieur Bari. The detachment is followed by twenty-eight bulldogs. These reinforcements should enable you to bring your operations to a successful close. I must not fail to inform you that no ration or allowance of any kind will be allowed for the maintenance of these dogs. You are to feed Negroes to them.*

But irresponsible power is unpredictable. The favorites of today may become the victims of tomorrow. The white inhabitants lost all enthusiasm for Rochambeau when he began to levy heavy toll upon them. If a colonist failed to pay he ran the risk of being shot. Sometimes he was shot anyway. A colonist named Feydon was imprisoned for failing to pay 20,000 francs demanded of him. His family was told that if the money was not forthcoming by three o'clock the following day Feydon would face a firing squad. They raised the ransom and brought it to Rochambeau. He accepted it and then informed them that the sentence had already been carried out.

* Perhaps we should not be too hard on Rochambeau. His methods were more bizarre, but hardly less inhuman than those of other white men warring against one of the colored races. Thus, in 1763, the British Commander in Chief in America, General Amherst, wished to send blankets inoculated with smallpox to the American Indians, "to extirpate this execrable race," and wished to hunt them down with dogs. John Penn, Governor of Pennsylvania, grandson of William Penn, proclaimed a bounty for Indian scalps, male or female.

## 4

In the meantime the Negroes were giving blow for blow. Less imaginative in their cruelty than Rochambeau, they were just as merciless and there was no longer a Toussaint Louverture to keep them in check. Rochambeau's army melted as had Leclerc's, and France being again at war with England it was impossible to send reinforcements. In November 1803 Rochambeau was besieged at Le Cap by Dessalines, while a British squadron lay in the offing. He offered to surrender the city if allowed to embark unhindered, i.e. to become a prisoner of the British. The offer was accepted, and on November 28 the Negro forces entered Le Cap.

Napoleon's colonial adventure was at an end. It had cost the lives of 63,000 Frenchmen and probably of double that number of Negroes. It would eventually cost the lives of all but a few of the white inhabitants, massacred by order of Dessalines. The material loss ran into hundreds of millions of francs. There was still another loss to deplore: Dessalines sat in the place once occupied by Toussaint.

But in April of that year Napoleon, despairing of conquering St. Domingo, had sold the Louisiana Territory, no longer needed as a supply base for the more valuable colony. Are we not justified in saying that this door to destiny was opened to the people of America as a direct result of the heroism of Toussaint Louverture and the Negroes and mulattoes of St. Domingo?

# APPENDIX

## Toussaint's Parentage and Date of Birth

TOUSSAINT's son, Isaac Louverture, has asserted that Pierre Baptiste Simon was not Toussaint's father, but his godfather. Toussaint's father, he informs us, was the second son of an African chieftain named Gaou-Ginou. Having been captured with his wife, Affiba, and their two children during a raid, he was separated from his family, taken to the slave market at Whyda, in Dahomey, transported to St. Domingo and sold to the manager of the Bréda plantation. A neighboring planter purchased Affiba and the two children, who arrived in the colony in a different vessel. When Toussaint's father married again, Affiba, hearing of the merrymaking on the Bréda plantation on the occasion of the marriage of a chieftain's son, went to look and recognized her husband in the bridegroom. She slunk off and, we are told, died of grief a short time later, which, considering that she was an African Negress accustomed to polygamy, seems strange.

There are excellent reasons for doubting this romantic tale. The principal one is that Toussaint, on two occasions, refers in his correspondence to Pierre Baptiste as his father and never makes the least mention of any other sire. In his memorandum to Napoleon he says: "I am separated from all that I hold dearest in the world – from a venerable father, one hundred and five years old, who needs my assistance."

Now, according to Isaac, Toussaint's father had died long before. The man one hundred and five years old was Pierre Baptiste.

On October 8, 1802, Toussaint writes to Bonaparte: "I am uneducated, I am ignorant, but my father, who is blind at present, has pointed out to me the road to probity and virtue."

The man "blind at present" was Pierre Baptiste, living on Toussaint's plantation at Ennery.

The fact that Toussaint was a devout Catholic, hated the voodoo religion and tried to suppress it, makes it appear certain that from earliest childhood he had been reared by someone devoted to the Catholic faith. Pierre Baptiste was such a man; the son of an African chieftain who had come to the colony at a mature age definitely would not have been.

## 2

Gragnon-Lacoste, a friend of Isaac's widow, Louise Chancy, corroborates Isaac, basing himself on "secret and historical documents," which he never saw fit to publish. Gragnon-Lacoste is, however, an exceedingly unreliable witness. In his book, published in 1877, he says: "Monsieur Isaac Louverture had his father's remains exhumed under the Restoration. His widow has entrusted them to me."

An official inquiry, conducted in 1921 and 1922 by the French authorities at the request of the Haitian Government, conclusively proved that Toussaint's remains never had been exhumed, which, however, had not prevented Gragnon-Lacoste from opening up a public subscription to bury the supposed remains by the side of those of the son. Whoever was responsible for the hoax, it is evident that Gragnon-Lacoste is not sufficiently reliable to be believed without supplementary evidence.

Still basing himself on the "secret and historical documents," Gragnon-Lacoste asserts that Toussaint was born on May 20, 1746. Toussaint himself does not appear to have known the date of his birth. In a letter to the French Directory, dated August 26, 1797, he says that he was fifty years old at the outbreak of the French Revolution, which means that he was born in 1739. In the prison register of the Fort de Joux, his age, undoubtedly given by himself, was entered, in 1802, as fifty-eight, which gives 1744 as the date of his birth. The plain truth is that we do not know when Toussaint was born, but that 1744 appears the most probable year.

That Toussaint's father had two children from a previous union we know from a legal action undertaken by their descendants for a share in the Negro leader's inheritance.

## The Meeting in the Bois Caïman

THE original documents from which the principal details of the meeting are taken can be found in the French Colonial Archives. The documents (reprinted, in part, in the first volume of Garran-Coulon's four-volume report to the French National Assembly, published in 1792) consist of a series of confessions made by a number of the delegates, who were arrested on August 20, two days before the outbreak of the rebellion. The preciseness of the information may be judged from this deposition of the Negro François, arrested for setting fire, on August 11, to the Chabaud plantation: –

"On Sunday, August 14, 1791, there took place on the Lenormand estate, at Morne-Rouge, a delegate meeting of Negroes. Two delegates were present from every plantation at Port-Margot, Limbé, Acul, Petite-Anse, Limonade, Plaine-du-Nord, Quartier Morin, Morne-Rouge, etc. The meeting was held for the purpose of agreeing on a date for the insurrection, which had been contemplated for a long time. At first it was the opinion of those present that the insurrection should start that night, but the Negroes reconsidered, as this would not allow sufficient time for preparation."

Others gave information concerning the number of delegates present, the presence of the mulatto, the reading of the spurious documents, etc. It is interesting to note that although the confessions were undoubtedly obtained by means of torture, the Negroes did not betray the name of any delegate. That the leading role was played by Boukmans became known after the outbreak of the rebellion.

# Index